21314

What's Wrong With
My Vegetable Garden?

What's Wrong With My Vegetable Garden?

100% ORGANIC SOLUTIONS FOR ALL YOUR VEGETABLES,
FROM ARTICHOKES TO ZUCCHINI

David Deardorff and Kathryn Wadsworth

TIMBER PRESS
Portland * London

Photo credits: John W. Bickley, pages 126 (cabbage maggots), 127 (slugs or snails), 131 (asparagus beetles), 143 (aphids), 156 (root rot), 178 (rust); Lindsey J. du Toit, page 129 (clubroot); Les Jones, page 147 (smut). All other photographs are by the authors.

Published in 2011 by Timber Press, Inc.

The Haseltine Building
133 S.W. Second Avenue, Suite 450
Portland, Oregon 97204-3527
www.timberpress.com

2 The Quadrant
135 Salusbury Road
London NW6 6RJ
www.timberpress.co.uk

Printed in China

Library of Congress Cataloging-in-Publication Data

Deardorff, David C.
  What's wrong with my vegetable garden? : 100% organic
  solutions for all your vegetables, from artichokes to
  zucchini / David Deardorff and Kathryn Wadsworth. —
  1st ed.
    p. cm.
  Includes bibliographical references and index.
  ISBN 978-1-60469-283-9 (hardcover)
  ISBN 978-1-60469-184-9 (pbk.)
  1. Organic gardening. 2. Vegetable gardening. 3.
  Vegetables—Diseases and pests—Control. I. Wadsworth,
  Kathryn B. II. Title.
  SB324.3D43 2012
  635—dc23   2011018443

A catalog record for this book is available from the British Library.

For all who cherish nature,
who celebrate the wild,
and, most importantly,
who hear the whispers of plants
and choose to nurture them.

Contents

Prepare for Success

THIS BOOK IS ALL ABOUT GROWING HEALTHY, ORGANIC vegetables at home, something that more and more of us are doing these days. We seek the satisfaction of nurturing amazing plants that become our platter of gourmet vegetables. We crave that moment when the flavor of a freshly picked tomato explodes in our mouths. Above all, by growing our own food, we know it is safe, clean, and chemical-free.

But we don't wish to waste time, energy, and money getting our "locally grown" vegetables. Here's the simple truth—the most effective way to grow healthy food in our own yards is to create gardens that replicate nature. By gardening in concert with the natural world, we garner many rewards. We profit from mutually beneficial transactions with the other creatures on earth. From the earthworm that enriches the soil to the bee that pollinates our crops, wild creatures work hard for our benefit. In return, let's provide them with a safe and healthy habitat. Creating an intact, albeit artificial, ecosystem that functions the way a natural ecosystem does just makes sense. Nature is the silent partner who makes your garden work. And this book will help you to enjoy the bounty.

Following this Introduction, we present plant portraits of popular vegetables in alphabetical order. Each plant portrait gives you all the information you need to grow that beautiful, sumptuous vegetable and its kin: a description, including growth habit; information on the plant's season; temperature, soil, light, and water requirements; and best garden uses and planting techniques. This part of the book helps you decide which plants you can grow, and how to plant them, as well as guiding you in their proper care. Fine-tune your choice of cultivar by having a look at the Appendix.

In each portrait, we stress the polyculture approach, where each plant's nearest neighbor is different from itself. This is one of the most important things you can do to keep your plants pest- and disease-free. In the polyculture garden, pests have a difficult time finding their vegetable of choice, and diseases have trouble spreading from plant to plant.

If pests or diseases are already visiting your favorite vegetable, consult the Family Problem-Solving Guides. Each vegetable portrait directs you to the proper one. These visual guides will help you identify and eliminate pests and diseases in the garden. We supply you with a photograph of the problem, symptom descriptions, diagnoses, and page numbers to find solutions.

The final part of the book, "Organic Solutions to Common Problems," presents in detail every solution listed in the problem-solving guides. Here you will learn how to change growing conditions to solve problems, and be introduced to organic techniques and remedies for garden pests and diseases, from deer to fungi. We urge you to use organic solutions and remedies for growing condition, pest, and disease challenges for three reasons. First, organic remedies are just as effective as synthetic ones. Second, we want everyone to have access to healthy, affordable, chemical-free food. And third, we want to protect and enhance the natural ecosystems that surround us. What works in nature will work for you.

Four essential physical factors affect how successful your garden will be: temperature, soil, light, and water. No matter where you live, you can modify or improve each of these somewhat unpredictable factors to an extent, and give each vegetable the best growing conditions possible. Considering these factors from the beginning will take you a long way toward the delicious harvest of your dreams.

(opposite, top) Heirloom tomatoes burst with flavor— one of the many rewards of growing your own vegetables.

(opposite, bottom) Corn appreciates warm temperatures, fertile soil, full sun, and regular water.

(opposite) California poppies, chives, and artichokes thrive in this healthy garden ecosystem.

(above) In the polyculture garden each plant's nearest neighbor is different from itself, so pests can't find their favorite food, and diseases don't run rampant through the garden.

TEMPERATURE

Most vegetables are annuals, so temperature during the growing season is essential information. For perennial vegetables, tolerance of winter cold is key. And some plants are sensitive to heat, which also affects whether and how to grow them in your climate. Determine the average daytime highs in your garden, and use this information to choose plants that are easy to grow where you live. Keep a record of both the highs and lows, if you can. Thermometers that measure minimum and maximum temperatures are extremely handy for this purpose.

Plant labels and catalog descriptions give you your first tool for discovering the temperature needs of your plants. Temperature requirements are sometimes expressed as a specific minimum temperature that the plant can withstand, also known as its hardiness. Other tag or catalog descriptions list the United States Department of Agriculture (USDA) hardiness zone number for that plant. The USDA has created a map of North America based on average annual winter low temperatures in ten-degree increments. This zone system tells you only a plant's ability to withstand cold, but this is important when you want to grow perennial vegetables like artichoke, asparagus, or rhubarb.

Get to know your local average dates for the last killing frost in springtime and the first killing frost in the fall. The growing season in your garden is the number of days between these two events. Growing seasons vary from 365 days to less than 90. If you live in a short, cool growing season, then you need to select cultivars with the shortest days to maturity. Vegetable seed packets and plant labels always give you the days to maturity for the crop. This information helps you plan what to grow and when to grow it.

How to Recognize Temperature-Related Problems Chart, page 16

SOIL

Soil is alive. It is home to a community of organisms: bacteria, fungi, nematodes, insects, worms, and other creatures that all feed on dead plant material and each other. This community helps maintain a constant source of nutrients for your plants as well as consistent soil moisture. Both services keep plants stress-free. And, perhaps even better, these microbes outcompete destructive soil pathogens (other bacteria and fungi) and pests. The basis of this food chain in your garden is dead or dying, but not diseased, plant material: compost, organic fertilizers, composted manure, and organic mulch.

Nurturing this living community in your garden is one of the most effective steps you can take to guard against plant problems. No matter what the configuration will be, preparing the place for your veggies to bed down is especially important if you are starting your first vegetable garden. In addition, renewing the soil in standard garden plots each season gives you a running start for abundant production. Begin these preparations two weeks before planting anything outside.

We highly recommend that you do not till your soil. Tilling is like plowing and turns the soil over to redistribute it. It disturbs the community of organisms that makes up biologically active soil and encourages dormant weed seeds to germinate. An even better reason to avoid tilling? It is unnecessary, back-breaking labor. Skip it.

How to Recognize Soil-Related Problems Chart, page 18

LIGHT

Without sunlight, plants would not be able to survive, much less thrive. Thus light, and the quality of that light, is essential. Through photosynthesis plants harvest solar energy and convert it to chemical energy. The plant uses these chemicals for growth and reproduction. The excess chemical energy is stored in leaves, roots, stems, and fruits for later use. This excess is also what we harvest to eat.

Most vegetables appreciate a full day of sun—that means six to 12 hours per day. But let's be realistic, almost no one has that kind of light. If you do, great, but if you don't, don't despair. To begin with, however, choose varieties of vegetables that grow well in light conditions that prevail in your location.

Keep in mind that as the season progresses and the earth's location and axis shift in relationship to the sun, the amount and quality of light that reaches your yard changes. If you have the opportunity, observe the shadows cast by your house, trees, fences, and other structures for an entire year. If it is the beginning of the season and you are raring to go, then estimate what structures and plants will cast shadows, and note what time of day your vegetable garden will be in shade. Try to locate your veggies where there are no shadows, or where the shade occurs in the afternoon. Morning light is best.

Some vegetables that do not like heat grow well in partial shade. Partial shade alters the duration or intensity of light. A half day of sun, at least three hours, qualifies as partial shade. So does the dappled light available under an overhanging tree, shrub, or trellis. You can also create partial shade by using 50 percent shade cloth.

How to Recognize Light-Related Problems Chart, page 21

WATER

As the old Spanish proverb says, *El agua es la vida*—"water is life." Nowhere is this more true than in the vegetable garden. Thus, first and foremost, make sure that you have access to water for your plants. The second most important adage comes from plant pathology: water the soil, not the foliage. This practice helps keep your plants disease-free, because many agents of destruction—fungal, bacterial, and viral—use moisture on the foliage as a passageway to infect plants.

What is the source of the water you use for the garden? For most of us, it is the spigot, either on the side of the house, or one that is freestanding in the garden. Water may also come from rain, as a gentle shower or a real gullywasher, and how it behaves on your property is important to note. So take some time to observe how surface water from rain or runoff from the neighborhood behaves. Where does it come from? Where does it flow as it crosses your property? And where does it go when it leaves? Or, does it stay and create wet, boggy areas? If so, try to locate your vegetable garden somewhere other than the dismal swamp. On the other hand, does it run across your property and spill into the street and storm drain, when you wish it would stay and water your plants? Put a water management plan in place as soon as it is convenient. You won't regret it.

How to Recognize Water-Related Problems Chart, page 22

How to Recognize Temperature-Related Problems

Symptom	Diagnosis	Solution
Germination is erratic. Seedlings grow very slowly. Leaves turn yellow.	**Cold soil**	Cool- and warm-season crops, page 192 Modify effects of temperature, page 193
Leaves turn brown at the tips and along the edges.	**Leaf scorch: too hot combined with insufficient water**	Modify effects of temperature, page 193 Manage water, page 199
Leaves are brown or black and melt away at the tips.	**Frost damage: too cold**	Cool- and warm-season crops, page 192 Modify effects of temperature, page 193
Plants are stunted. Crops are undersized. Yields are small. Produce may be strongly flavored.	**Environmental stress: too hot, too dry**	Cool- and warm-season crops, page 192 Modify effects of temperature, page 193 Manage water, page 199

Symptom	Diagnosis	Solution
Tomatoes fail to ripen and stay green at the stem end of the fruit.	**Greenback: too cold**	Cool- and warm-season crops, page 192 Modify effects of temperature, page 193
Beet roots develop a bull's-eye pattern of light and dark rings.	**Too hot combined with irregular watering**	Cool- and warm-season crops, page 192 Modify effects of temperature, page 193 Manage water, page 199
Onion bulbs turn gray on the outer scales.	**Too hot combined with irregular watering**	Cool- and warm-season crops, page 192 Modify effects of temperature, page 193 Manage water, page 199
Plants flower prematurely (bolt).	**Too hot or too cold**	Cool- and warm-season crops, page 192 Modify effects of temperature, page 193

How to Recognize Soil-Related Problems

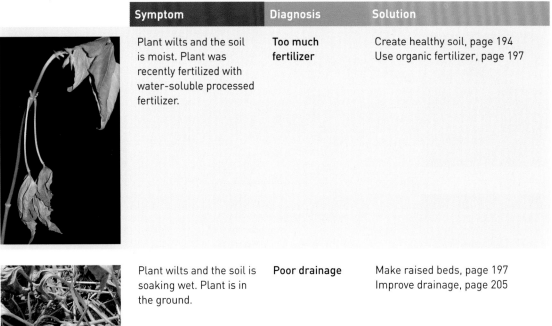

Symptom	Diagnosis	Solution
Plant wilts and the soil is moist. Plant was recently fertilized with water-soluble processed fertilizer.	**Too much fertilizer**	Create healthy soil, page 194 Use organic fertilizer, page 197

Symptom	Diagnosis	Solution
Plant wilts and the soil is soaking wet. Plant is in the ground.	**Poor drainage**	Make raised beds, page 197 Improve drainage, page 205

Symptom	Diagnosis	Solution
Lower leaves turn completely yellow and drop off. Soil is soaking wet. Plant is in the ground.	**Poor drainage**	Make raised beds, page 197 Improve drainage, page 205

Symptom	Diagnosis	Solution
 Lower leaves turn yellow, veins stay green. Leaves do not drop off.	**Nitrogen or magnesium deficiency**	Create healthy soil, page 194 Use organic fertilizer, page 197
 New leaves turn yellow, veins stay green. Leaves do not drop off.	**Iron or manganese deficiency**	Create healthy soil, page 194 Use organic fertilizer, page 197
 Leaf edges turn yellow with brown spots. Leaves turn brown and die.	**Potassium deficiency**	Create healthy soil, page 194 Use organic fertilizer, page 197
Leaves look purplish. Veins turn purple.	**Phosphorus deficiency**	Create healthy soil, page 194 Use organic fertilizer, page 197

Symptom	Diagnosis	Solution
 Tomatoes, squash, peppers, and other fruits develop a brown-black circular lesion on the blossom end.	**Blossom-end rot: calcium deficiency, irregular watering**	Manage water, page 199 Improve drainage, page 205 Use organic fertilizer, page 197
Carrots or parsnips are forked or twisted.	**Rocky, lumpy soil**	Create healthy soil, page 194 Make raised beds, page 197

How to Recognize Light-Related Problems

	Symptom	Diagnosis	Solution
	Plant wilts and soil is moist. Plant was recently transplanted.	**Transplant shock**	Modify the site: provide temporary shade, page 199
	Leaves or fruit have large brown to black burned patches.	**Sunburn**	Modify the site: provide shade, page 199
	Leaves are pale green, plants tall and spindly.	**Not enough sunlight**	Modify the site: provide full sun, page 199
	Leaves turn brown at the tips and along the edges.	**Leaf scorch: too much light, heat, too little water**	Modify the site: provide shade, page 199 Manage water, page 199

How to Recognize Water-Related Problems

Symptom	Diagnosis	Solution
 Plant wilts and the soil is bone dry.	**Too little water**	Manage water, page 199
 Plant wilts, recovers when watered, then quickly wilts again. Plant is in a container.	**Rootbound in container**	Put the plant in a bigger pot
 Plant wilts and the soil is soaking wet. Plant is in a container with a saucer underneath.	**Overwatering**	Watering the container garden, page 205
 Plant wilts and the soil is soaking wet. Plant is in the ground.	**Poor drainage**	Make raised beds, page 197 Improve drainage, page 205

Symptom	Diagnosis	Solution
 Leaves at the base of stems turn completely yellow and drop off. Soil is soaking wet. Plant is in a container.	Overwatering	Watering the container garden, page 205
 Leaves turn brown at the tips and along the edges.	Leaf scorch: insufficient water and too hot	Manage water, page 199 Modify effects of temperature, page 193
 Plants are stunted. Crops are undersized, yields small, and produce may be strongly flavored.	Environmental stress: too hot, and too dry	Manage water, page 199 Cool- and warm-season crops, page 192 Modify effects of temperature, page 193
 Green beans, squash, tomatoes, and other fruits get brown, scabby, corky patches.	Russeting or edema: too much water	Manage water, page 199

Symptom	Diagnosis	Solution
Tomatoes, other fruits, and fleshy roots crack.	**Irregular watering with cycling from very dry to very wet**	Manage water, page 199
Potatoes are lumpy, mis-shapen.	**Irregular watering with cycling from very dry to very wet**	Manage water, page 199
Beet roots develop a bull's-eye pattern of light to dark rings.	**Too hot combined with irregular watering**	Cool- and warm-season crops, page 192 Modify effects of temperature, page 193 Manage water, page 199
Onion bulbs turn gray on outer scales.	**Too hot combined with irregular watering**	Cool- and warm-season crops, page 192 Modify effects of temperature, page 193 Manage water, page 199

Plant Portraits

Artichokes

Cynara cardunculus Scolymus Group

Family Problem-Solving Guide, page 118

DESCRIPTION. Artichokes are shrubby perennials where summer daytime high temperatures average 60 to 75°F, and winter nighttime low temperatures average higher than 25°F. They grow 3 to 5 feet tall and wide. Choose the right cultivar for your climate and taste. For help with this decision, see the Appendix.

SEASON. A cool-season crop. Plant in early spring or early fall, depending on temperatures where you live.

TEMPERATURE. Artichokes thrive where summer daytime high temperatures average 60 to 65°F. They will grow, and make flower buds, in climates where temperatures are higher during the growing season, but they will need afternoon shade. Where summer highs average 85°F or above, plant them in the fall to harvest in the spring (assuming that your winters are not too cold). It is too cold for artichokes where winter nighttime lows average 25°F or below, unless you cut them to the ground and mulch with 6 inches of straw. Where winter temperatures drop to 15°F, plants will be killed regardless of the mulch. You might want to try growing them in containers if you live in a cold climate, but bring them indoors in winter and store them in a frost-free location.

SOIL. Start with well-drained, biologically active soil that is rich in organic matter. To learn how to create such healthy soil, see page 194. Feed the soil with high-nitrogen organic fertilizer, composted manure, and/or compost at the beginning of each growing season. Spread mulch over the ground to a depth of 3 inches. These amendments should last the entire season. A soil pH of 6.5, which is slightly acid, allows artichokes to take up nutrients most efficiently.

LIGHT. Artichokes need six to 12 hours of direct sun per day. If you live where summer days are hot (average highs over 75°F), they will appreciate afternoon shade.

WATER. While artichoke plants are very tolerant of drought, they will not flower without plenty of water. Since the flower is the part you'll relish eating, water plants diligently—deeply and regularly. Give each plant 1 inch of water per week, remembering to water the root zone, not the foliage.

GARDEN USES AND PLANTING TECHNIQUES. If artichokes overwinter in your climate (because it is warm enough for them), use them as ornamental plants in your perennial border or with other perennial vegetables, such as asparagus. Because of their size, artichokes can provide a shaded microhabitat on their north sides. Annuals that appreciate shade will thrive here. Once established, artichoke roots go down 4 feet, so they grow well with shallow-rooted, cool-season plants with similar temperature, soil, light, and water requirements. Examples include cabbage and its relatives, lettuce, beets, carrots, violets, violas, Johnny-jump-ups, and pansies.

START SEEDS. Choose a place indoors where the temperature remains about 65°F. Eight weeks before your estimated last spring frost, fill 4-inch pots with the container soil mix you prepared. Poke two or three seeds about ½ inch deep into this potting mix. Once the seeds germinate, remove the weaker seedlings, leaving one strong seedling per pot. Keep the remaining seedlings in full sun. After the last spring frost, plant your seedlings in the ground or in containers outdoors.

PLANT SEEDLINGS. In the ground: Space plants about 3 feet apart in full sun. Dig a hole the same height and depth as the seedling's container. Slide both plant and potting soil out of the container and into the hole, roots down. The top surface of the seedling's potting mix should be at the same level as the ground. Do not bury any leaves. If you can see vegetative buds at the base of the plant, make sure they too are at ground level. Fill the hole with additional soil mix as needed, press gently all around the plant to create a shallow basin, and fill it with water. Once the water has drained away, spread mulch 3 inches deep around the plant and about 1 inch away from its stem. **In containers:** Use a 5-gallon pot with a drainage hole. Place a small square of window screen over the hole, inside the pot, and add ½ inch of gravel. Fill the pot with the container soil mix you prepared. Follow directions for planting in the ground, except use the container soil mix when additional soil is needed. Be sure to top-dress, as mulch is called when applied to pots.

PLANT DORMANT ROOTS. In the ground: Dig a hole about 18 inches wide and deep. Fill the hole with the in-ground soil mix you prepared. Use a trowel, or your hands, to dig a hole the same size as the root, and insert the root into this hole with its vegetative buds up. Make sure all these buds are at soil level, not buried. Press down on the soil mix gently to form a shallow basin and fill it with water. Once the water has drained away, spread mulch 3 inches deep around the plant and about 1 inch away from the stem. **In containers:** As with seedlings, use a 5-gallon pot and fill the container with the container soil mix you prepared. Follow the steps for planting dormant roots in the ground, except use the container soil mix to fill the hole. Be sure to top-dress.

PROBLEM-SOLVING. Many solutions to problems lie in garden preparation, so please read the Introduction to avoid trouble in the first place. Also refer to "Change Growing Conditions to Solve Problems" on page 192. We have grown artichokes in the Pacific Northwest and the Desert Southwest, and encountered very few problems. If you meet their nutritional and water needs, and protect them from winter cold, you should have the same success. Aphids were always our biggest problem. They love to hide between the bracts on the flower buds. If you encounter these or any other pests or diseases, consult the Family Problem-Solving Guide on page 118.

Arugula

Eruca vesicaria subsp. *sativa*

Family Problem-Solving Guide, page 124

DESCRIPTION. Arugula (aka rocket) is a quick-growing annual that grows 1 to 3 feet tall, maturing in six weeks. It reseeds freely and can become weedy. See that it does not spread throughout your garden.

SEASON. A cool-season crop. Plant in spring or early fall, depending on temperatures where you live.

TEMPERATURE. Arugula prefers cool weather and thrives at daytime high temperatures of 40 to 60°F. It will produce tasty flowers in hot weather (greater than 70°F), but the leaves become inedible.

SOIL. Start with well-drained, biologically active soil that is rich in organic matter. To learn how to create such healthy soil, see page 194. Feed the soil with a complete, balanced organic fertilizer, composted manure, and/or compost at the beginning of each growing season. These amendments should last the entire season. Best soil pH range is 6 to 7.

LIGHT. As long as the cool weather (40 to 60°F) holds, plant arugula in six to 12 hours of direct sun per day. Providing light shade in hot weather (above 70°F) may prolong edibility of the foliage.

WATER. Arugula is not drought-tolerant and needs regular water, about 1 inch a week. Apply water to the root zone, not the foliage.

GARDEN USES AND PLANTING TECHNIQUES. Grow arugula in a baby greens (aka mesclun) mix that you harvest with scissors for salads. Choose late- and early-harvesting types to extend the season of this mix. These mixtures perform as well in large, shallow pots as they do in the garden bed. Sow a small amount of seeds in little patches among plants that require similar growing conditions, such as lettuce, radishes, dill, parsnips, chives, basil, violas, and calendula.

START SEEDS. Begin indoors in 4-inch pots and plant out in the garden or in larger containers when seedlings have four or five leaves. Sow seeds ½ inch deep, two or three seeds to a pot, and thin to the strongest seedling. Eat the thinnings as baby greens. You can also sow seeds directly in the garden; plant seeds 2 inches apart in rows 16 inches apart. To keep your arugula coming, start new patches every couple of weeks. Thin seedlings to 6 inches apart.

PLANT SEEDLINGS. In the ground: Space plants about 6 inches apart in full sun. Dig a hole the same height and depth as the seedling's container. Slide both plant and potting soil out of the container and into the hole, roots down. The top surface of the seedling's potting mix should be at the same level as the ground. Do not bury any leaves. Fill the hole with additional soil mix as needed, press gently all around the plant to create a shallow basin, and fill it with water. Once the water has drained away, spread mulch 3 inches deep around the plant and 1 inch away from the base of the plant. **In containers:** Use a one-gallon pot with a drainage hole. Place a small square of window screen over the hole, inside the pot, and add ½ inch of gravel. Fill the pot with the container soil mix you prepared. Follow directions for planting in the ground, except use the container soil mix when additional soil is needed. Be sure to mulch (top-dress).

PROBLEM-SOLVING. Hardy and prolific, arugula is a cinch to grow. Still, problems can crop up. Please read the Introduction to avoid trouble in the first place. Also refer to "Change Growing Conditions to Solve Problems" on page 192. If you encounter pests or diseases, consult the Family Problem-Solving Guide on page 124.

Asparagus

Asparagus officinalis

Family Problem-Solving Guide, page 131

DESCRIPTION. An edible and ornamental perennial, asparagus produces fern-like foliage 3 to 8 feet tall and 2 to 4 feet wide. Choose the right cultivar for your climate and taste. For help with this decision, see the Appendix.

SEASON. A cool-season crop. Plant in early spring. Early fall planting is appropriate if you live where winter lows average 15°F or warmer.

TEMPERATURE. Asparagus grows best when day-time highs average 60 to 75°F during the growing season. It is quite hardy, withstanding temperatures to -30°F. However, it is best to protect the crowns (dormant roots) with 6 inches of mulch when temperatures drop below freezing.

SOIL. Start with well-drained, biologically active soil that is rich in organic matter. To learn how to create such healthy soil, see page 194. At the beginning of the growing season, spread plenty of compost (2 to 3 inches) on top of and around the existing asparagus crowns. To encourage new shoots, do not mulch over the compost. Cover the soil with more compost and 3 inches of mulch, when you stop harvesting. Best soil pH range is 6 to 8.

LIGHT. Asparagus needs six to 12 hours of direct sun per day.

WATER. Asparagus is not drought-tolerant and needs about 2 inches of water weekly. Your climate and rainfall will determine how much supplemental water the plant needs, as well as how often you need to provide it. Water the roots so that the water soaks deeply into the soil whenever the soil has dried out.

GARDEN USES AND PLANTING TECHNIQUES. Asparagus does well in a border with other perennials, as long as it receives the proper nutrients, temperature, light, and water. Its roots are shallow, meaning you can pair it with artichokes and other deep-rooted perennial vegetables. For color and the benefits of polyculture, sow seeds of lupine, bush beans, crimson clover, and other nitrogen-fixing, low-growing annuals around the asparagus.

START SEEDS. Soak seeds in water for a couple of hours before planting to enhance germination. In late winter or early spring, sow seeds indoors in 4-inch pots. Plant two or three soaked seeds 2 inches deep in each pot. After germination, thin to the most robust seedling per pot. Plant seedlings out in the garden or in larger containers after all danger of frost is past. You can also sow seeds directly in the garden, 2 inches apart and deep, after the last spring frost. When seedlings are 6 inches tall, thin them to 12 inches apart.

PLANT DORMANT ROOTS. This is the easiest and the most common way to plant asparagus. Crowns, as these dormant roots are called, are widely available from nurseries and garden centers. In the ground: Dig a hole 8 inches deep and 5 inches wide. Place one crown in the hole, taking care to spread the roots horizontally along the bottom. Space the crowns about a foot apart. Cover the roots with 3 inches of sifted, rich compost. Water thoroughly. Through the season, as the stems grow, continue to add some of the in-ground soil mix you prepared, until the hole is full. Do not bury the growing tips. In containers: Use a 5-gallon pot with a drainage hole. Place a small square of window screen over the hole, inside the pot, and add ½ inch of gravel. Put the container in full sun, and follow directions for planting in the ground. Mulch, aka top-dress, after you stop harvesting.

PROBLEM-SOLVING. Asparagus needs lots of nutrients and lots of water. If you follow the guidelines just given, you should not run into too many problems. Please read the Introduction to avoid trouble in the first place. Also refer to "Change Growing Conditions to Solve Problems" on page 192. If you encounter pests or diseases, consult the Family Problem-Solving Guide on page 131.

Beets

Beta vulgaris

Family Problem-Solving Guide, page 134

DESCRIPTION. Beets are biennials grown as annuals in the garden. Choose the right cultivar for your climate. For help with this decision, see the Appendix.

SEASON. A cool-season crop. Plant in early spring for best performance. Plant in late summer if you live where summers are hot (regularly above 75°F), but winters are mild (daytime highs above 50°F).

TEMPERATURE. Beets prefer daytime high temperatures of 60 to 65°F. Once the weather turns hot (above 75°F), beets languish, and the roots lose flavor and tenderness. Beets tolerate freezing, but if temperatures drop below 50°F for three weeks, the plants will flower, bolt, and produce seeds.

SOIL. Start with well-drained, biologically active soil that is rich in organic matter. To learn how to create such healthy soil, see page 194. At planting time, add 1 cup of bone meal to every 2 gallons of the soil mix you prepared. Feed beets with a complete, balanced organic fertilizer, composted manure, and/or compost at the beginning of each growing season. These amendments should last the entire season. Take care to remove lumps and rocks. The soil should be loose to give the beet roots room to develop. Best soil pH range is 6.2 to 7. If pH is not within this range, beets can suffer from boron deficiency.

LIGHT. Beets need six to 12 hours of direct sun per day. If you grow beets for their greens only, provide light, dappled shade, so that the greens don't become bitter.

WATER. Beets need 1 inch of water each week. Apply water to the root zone, not the foliage, and maintain consistent moisture to keep the roots tender.

GARDEN USES AND PLANTING TECHNIQUES. Healthy beet leaves are attractive in an ornamental garden. If you add annuals to your perennial border, consider including beets. Keep in mind, however, that the bulbous roots need room to develop, and their taproot descends about a foot into the earth. In the vegetable bed they do well in a polyculture mix with scallions, peas, and members of the cabbage family. For containers, choose "baby beet" varieties, and plant them with other small vegetables and flowers such as lettuce and violas.

START SEEDS. Soak seeds for an hour before planting. Two weeks before the anticipated last spring frost, plant seeds directly in the ground or in 4-inch pots. Space the seeds 1 inch apart, and cover with ½ inch of your prepared soil mix. When the seedlings are 2 to 3 inches tall, thin them so that the strong healthy ones remain 4 to 6 inches apart. Eat and enjoy the tender shoots you thinned out. Spread 3 inches of mulch on the seedlings when they are about 5 inches tall. You can also plant seeds four to eight weeks before the anticipated first fall frost, using the techniques just described.

PLANT SEEDLINGS. In the ground: Space plants about 6 inches apart in full sun. Dig a hole the same height and depth as the seedling's container. Put 1 cup of bone meal into the hole and mix it with the soil. Slide both plant and potting soil out of the pot and into the hole, roots down. The top surface of the seedling's potting mix should be at the same level as the ground. Do not bury any leaves. Fill the hole with additional soil mix as needed, press gently all around the plant to create a shallow basin, and fill it with water. Once the water has drained away, spread mulch 3 inches deep around the plant and about 1 inch away from its stem. In containers: For an individual beet plant, use a one-gallon container. If you want to plant several beets, or beets with other vegetables, use a half whiskey barrel or a 5-gallon container. Whichever pot you choose, make sure there is a drainage hole. Place a small square of window screen over the hole, inside the pot, and add ½ inch of gravel. Fill the pot with the container soil mix you prepared. Follow directions for planting in the ground, except use the container soil mix when additional soil is needed. Be sure to mulch (top-dress).

PROBLEM-SOLVING. Satisfying and easy to grow, beets rarely have problems in the garden. Nevertheless, sometimes despite your best efforts, something does go wrong. Please read the Introduction to avoid trouble in the first place. Also refer to "Change Growing Conditions to Solve Problems" on page 192. If you encounter pests or diseases, consult the Family Problem-Solving Guide on page 134.

Bok choy

Brassica rapa Chinensis Group

Family Problem-Solving Guide, page 124

DESCRIPTION. A biennial grown as an annual, with plants from 6 inches to 2 feet tall and 1 foot wide, depending on the cultivar. For help choosing the right cultivar for your circumstances, see the Appendix.

SEASON. A cool-season crop. Plant in early spring for an early summer harvest, or in early fall for an early winter harvest. Where winter daytime temperatures average in the 60s, bok choy is a great winter vegetable.

TEMPERATURE. Bok choy does best when daytime high temperatures are between 55 and 70°F. When daytime highs average above 75°F or below 55°F, plants often bolt, and above 75°F, the leaf tips may burn. For seed germination, the optimum ambient temperature is 50 to 80°F.

SOIL. Start with well-drained, biologically active soil that is rich in organic matter. To learn how to create such healthy soil, see page 194. At the beginning of the growing season, add organic compost or fertilizer that is slightly higher in nitrogen (N) than it is in phosphorus (P) or potassium (K). Use a fertilizer with a ratio of 10-7-7 or something similar, or add extra nitrogen (in the form of chicken manure, for instance) to a balanced fertilizer or compost. The higher nitrogen helps plants grow quickly and produce tastier leaves. Add a dose of this fertilizer again about two to three weeks after sowing, at the time you thin the seedlings. Best soil pH range is 6 to 7.5. Adding lime to raise the pH to 7.2 helps control clubroot.

LIGHT. When temperatures are moderate, as it prefers, bok choy needs six to 12 hours of direct sun per day. Where daytime temperatures are hot (above 75°F), provide dappled/filtered shade. Bok choy is sensitive to light periods. Long days, 16 hours or more of daylight every day for a month, cause plants to flower and the leaves to become bitter.

WATER. Bok choy likes consistent moisture and an average of 1 inch of water per week. Do not let the soil dry out or become waterlogged. Remember to water the soil, not the foliage.

GARDEN USES AND PLANTING TECHNIQUES. With its lovely, deep green foliage, bok choy works very well as an ornamental, scattered through a garden or in a container mix of annual flowers. It is appropriate with other low- to medium-growing flowers and spring bulbs. In the polyculture garden, sow a few seeds in a small patch among plants that require similar growing conditions. Do not put bok choy in the same bed or container where it, or any cabbage relative, grew in the past three years.

START SEEDS. Because bok choy is susceptible to transplant shock, the best way to get it going is to sow seeds directly where you want plants to grow. Prepare the garden bed with the good soil mix you made. Or, to grow in a container, use a one-gallon pot with a drainage hole. Place a small square of window screen over the hole, inside the pot, and add ½ inch of gravel. Then fill the pot with the container soil mix you made. After the last spring frost, sow the seeds about 2 inches apart and about ¼ to ½ inch deep. Water immediately and keep the soil moist but not soggy until seeds germinate, which should occur in four to seven days. As the seedlings appear, thin them to 4 to 8 inches apart, further if you chose a large cultivar. After thinning, mulch 1 to 3 inches deep, depending on the size of the plants, to control weeds and to retain consistent soil moisture.

PROBLEM-SOLVING. Bok choy is easy to grow. It can have some of the many problems that plague the cabbage family, but if you keep its requirements in mind, you should encounter few of them. Please read the Introduction to avoid trouble in the first place. Also refer to "Change Growing Conditions to Solve Problems" on page 192. If you encounter pests or diseases, consult the Family Problem-Solving Guide on page 124.

Broccoli

Brassica oleracea Italica Group

Family Problem-Solving Guide, page 124

DESCRIPTION. Broccoli, including broccoli raab and broccolini, is an annual that grows 2 to 3 feet tall and 6 to 24 inches wide, depending on the cultivar. For help choosing the right cultivar for your circumstances, see the Appendix.

SEASON. A cool-season crop. Plant in early spring, or, better yet, in late summer to take advantage of the cool fall weather. Where winter daytime temperatures average in the 60s, stagger plantings throughout the year to enjoy broccoli year-round.

TEMPERATURE. Broccoli grows best when daytime temperatures average 60 to 65°F. For seed germination, the optimum ambient temperature is 50 to 85°F.

SOIL. Start with well-drained, biologically active soil that is rich in organic matter. To learn how to create such healthy soil, see page 194. Feed twice during the growing season. When you plant the seedlings, add ½ cup of balanced, organic fertilizer to the planting hole. When the main flower head forms, feed again: pull mulch away from each plant, and sprinkle ½ cup of complete, balanced organic fertilizer around it. Then replace the mulch. Mulch is particularly important to broccoli, which prefers cool soil temperatures. Best soil pH range is 6 to 7.5. Adding lime to raise the pH to 7.2 helps control clubroot.

LIGHT. Broccoli needs six to 12 hours of direct sun per day. Where daytime temperatures are hot (above 75°F), provide dappled/filtered shade.

WATER. Broccoli thrives with consistent moisture and an average of 1 inch of water per week. Do not let the soil dry out or become waterlogged. Remember to water the soil, not the foliage.

GARDEN USES AND PLANTING TECHNIQUES. Broccoli, especially the 'Romanesco' varieties, is particularly attractive in the flower garden. Interplant it among dill, nasturtium, rosemary, sage, and thyme to attract beneficial predators. This practice saves you a lot of work. For additional polyculture benefits, try planting it with beets, bush beans, chard, lettuce, and spinach. Do not put broccoli in the same bed or container where it, or any relative, grew within the past three years.

START SEEDS. Begin indoors six to eight weeks before the estimated last spring frost. Once seeds have germinated, set the plantlets outdoors during the warmest part of the day and bring them in at night for two weeks before transplanting them to their permanent outdoor location. In late summer or fall, sow seeds in the ground or container ten to 12 weeks before the estimated first fall frost.

PLANT SEEDLINGS. In the ground: Space plants about 1½ to 2 feet apart in full sun. Dig a hole 1 inch deeper than the seedling's container. Add ½ cup of balanced, organic fertilizer to the soil in the bottom of the hole, and mix well. Slide both plant and potting soil out of the container and into the hole, roots down. The top surface of the seedling's potting mix should be 1 inch lower than the ground. Do not bury any leaves. Fill the hole with the soil mix you prepared as needed, and press gently all around the plant to create a shallow basin. Place a cutworm collar around the stem. Now fill the basin with water. Once the water has drained away, spread mulch 3 inches deep around the plant and about 1 inch away from its stem. **In containers:** Use a 5-gallon pot with a drainage hole. Place a small square of window screen over the hole, inside the pot, and add ½ inch of gravel. Fill the pot with the container soil mix you prepared. Follow directions for planting in the ground, except use the container soil mix when additional soil is needed. Be sure to mulch (top-dress).

PROBLEM-SOLVING. Broccoli is actually very easy and satisfying to grow, despite the fact that it can suffer from many of the maladies that plague the cabbage family. Our best advice? Meet all nutrient requirements to keep plants growing quickly. Keep the garden weeded and mulched. Place row covers or other protection over the plants as soon as they are in the ground or containers. Finally, do not compost roots or other tissue of any cabbage relative. If your climate allows, it is also best to grow broccoli in the fall, when there are far fewer pests. Please read the Introduction to avoid trouble in the first place. Also refer to "Change Growing Conditions to Solve Problems" on page 192. If you do encounter pests or diseases, consult the Family Problem-Solving Guide on page 124.

Brussels sprouts

Brassica oleracea Gemmifera Group

Family Problem-Solving Guide, page 124

DESCRIPTION. A biennial grown as an annual. Plants grow 2 to 4 feet tall and 2 feet wide, depending on the cultivar. For help choosing the right cultivar for your climate and taste, see the Appendix.

SEASON. A cool-season crop. Plant in early spring, or, better yet, in late summer to take advantage of the cool fall weather. Where winter daytime temperatures average in the 60s, stagger plantings throughout the year to enjoy Brussels sprouts year-round.

TEMPERATURE. Brussels sprouts grow best when daytime temperatures average 60 to 65°F. Ten or more days of cool temperatures (35 to 45°F) will cause the plants to bolt; excessively hot temperatures (above 75°F) may do the same. Seeds germinate most efficiently when the ambient temperature is 50 to 80°F.

SOIL. Start with well-drained, biologically active soil that is rich in organic matter. To learn how to create such healthy soil, see page 194. Feed twice during the growing season. When you plant the seedlings, add ½ cup of balanced, organic fertilizer to the planting hole. When the plants are half of their mature size, feed again: pull mulch away from each plant, and sprinkle ½ cup of complete, balanced organic fertilizer around it; then replace the mulch. Mulch is particularly important to Brussels sprouts, which prefer cool soil temperatures. Best soil pH range is 6 to 7.5. Adding lime to raise the pH to 7.2 helps control clubroot.

LIGHT. Brussels sprouts need six to 12 hours of direct sun per day. Where daytime temperatures are hot (above 75°F), provide dappled/filtered shade.

WATER. Brussels sprouts thrive with consistent moisture and an average of 1 inch of water per week. Do not let the soil dry out or become water-logged. Be sure to water the soil, not the foliage.

GARDEN USES AND PLANTING TECHNIQUES. Brussels sprouts, especially the red varieties, add an attractive note to the flower garden. Interplant them among dill, nasturtium, rosemary, sage, and thyme to attract beneficial predators. This practice saves you a lot of work. For additional polyculture benefits, try planting with beets, bush beans, chard, lettuce, and spinach. Do not put Brussels sprouts in the same bed or container where they or any cabbage relative grew within the past three years.

START SEEDS. Begin indoors six to eight weeks before the estimated last spring frost. Once seeds have germinated, set the plantlets outdoors during the warmest part of the day and bring them in at night for two weeks before transplanting them to their permanent outdoor location. In late summer or fall, sow the seeds in the ground or container ten to 12 weeks before the estimated first fall frost.

PLANT SEEDLINGS. In the ground: Space the plants about 1½ feet apart in full sun. Dig a hole 1 inch deeper than the seedling's container. Add a ½ cup of balanced, organic fertilizer to the soil in the bottom of the hole, and mix well. Slide both plant and potting soil out of the container and put it in the hole, roots down. The top surface of the seedling's potting mix should be 1 inch lower than the ground. Do not bury any leaves. Fill the hole with the soil mix you prepared as needed, and press gently all around the plant to create a shallow basin. Place a cutworm collar around the stem. Now fill the basin with water. Once the water has drained away, spread mulch 3 inches deep around the plant and about 1 inch away from its stem. **In containers:** Use a 5-gallon pot with a drainage hole. Place a small square of window screen over the hole, inside the pot, and add ½ inch of gravel. Fill the pot with the container soil mix you prepared. Follow directions for planting in the ground, except use the container soil mix when additional soil is needed. Be sure to mulch (top-dress).

PROBLEM-SOLVING. Brussels sprouts are as easy to grow as the rest of the cabbage family. They also suffer many of the same maladies. Our best advice? Meet all their nutrient requirements to keep plants growing quickly. Keep the garden weeded and mulched. Place row covers or other protection over the plants as soon as they are in the ground or containers. Do not compost roots or other tissue of cabbage relatives. If your climate allows, it is also best to grow Brussels sprouts in the fall, when there are far fewer pests. In addition, their flavor is improved by frost. Please read the Introduction to avoid trouble in the first place. Also refer to "Change Growing Conditions to Solve Problems" on page 192. If you encounter pests or diseases, consult the Family Problem-Solving Guide on page 124.

Cabbage

Brassica oleracea Capitata Group

Family Problem-Solving Guide, page 124

DESCRIPTION. A biennial grown as an annual. Plants grow 12 to 15 inches tall and 2 to 3 ½ feet wide, depending on the cultivar. For help choosing the right cultivar for your circumstances, see the Appendix.

SEASON. A cool-season crop. Plant in early spring, or, better yet, in late summer to take advantage of the cool fall weather. Where winter daytime temperatures average in the 60s, stagger plantings throughout the year to enjoy cabbage year-round.

TEMPERATURE. Cabbage grows best when daytime temperatures are between 40 and 75°F. Ten or more days of cool temperatures (35 to 45°F) will cause the plants to bolt; excessively hot temperatures (above 75°F) may do the same. Seeds germinate most efficiently when the ambient temperature is 45 to 95°F.

SOIL. Start with well-drained, biologically active soil that is rich in organic matter. To learn how to create such healthy soil, see page 194. Feed twice during the growing season. When you plant the seedlings, add ½ cup of balanced, organic fertilizer to the planting hole. When the main head begins to form, feed again: pull mulch away from each plant, and sprinkle ½ cup of complete, balanced organic fertilizer around it; then replace the mulch. Mulch is particularly important to cabbage, which prefers cool soil temperatures. Best soil pH range is 6 to 7.5. Adding lime to raise the pH to 7.2 helps control clubroot.

LIGHT. Cabbage needs six to 12 hours of direct sun per day. Where daytime temperatures are hot (above 75°F), provide dappled/filtered shade.

WATER. Cabbage thrives with consistent moisture and an average of 1 inch of water per week. Do not let the soil dry out or become waterlogged. Be sure to water the soil, not the foliage.

GARDEN USES AND PLANTING TECHNIQUES. We like cabbage, especially the red varieties, in our flower garden. Its large leaves and coarse texture lend an almost tropical note. Interplant it among dill, nasturtium, rosemary, sage, and thyme to attract beneficial predators. Doing so will save you a lot of work. For additional polyculture benefits, plant it with beets, bush beans, chard, lettuce, and spinach. Do not put cabbage in the same bed or container where it, or any relative, grew within the past three years.

START SEEDS. Begin indoors six to eight weeks before the estimated last spring frost. Once seeds have germinated, set the plantlets outdoors during the warmest part of the day and bring them in at night for two weeks before transplanting them to their permanent outdoor location. In the fall, sow seeds in the ground or container ten to 12 weeks before the estimated first fall frost.

PLANT SEEDLINGS. In the ground: Space plants about 1½ feet apart in full sun. Dig a hole 1 inch deeper than the seedling's container. Add ½ cup of balanced, organic fertilizer to the soil in the bottom of the hole, and mix well. Slide both plant and potting soil out of the container and into the hole, roots down. The top surface of the seedling's potting mix should be 1 inch lower than the ground. Do not bury any leaves. Fill the hole with the soil mix you prepared as needed, and press gently all around the plant to create a shallow basin. Place a cutworm collar around the stem. Now fill the basin with water. Once the water has drained away, spread mulch 3 inches deep around the plant and about 1 inch away from its stem. **In containers:** Use a 5-gallon pot with a drainage hole. Place a small square of window screen over the hole, inside the pot, and add ½ inch of gravel. Fill the pot with the container soil mix you prepared. Follow directions for planting in the ground, except use the container soil mix when additional soil is needed. Be sure to mulch (top-dress).

PROBLEM-SOLVING. Cabbage is fairly easy and very satisfying to grow, but it suffers from many of the pests and diseases that afflict its family. Our best advice? Meet all nutrient requirements to keep plants growing quickly. Keep the garden weeded and mulched. Place row covers or other protection over the plants as soon as they are in the ground or containers. Do not compost roots or other tissue of cabbage relatives. If your climate allows, it is also best to grow cabbage in the fall, when there are far fewer pests. Sometimes despite your best efforts, problems crop up. Please read the Introduction to avoid trouble in the first place. Also refer to "Change Growing Conditions to Solve Problems" on page 192. If you encounter pests or diseases, consult the Family Problem-Solving Guide on page 124.

Carrots

Daucus carota

Family Problem-Solving Guide, page 139

DESCRIPTION. Carrots are biennials, grown as annuals in the garden. For help choosing the right cultivar for your climate and taste, see the Appendix.

SEASON. A cool-season crop. Plant in early spring or late summer.

TEMPERATURE. Carrots thrive when daytime high temperatures are between 60 and 70°F.

SOIL. Start with well-drained, biologically active soil that is rich in organic matter. To learn how to create such healthy soil, see page 194. Rocks or other obstructions cause carrots to distort; soil should be light and loose to avoid this problem. At planting time, add an organic fertilizer or compost with an N-P-K ratio of 1-2-2 to the garden bed or container. These nutrients should last the entire season and will be most accessible if the soil pH is 6 to 6.8. When seedlings are taller than 3 inches, spread at least 3 inches of organic mulch.

LIGHT. Carrots thrive in full sun, so place them where they get six to 12 hours of sunlight every day. If temperatures average above 75°F, carrots appreciate dappled shade.

WATER. This is one of the most important aspects of growing carrots successfully. They want an average of 1 inch of water per week, but if they dry out between waterings they become tough and somewhat bitter. If the soil is waterlogged, they can crack or fork. Vigilance and mulch help ensure consistent moisture, a key to carrot happiness.

GARDEN USES AND PLANTING TECHNIQUES. Carrots are an especially good choice for raised beds and containers, because it is much easier to create the kind of loose soil they like in these circumstances. Plant them with radishes, which germinate more quickly, thus keeping the soil from forming a crust on top. The graceful, ferny foliage of carrots complements many flowers and herbs in the garden or a mixed container. Plant them with violas, calendula, bachelor buttons, California poppies, peas, bush beans, leeks, peppers, and tomatoes.

START SEEDS. Prepare the garden bed with the good soil mix you made. Or, to grow in a container, start with either a 5-gallon pot or a half whiskey barrel. Make sure there is a drainage hole. Place a small square of window screen over the hole, inside the pot, and add ½ inch of gravel. Then fill the pot with the container soil mix you made. Add an organic fertilizer or compost with an N-P-K ratio of 1-2-2 to the garden bed or container. Carrot seeds are very small; the easiest way to sow them is to mix them with a light potting soil, vermiculite, or sifted compost. Sprinkle the seeds where you want them to grow, and then cover with ¼ inch of the light soil mix. If you are growing radishes with your carrots, mix the radish seeds into the seed mix as well. Do not tamp down the soil, but water very gently, taking care not to wash the seeds away. Carrot seeds take three weeks to germinate, so keep an eye out and be patient. Keep the soil moist to encourage germination; this may require daily watering. Harvest the radishes as they germinate to give the carrots room to grow. When the carrots are 1 to 2 inches tall, thin the plantlets so that the strongest shoots are about 2 inches apart. Two weeks later, thin them again to 4 to 6 inches apart, depending on the mature size of the cultivar you selected. Spread at least 3 inches of organic mulch to keep weeds from growing and to maintain consistent soil moisture. Do not transplant carrots.

PROBLEM-SOLVING. Carrots are somewhat finicky about their need for loose soil and consistent moisture, but they are otherwise easy to grow. If you've followed these guidelines, you should have few problems. Observation and prevention are the best medicine for avoiding plant problems. The Introduction will help you skirt trouble in the first place. Also see "Change Growing Conditions to Solve Problems" on page 192. Placing barriers, such as row covers, early on always helps to avoid pest and diseases. However, if you encounter pests or diseases, consult the Family Problem-Solving Guide on page 139.

Cauliflower

Brassica oleracea Botrytis Group

Family Problem-Solving Guide, page 124

DESCRIPTION. A biennial grown as an annual. Plants grow 1½ to 2 feet tall and 2 to 2 ½ feet wide, depending on the cultivar. For help choosing the right cultivar for your circumstances, see the Appendix.

SEASON. A cool-season crop. Plant in early spring, or, better yet, in late summer to take advantage of the cool fall weather. Where winter daytime temperatures average in the 60s, stagger plantings throughout the year to enjoy cauliflower year-round.

TEMPERATURE. Cauliflower grows best when daytime temperatures average 60 to 70°F. Excessively hot temperatures (above 85°F) may cause the plants to bolt or develop leaves inside the heads. Seeds germinate most efficiently when the ambient temperature is 45 to 85°F.

SOIL. Start with well-drained, biologically active soil that is rich in organic matter. To learn how to create such healthy soil, see page 194. Feed twice during the growing season. When you plant the seedlings, add ½ cup of balanced, organic fertilizer to the planting hole. When the main head begins to form, feed again: pull mulch away from each plant, and sprinkle ½ cup of complete, balanced organic fertilizer around it; then replace the mulch. Mulch is particularly important to cauliflower, which prefers cool soil temperatures. Best soil pH range is 6 to 7.5. Adding lime to raise the pH to 7.2 helps control clubroot.

LIGHT. Cauliflower needs six to 12 hours of direct sun per day. Where daytime temperatures are hot (above 75°F), provide dappled/filtered shade.

WATER. Cauliflower thrives with consistent moisture and an average of 1 inch of water per week. Do not let the soil dry out or become waterlogged. Be sure to water the soil, not the foliage.

GARDEN USES AND PLANTING TECHNIQUES. Cauliflower needs quite a bit of room but still works well in a polyculture garden. Plant it with beets, bush beans, chard, lettuce, and spinach. Interplant it among dill, nasturtium, rosemary, lavender, sage, and thyme to attract beneficial predators. This practice saves you a lot of work. Do not put cauliflower in the same bed or container where it, or any relative, grew within the past three years.

START SEEDS. Begin indoors six to eight weeks before the estimated last spring frost. Once seeds have germinated, set the plantlets outdoors during the warmest part of the day and bring them in at night for two weeks before transplanting them to their permanent outdoor location. In the fall, sow seeds in the ground or container ten to 12 weeks before the estimated first fall frost.

PLANT SEEDLINGS. In the ground: Space plants about 1½ feet apart in full sun. Dig a hole 1 inch deeper than the seedling's container. Add ½ cup of balanced, organic fertilizer to the soil in the bottom of the hole, and mix well. Slide both plant and potting soil out of the container and into the hole, roots down. The top surface of the seedling's potting mix should be 1 inch lower than the ground. Do not bury any leaves. Fill the hole with the soil mix you prepared as needed, and press gently all around the plant to create a shallow basin. Place a cutworm collar around the stem. Now fill the basin with water. Once the water has drained away, spread mulch 3 inches deep around the plant and about 1 inch away from its stem. **In containers:** Use a 5-gallon pot with a drainage hole. Place a small square of window screen over the hole, inside the pot, and add ½ inch of gravel. Fill the pot with the container soil mix you prepared. Follow directions for planting in the ground, except use the container soil mix when additional soil is needed. Be sure to mulch (top-dress).

PROBLEM-SOLVING. Cauliflower is relatively easy and satisfying to grow, but it is vulnerable to many of the maladies that plague the cabbage family. Our best advice? Meet all its nutrient requirements to keep plants growing quickly. Keep the garden weeded and mulched. Place row covers or other protection over the plants as soon as they are in the ground or containers. Do not compost roots or other tissue of any cabbage relative. If your climate allows, it is also best to grow cauliflower in the fall: there are far fewer pests then, and cauliflower's tendency to bolt in hot weather can be avoided. We have found that deer love cauliflower, and they seem to know exactly when it is ready to harvest; protect your crop from deer, if you can. Please read the Introduction to avoid trouble in the first place. Also refer to "Change Growing Conditions to Solve Problems" on page 192. If you encounter pests or diseases, consult the Family Problem-Solving Guide on page 124.

Chard

Beta vulgaris subsp. *cicla*

Family Problem-Solving Guide, page 134

DESCRIPTION. Chard (aka Swiss chard) is another biennial grown as an annual. It grows to 1½ feet tall and wide. Some varieties have white stalks. Others are multi-colored. For help choosing a good cultivar, see the Appendix.

SEASON. A cool-season crop. Plant in early spring for best performance, or in late summer if you live where summers are hot (regularly above 75°F) but winters are mild (average daytime temperatures in the 60s).

TEMPERATURE. Chard prefers daytime high temperatures of 60 to 65°F. Once the weather turns hot (above 75°F), it languishes. It tolerates freezing, but if temperatures drop below 50°F for three weeks, plants will bolt and produce seeds. Seeds germinate most efficiently when the ambient temperature is 70°F.

SOIL. Start with well-drained, biologically active soil that is rich in organic matter. To learn how to create such healthy soil, see page 194. Feed with a complete, balanced organic fertilizer, composted manure, and/or compost at the beginning of each growing season. These amendments should last the entire season. Best soil pH range is 6.2 to 7. If pH is not within this range, chard can suffer from boron deficiency.

LIGHT. Plant in full sun (six to 12 hours daily) or light, dappled shade.

WATER. Chard needs 1 inch of water each week. Apply water to the root zone, not the foliage, and maintain consistent moisture.

GARDEN USES AND PLANTING TECHNIQUES.
Healthy chard leaves, with their brightly colored stalks, are an attractive addition to an ornamental garden. If you add annuals to your perennial garden bed, be sure to include chard. In the vegetable bed, it does well in a polyculture mix with scallions, peas, and members of the cabbage family. Choose 'Bright Lights' or some other "rainbow" cultivar with red, orange, or yellow stalks for containers, and plant them with other small vegetables and flowers such as lettuce and violas.

START SEEDS. To jumpstart the germination process, soak seeds for an hour before planting. Two weeks before the anticipated last spring frost, plant seeds directly in the ground or in an outdoor container. Space the seeds 1 inch apart, and cover with ½ inch of your prepared soil mix. When the seedlings are 2 to 3 inches tall, thin them so that the strong healthy ones remain 4 to 6 inches apart. Enjoy the tender, edible shoots in your next salad. Spread at least 3 inches of mulch around the seedlings. You can also plant seeds four to eight weeks before the anticipated first fall frost, using the techniques just described.

PLANT SEEDLINGS. In the ground: Space plants about 6 inches apart in full sun for best performance. Dig a hole the same height and depth as the seedling's container. Slide both plant and potting soil out of the pot and into the hole, roots down. The top surface of the plant's potting mix should be at the same level as the ground. Do not bury any leaves. Fill the hole with additional soil mix as needed, press gently all around the plant to create a shallow basin, and fill it with water. Once the water has drained away, spread mulch 3 inches deep around the plant and about 1 inch away from its stem.

In containers: For an individual chard plant, use at least a one-gallon pot. If you want to plant chard with other vegetables, use either a 5-gallon pot or a half whiskey barrel. Make sure there is a drainage hole. Place a small square of window screen over the hole, inside the pot, and add ½ inch of gravel. Fill the pot with the container soil mix you prepared. Follow directions for planting in the ground, except use the container soil mix when additional soil is needed. Be sure to mulch (top-dress).

PROBLEM-SOLVING. Chard rarely has problems. It is easy to grow, and the colorful varieties work well in any garden. Nevertheless, there is a surprisingly long list of problems that occasionally appear. Please read the Introduction to avoid trouble in the first place. Also refer to "Change Growing Conditions to Solve Problems" on page 192. If you encounter pests or diseases, consult the Family Problem-Solving Guide on page 134.

Chicory and radicchio

Cichorium intybus

Family Problem-Solving Guide, page 118

(top) Radicchio. (bottom) Belgian endive.

DESCRIPTION. Both plants, as well as Belgian endive, French endive, and Witloof chicory, are perennials. Chicory grows 12 to 15 inches tall and 24 to 40 inches wide, depending on the cultivar. Radicchio grows 6 inches tall and wide. For help choosing the right cultivar for your circumstances, see the Appendix.

SEASON. Both are cool-season crops. Plant in early spring, or, better yet, in late summer to take advantage of the cool fall weather. Where winter daytime temperatures average in the 60s, stagger plantings throughout the year to enjoy chicory and radicchio year-round.

TEMPERATURE. Chicory and radicchio grow best when daytime temperatures are between 40 and 75°F. Ten or more days of cool temperatures (35 to 45°F) or excessively hot temperatures (above 75°F) will cause plants to bolt. Seeds germinate most efficiently when the ambient temperature is 45 to 95°F.

SOIL. Start with well-drained, biologically active soil that is rich in organic matter. To learn how to create such healthy soil, see page 194. Feed twice during the growing season. When you plant the seedlings, add ½ cup of a balanced, organic fertilizer to the planting hole. When the main head begins to form, feed again: pull mulch away from each plant, and sprinkle ½ cup of complete, balanced organic fertilizer around it; then replace the mulch. Mulch is particularly important to both plants, both of which prefer cool soil temperatures. Best soil pH range is 6 to 7.5.

LIGHT. Chicory and radicchio need six to 12 hours of direct sun per day. Where daytime temperatures are hot (above 75°F), provide dappled/filtered shade.

WATER. Chicory and radicchio thrive with consistent moisture and an average of 1 inch of water per week. Do not let the soil dry out or become waterlogged. Be sure to water the soil, not the foliage.

GARDEN USES AND PLANTING TECHNIQUES. These perennials, especially the red varieties of radicchio, are particularly attractive in the flower garden. Chicory flowers make a lovely addition to a cottage garden. Interplant them among catmint, fennel, dill, nasturtium, rosemary, sage, and thyme to attract beneficial predators. This practice saves you a lot of work. For additional polyculture benefits, mix in some scallions, beets, bush beans, chard, onions, and spinach. Do not put chicory or radicchio in the same bed or container where it, or any relative, grew within the past three years.

START SEEDS. Begin indoors six to eight weeks before the estimated last spring frost. Once seeds have germinated, set the plantlets outdoors during the warmest part of the day and bring them in at night for two weeks before transplanting them to their permanent outdoor location. In the fall, sow seeds in the ground or container ten to 12 weeks before the estimated first fall frost.

PLANT SEEDLINGS. In the ground: Space plants about 1½ feet apart in full sun. Dig a hole 1 inch deeper than the seedling's container. Add ½ cup of balanced, organic fertilizer to the soil in the bottom of the hole, and mix well. Slide both plant and potting soil out of the container and into the hole, roots down. The top surface of the seedling's potting mix should be 1 inch lower than the ground. Do not bury any leaves. Fill the hole with the soil mix you prepared as needed, press gently all around the plant to create a shallow basin, and fill it with water. Once the water has drained away, spread mulch 3 inches deep around the plant and about 1 inch away from its stem. **In containers:** Use a 5-gallon pot with a drainage hole. Place a small square of window screen over the hole, inside the pot, and add ½ inch of gravel. Fill the pot with the container soil mix you prepared. Follow directions for planting in the ground, except use the container soil mix when additional soil is needed. Be sure to mulch (top-dress).

PROBLEM-SOLVING. Both chicory and radicchio, although very easy and satisfying to grow, suffer from many of the maladies that afflict lettuce and other members of the daisy family. Our best advice? Keep the garden weeded and mulched, and, if your climate allows, grow these veggies in the fall, when there are far fewer pests. Please read the Introduction to avoid trouble in the first place. Also refer to "Change Growing Conditions to Solve Problems" on page 192. If you encounter pests or diseases, consult the Family Problem-Solving Guide on page 118.

Chinese cabbage

Brassica rapa Pekinensis Group

Family Problem-Solving Guide, page 124

DESCRIPTION. Chinese cabbage (aka napa, michihili) is a biennial grown as an annual. Plants grow 6 to 24 inches tall and 12 inches wide, depending on the cultivar. For help choosing the cultivar that works best for you, see the Appendix.

SEASON. A cool-season crop. Plant in early spring for an early summer harvest, or in early fall for an early winter harvest. If you live where winter daytime temperatures average in the 60s, Chinese cabbage is a great winter vegetable.

TEMPERATURE. Chinese cabbage does best when daytime high temperatures are between 55 and 70°F. When daytime highs average above 75°F or below 55°F, plants often bolt, and above 75°F, the leaf tips may burn. Seeds germinate best when the ambient temperature is 50 to 80°F.

SOIL. Start with well-drained, biologically active soil that is rich in organic matter. To learn how to create such healthy soil, see page 194. At the beginning of the growing season, add organic compost or fertilizer that is slightly higher in nitrogen (N) than it is in phosphorus (P) or potassium (K). Use a fertilizer with a ratio of 10-7-7 or something similar, or add extra nitrogen (in the form of chicken manure, for instance) to a balanced fertilizer or compost. The higher nitrogen helps plants grow quickly and produce tastier leaves. Add a dose of this fertilizer again about two to three weeks after sowing, at the time you thin the seedlings. Best soil pH range is 6 to 7.5.

LIGHT. When temperatures are moderate, as Chinese cabbage prefers, it needs six to 12 hours of direct sun per day. Where daytime temperatures are hot (above 75°F), provide dappled/filtered shade. Chinese cabbage is sensitive to light periods; long days (16 hours or more of daylight every day for a month) cause plants to flower and the leaves to become bitter.

WATER. Chinese cabbage likes consistent moisture and an average of 1 inch of water per week. Do not let the soil dry out or become waterlogged. Remember to water the soil, not the foliage.

GARDEN USES AND PLANTING TECHNIQUES. With its attractive foliage, Chinese cabbage works very well scattered through an ornamental garden or in a container mix of annual flowers. It is most appropriate with other low- to medium-growing flowers and spring bulbs; sow a small amount of seeds in a small patch among plants that require similar growing conditions. Reap polyculture benefits by planting it among violas, marigolds, bachelor buttons, calendula, lettuce, scallions, and radishes. Do not put Chinese cabbage in the same bed or container where it, or any relative, grew in the past three years.

START SEEDS. Because Chinese cabbage is prone to transplant shock, it is best to sow seeds directly where you want plants to grow. Prepare the garden bed with the good soil mix you made. Or, to grow in a container, start with a one-gallon pot with a drainage hole. Place a small square of window screen over the hole, inside the pot, and add ½ inch of gravel. Then fill the pot with the container soil mix you made. After the last spring frost, sow seeds about 2 inches apart and ¼ to ½ inch deep. Water immediately and keep the soil moist but not soggy until the seeds germinate, which should occur in four to seven days. As the seedlings appear, thin them to 4 to 8 inches apart, further if you chose a large cultivar. After thinning, mulch 1 to 3 inches deep, depending on the height of the plants, to control weeds and to retain consistent soil moisture.

PROBLEM-SOLVING. Chinese cabbage is quite easy to grow, so providing the right growing conditions is not a challenge. However, as a cabbage, it can develop some of the many problems that plague that family. Close observation will help nip these in the bud. Please read the Introduction to avoid trouble in the first place. Have a look at "Change Growing Conditions to Solve Problems" on page 192. If you encounter pests or diseases, consult the Family Problem-Solving Guide on page 124.

Corn

Zea mays

Family Problem-Solving Guide, page 143

DESCRIPTION. Corn (aka sweet corn, maize, popcorn) is a frost-sensitive tropical grass that grows 8 to 10 feet tall or more.

SEASON. A warm-season crop. Plant in late spring or early summer after all danger of frost is past. Days to maturity are 55 to 110, depending on the cultivar. For help choosing the right cultivar for your climate and taste, see the Appendix.

TEMPERATURE. Corn thrives where summer daytime high temperatures average 60 to 75°F and the soil temperature is 60°F. Seeds planted in soil that is too cool generally fail to germinate and rot, so wait to plant until the soil is warm enough. Make sure your summer planting allows enough time for the ears to mature before the first frost of autumn. Corn is killed by frost.

SOIL. Start with well-drained, biologically active soil that is rich in organic matter. To learn how to create such healthy soil, see page 194. Feed with a complete, balanced organic fertilizer and compost at the beginning of each growing season. Feed with additional organic fertilizer when the plants are 1 foot tall and again when they are 2 feet tall. Gently rake the nutrients into the soil around the plants. Corn is shallow-rooted, so do your raking and hoeing carefully to avoid damaging its root system. Control weeds and conserve moisture by spreading mulch to a depth of 3 inches when plants are a foot tall and after applying fertilizer.

LIGHT. Corn needs full sun (six to 12 hours daily) to do its best.

WATER. Corn requires regular water. Give it 1 inch per week, watering the root zone, not the foliage. The planting site must be well drained; use raised beds or large containers if your drainage is poor or the water table is high.

GARDEN USES AND PLANTING TECHNIQUES. Because of its size, corn provides a shaded microhabitat on its north side; annuals that appreciate midsummer shade will thrive there. In the polyculture garden, sow a few seeds in a small patch among plants that require similar growing conditions. Corn plays especially well with squash and beans. Indigenous peoples of Central America and Mexico developed this famous plant guild, and this technique spread throughout North America, where it became known as the "Three Sisters."

START SEEDS. Because corn seedlings are susceptible to transplant shock, the best planting technique is to sow seeds directly where you want plants to grow. Prepare the garden bed with the good soil mix you made. Or, to grow dwarf cultivars in a container, start with a half whiskey barrel. Make sure there is a drainage hole. Place a small square of window screen over the hole, inside the pot, and add ½ inch of gravel. Then fill the pot with the container soil mix you made. After the last spring frost, water the soil (either in the garden or in the container) thoroughly before sowing. Be sure the soil is loose. Sow the seeds 12 to 18 inches apart and 1 to 2 inches deep. Corn is wind-pollinated, so avoid planting it in long, skinny rows. Plants that are in a block of short rows will pollinate each other more efficiently, and you'll get a much better crop. In a container, plant them in a circle. Seeds should germinate in four to seven days. Sow small amounts of seed every two or three weeks for a continuous harvest.

PROBLEM-SOLVING. There's just about nothing better than freshly picked corn, and it is generally prolific and easy to grow. It is not without problems, however. Close observation will help nip these in the bud. Please read the Introduction to avoid trouble in the first place. "Change Growing Conditions to Solve Problems" on page 192 will guide you through any necessary adjustments. If you encounter pests or diseases, consult the Family Problem-Solving Guide on page 143.

Cucumbers

Cucumis sativus

Family Problem-Solving Guide, page 149

DESCRIPTION. Plants are frost-sensitive, herbaceous, annual vines with tendrils. Cucumber vines grow big, sprawling over 25 square feet; they can climb a 6-foot trellis or crawl across the ground. Compact bush types, which do well in containers, are also available. For help choosing the right cultivar for your circumstances, see the Appendix. Each plant makes male (pollen-bearing) and female (fruit-bearing) flowers. The first flowers will always be male and cannot produce fruit. Be patient. As the plant gets a little older, it will make female flowers and produce a generous crop of fruit after the bees have done their job.

SEASON. A warm-season crop. Plant in late spring or early summer after all danger of frost is past.

TEMPERATURE. Cucumbers thrive where summer daytime high temperatures average 65 to 75°F and the soil temperature is at least 60°F. Seeds planted in soil that is too cool generally fail to germinate and rot, so wait to plant until the soil is warm enough. Make sure your summer planting allows enough time for plants to mature before the first frost of autumn. Frost kills cucumbers.

SOIL. Start with well-drained, biologically active soil that is rich in organic matter. To learn how to create such healthy soil, see page 194. Feed with a complete, balanced organic fertilizer and compost at the beginning of each growing season. Avoid high-nitrogen fertilizers, as cucumbers will respond with lush vegetative growth and few flowers and fruits. Feed them additional organic fertilizer during the growing season, gently raking the nutrients into the soil around the plants. Control weeds, conserve moisture, and protect fruit lying on the ground by mulching to a depth of 3 inches once plants are growing well. Maintain a pH of 6 to 6.5.

LIGHT. Cucumbers need full sun (six to 12 hours daily) to do their best.

WATER. Cucumbers require regular water. Give them 1 inch per week, watering the root zone, not the foliage. Increase the amount of water to as much as 2 inches a week when the vines support a heavy fruit crop. The planting site must be well drained; use raised beds or large containers if your drainage is poor or the water table is high.

GARDEN USES AND PLANTING TECHNIQUES. Prepare the structure cucumber vines are going to climb before you plant seeds. You can use twine, tripods of bamboo, limbs of trees arranged in a teepee fashion, or you can grow them on a net or trellis. These support structures offer a shaded microhabitat on their north side, and annuals that appreciate midsummer shade will thrive there. Since they can be very large, using cucumbers in an ornamental garden can be problematic; however, they look very nice growing along a fence and can provide summertime privacy for your garden. In the polyculture garden, sow a few seeds in a small patch among other warm-season vegetables, herbs, and flowers. Good choices include beans, tomatoes, corn, okra, fennel, rosemary, sunflowers, and echinacea.

START SEEDS. Because cucumber seedlings are prone to transplant shock, it is best to sow seeds directly where you want the vines to grow. Prepare the garden bed with the good soil mix you made. Or, to grow in a container, start with either a 5-gal-lon pot or a half whiskey barrel. Make sure there is a drainage hole. Place a small square of window screen over the hole, inside the pot, and add ½ inch of gravel. Then fill the pot with the container soil mix you made. After the last spring frost, water the soil (either in the garden or in the container) thoroughly before sowing. Be sure the soil is loose. Sow the seeds about 1 inch deep. Put two or three seeds in each hole, and space the planting holes 1 to 2 feet apart. Alternatively, plant two or three seeds in each container you have prepared. Seeds should germinate in four to seven days. Thin to one robust seedling per planting hole.

PROBLEM-SOLVING. Cucumbers are easy to grow, and we doubt you will encounter serious problems. As members of the squash family, they do share some of the family weaknesses, but if you spend time with your plants and keep a watchful eye, you can nip problems in the bud. Please read the Introduction to avoid trouble in the first place, as well as "Change Growing Conditions to Solve Problems" on page 192. If you encounter pests or diseases, consult the Family Problem-Solving Guide on page 149.

Eggplant

Solanum melongena

Family Problem-Solving Guide, page 157

DESCRIPTION. Eggplants (aka aubergine, brinjal) are bushy annuals usually grown as freestanding shrubby plants, 2 to 3 feet tall and 3 to 4 feet wide. For help choosing the right cultivar for your circumstances, see the Appendix.

SEASON. A warm-season crop. Plant in late spring or early summer after all danger of frost is past.

TEMPERATURE. Eggplants thrive where summer daytime high temperatures average 70 to 85°F and the soil temperature is at least 75°F. Seeds planted in soil that is too cool generally fail to germinate and rot, so wait until the soil is warm enough. Seeds germinate most efficiently when the ambient temperature is 70 to 90°F. Make sure your summer planting allows enough time for the fruit to mature before the first frost of autumn. Check the days to maturity on the cultivar label to be sure. Frost kills eggplants.

SOIL. Start with well-drained, biologically active soil that is rich in organic matter. To learn how to create such healthy soil, see page 194. Feed with a complete, balanced organic fertilizer and compost at the beginning of each growing season. Feed eggplants additional organic fertilizer during the growing season, gently raking the nutrients into the soil around the plants. Control weeds, conserve moisture, and protect fruit close to the ground by spreading mulch to a depth of 3 inches after plants are growing well. Maintain a slightly acid soil pH of 5.5 to 6.5.

LIGHT. Eggplants need full sun (six to 12 hours daily) to do their best.

WATER. Eggplants require a steady supply of moisture, not too dry and not too wet, to maintain their sweet, mild flavor. Give them 1 inch of water per week, watering the root zone, not the foliage. Avoid irregular watering, where conditions bounce back and forth between extremely dry and extremely wet. The planting site must be well drained; use raised beds or large containers if your drainage is poor or the water table is high.

GARDEN USES AND PLANTING TECHNIQUES. Eggplant foliage is often a bit bedraggled and full of holes, courtesy of flea beetles. As a result, eggplants are not always beautiful additions to the flower or container garden. They grow well in combination with beans and peppers, and always benefit from being interplanted with marigolds and other flowers in the daisy, carrot, and mint families. Plants in these families attract beneficial predators. In the polyculture garden, sow a few seeds in a small patch among plants that require similar growing conditions. Do not put eggplants in the same bed or container where they, or any relative, grew within the past three years.

START SEEDS. Indoors: Begin six to eight weeks before the estimated last spring frost. Set the plantlets outdoors during the warmest part of the day and bring them in at night for two weeks before transplanting them to their permanent outdoor location. Plant them outdoors after all danger of frost is past. **Outdoors:** Prepare the garden bed with the good soil mix you made. Or, to grow in a container, select a compact variety and start with either a 5-gallon pot or a half whiskey barrel. Make sure there is a drainage hole. Place a small square of window screen over the hole, inside the pot, and add ½ inch of gravel. Then fill the pot with the container soil mix you made. After the last spring frost, water the soil (either in the garden or in the container) thoroughly before sowing. Be sure the soil is loose. Sow the seeds about ¼ inch deep. Poke a hole in the soil with your finger or a stick, and put two or three seeds in the hole. In a garden bed, space the planting holes 2 feet apart, with 3 to 4 feet between rows. Seeds should germinate in five to ten days in warm soil. Thin to one robust seedling per planting hole.

PLANT SEEDLINGS. Prepare the garden bed or container following the instructions for starting seeds. Eggplants don't generally need a support. Choose a location in full sun. Space the plants 2 feet apart, with 3 to 4 feet between rows. Dig a hole 1 inch deeper than the seedling's container. Add ½ cup of balanced, organic fertilizer to the soil in the bottom of the hole, and mix well. Slide both plant and potting soil out of the container and into the hole, roots down. The top surface of the seedling's potting mix should be 1 inch lower than the ground. Do not bury any leaves. Fill the hole with the soil mix you prepared as needed, and press gently all around the plant to create a shallow basin. Place a cutworm collar around the stem. Now fill the basin with water. Once the water has drained away, spread mulch 3 inches deep around the plant and about 1 inch away from its stem.

PROBLEM-SOLVING. Except for their problems with flea beetles, eggplants are pretty easy to grow, and suffer from fewer problems than their cousin the tomato. Place row covers over the plants to keep pests at bay. Otherwise, you should not encounter serious problems, but sometimes, despite your best efforts, they do crop up. Please read the Introduction to avoid trouble in the first place, and have a look at "Change Growing Conditions to Solve Problems" on page 192. If you encounter pests or diseases, consult the Family Problem-Solving Guide on page 157.

Endive and escarole

Cichorium endivia

Family Problem-Solving Guide, page 118

(top) Escarole. **(bottom)** Endive.

DESCRIPTION. Endive and escarole are annuals that grow 12 to 15 inches tall and wide. Endive has curly narrow leaves. Escarole's are broader. For help selecting the cultivar that works for you, see the Appendix.

SEASON. Both are cool-season crops. Plant in early spring. You can also plant in late summer to take advantage of cool autumn weather. Where winter daytime temperatures average in the 60s, stagger plantings throughout the year to enjoy these leafy greens year-round.

TEMPERATURE. Endive and escarole grow best when daytime temperatures average 60 to 65°F. When temperatures exceed 75°F, plants tend to bolt. Escarole tolerates slightly colder temperatures, but if temperatures go below freezing for a day or two, endive does not survive. Seeds germinate most efficiently when the ambient temperature is 40 to 80°F.

SOIL. Start with well-drained, biologically active soil that is rich in organic matter. To learn how to create such healthy soil, see page 194. Feed twice during the growing season. When you plant seedlings, add ½ cup of balanced, organic fertilizer to the planting hole. After one month, feed again: pull mulch away from each plant, and sprinkle ½ cup of the organic fertilizer around it; then replace the mulch. Mulch is particularly important to endive and escarole, both of which prefer cool soil temperatures. Best soil pH range is 6 to 7.5.

LIGHT. Endive and escarole need six to 12 hours of direct sun per day. Where daytime temperatures are hot (above 75°F), provide dappled/filtered shade.

WATER. Endive and escarole thrive with consistent moisture and an average of 1 inch of water per week. Do not let the soil dry out or become waterlogged. Be sure to water the soil, not the foliage.

GARDEN USES AND PLANTING TECHNIQUES. Both endive and escarole make attractive additions to the flower garden. Interplant them with dill, nasturtium, rosemary, sage, and thyme to attract beneficial predators, thus saving yourself a lot of work. For additional polyculture benefits, try planting them with carrots, cucumber, onions, beets, and pole beans. Do not put endive or escarole in the same bed or container where it, or any relative, grew within the past three years.

START SEEDS. Begin indoors eight to ten weeks before the estimated last spring frost. Once seeds have germinated, set the plantlets outdoors during the warmest part of the day and bring them in at night for two weeks before transplanting them to their permanent outdoor location. In spring, sow seeds in the ground four to six weeks before the average date of the last spring frost. In the fall, sow seeds in the ground or container ten to 12 weeks before the estimated first fall frost.

PLANT SEEDLINGS. In the ground: Space plants about 12 inches apart in full sun. Dig a hole 1 inch deeper than the seedling's container. Add ½ cup of balanced, organic fertilizer to the soil in the bottom of the hole, and mix well. Slide both plant and potting soil out of the container and into the hole, roots down. The top surface of the seedling's potting mix should be 1 inch lower than the ground. Do not bury any leaves. Fill the hole with the soil mix you prepared as needed, press gently all around the plant to create a shallow basin, and fill it with water. Once the water has drained away, spread mulch 3 inches deep around the plant and about 1 inch away from its stem. **In containers:** Use a wide pot that is at least 6 inches deep. Make sure there is a drainage hole. Place a small square of window screen over the hole, inside the pot, and add ½ inch of gravel. Fill the pot with the container soil mix you prepared. Follow directions for planting in the ground, except use the container soil mix when additional soil is needed. Be sure to mulch (top-dress).

ADDITIONAL TECHNIQUES. Some people use blanching to counteract the occasional bitterness of endive and escarole. To blanch in this context means to keep a plant in the shade. The easiest way to blanch a plant is to put some kind of container over it two weeks before you harvest. The container can be a pot, a milk carton—anything that accommodates the foliage and provides shade.

PROBLEM-SOLVING. Endive and escarole are easy and satisfying to grow, but they suffer from many of the maladies that afflict the daisy family. Our best advice is to meet all the nutrient requirements to keep plants growing quickly; and keep the garden weeded and mulched. If your climate allows, it is also best to grow them in the fall, when there are far fewer pests. Please read the Introduction to avoid trouble in the first place. Also read "Change Growing Conditions to Solve Problems" on page 192. If you encounter pests or diseases, consult the Family Problem-Solving Guide on page 118.

Fava beans

Vicia faba

Family Problem-Solving Guide, page 167

DESCRIPTION. Fava beans (aka broad beans, horse beans) are herbaceous, bushy annuals in the pea family. They grow 2 to 4 feet tall and wide and are self-supporting. For help choosing the right cultivar for your circumstances, see the Appendix.

SEASON. A cool-season crop. Plant in early spring, as soon as the soil can be worked. The crop matures in 120 to 150 days. In other words, they require a long, cool growing season.

TEMPERATURE. Fava beans thrive where daytime high temperatures average 60 to 65°F. They can tolerate cold temperatures down to 15°F and are a good winter crop in many areas. Plant in summer for a fall crop. Pay attention to the number of days to maturity listed on the label.

SOIL. Start with well-drained, biologically active soil that is rich in organic matter. To learn how to create such healthy soil, see page 194. Feed with a complete, balanced organic fertilizer and compost at the beginning of each growing season. Avoid high-nitrogen fertilizers, as fava beans will respond with lush vegetative growth and few flowers and fruits, aka pods. Feed them an additional ½ cup of organic fertilizer during the growing season, gently raking the nutrients into the soil around the plants. Like all beans, fava beans are shallow-rooted, so do your raking and hoeing carefully to avoid damaging their root system. Control weeds and conserve moisture by spreading mulch to a depth of 3 inches after the plants are a foot tall.

LIGHT. Fava beans need full sun (six to 12 hours daily) to do their best.

WATER. Fava beans require regular water. Give them 1 inch per week, by watering the root zone, not the foliage. The planting site must be well drained. Use raised beds or large containers if your drainage is poor or the water table is high.

GARDEN USES AND PLANTING TECHNIQUES. Fava beans become lovely small shrubs as they grow up. We love them in the mixed border, where annuals with similar needs do well. Sow a few seeds in a small patch among such plants. For additional polyculture benefits, plant them with other annuals that attract beneficial predators. Herbs in the mint family (thyme, rosemary, catnip, sage, and mint itself) and in the carrot family (dill, fennel, coriander, parsley) make good choices. And don't forget flowers and vegetables in the daisy family. Shallow-rooted fava beans grow well with deep-rooted vegetables like carrots and beets. Because fava beans are cool-season, they are not useful in the bean, squash, corn triumvirate.

START SEEDS. Fava bean seedlings are prone to transplant shock, so it is best to sow seeds directly where you want plants to grow. Prepare the garden bed with the good soil mix you made. Or, to grow in a container, start with either a 5-gallon pot or a half whiskey barrel. Make sure there is a drainage hole. Place a small square of window screen over the hole, inside the pot, and add ½ inch of gravel. Then fill the pot with the container soil mix you made. Water the soil (either in the garden or in the container) thoroughly before sowing. Be sure the soil is loose. Sow the seeds 4 to 5 inches apart and about 1 inch deep. Thin seedlings to 8 to 10 inches apart. In a container, plant them in a circle. Seeds should germinate in four to seven days.

ADDITIONAL TECHNIQUES. You'll have better success with your beans if your seeds are inoculated with nitrogen-fixing bacteria. You can buy seeds that are already inoculated, or you can buy some inoculum and do it yourself, just before sowing, following instructions on the package. The bacteria and the bean plant form a symbiosis. The bacteria take nitrogen out of the air and feed it to the bean, while the bean makes carbohydrate and feeds it to the bacteria. Thus, fava beans create their own nitrogen fertilizer out of the air.

PROBLEM-SOLVING. As always, close observation will help you nip problems in the bud. If you use the guidelines just given, you should have few problems and plenty of delicious fava beans come harvest time. Please read the Introduction to avoid trouble in the first place. Also see "Change Growing Conditions to Solve Problems" on page 192. If you encounter pests or diseases, consult the Family Problem-Solving Guide on page 167.

Garlic
Allium sativum

Family Problem-Solving Guide, page 175

DESCRIPTION. Garlic is a bulb-forming perennial that is grown as an annual. You can easily save a few garlic bulbs every year and plant some cloves for an annual crop. Choose the best cultivar for your climate and taste. For help, see the Appendix.

SEASON. A cool-season crop. Garlic grows best when planted in autumn, about the same time you would plant tulips and daffodils. It can be planted in early spring but will frequently produce smaller bulbs, especially where summers are hot and dry.

TEMPERATURE. Garlic prefers daytime high temperatures between 55 and 75°F. Once the weather turns hot (above 75°F), garlic stops growing, the bulbs mature, and plants go dormant. Fall-planted garlic tolerates light freezing over the winter, but plan to protect the crop with mulch where winters are severe (below 28°F, for a week or more).

SOIL. Start with well-drained, biologically active soil that is rich in organic matter. To learn how to create such healthy soil, see page 194. At planting time, add 1 cup of bone meal to every 2 gallons of the soil mix you prepared. Add a complete, balanced organic fertilizer, composted manure, and/or compost to the garden bed at the beginning of each growing season. These amendments should last the entire season. Do not give garlic more fertilizer during the growing season because it can prevent proper maturation of the bulbs. Take care to remove lumps and rocks; the soil should be loose to give the garlic bulbs room to develop. Spread 3 inches of mulch over the ground after planting. Garlic tolerates a wide pH range, from 4.5 (acid) to 8.3 (alkaline).

LIGHT. Plant in six to 12 hours of direct sun per day.

WATER. Garlic requires 1 inch of water each week. Apply water to the root zone, not the foliage, and maintain consistent moisture. When the tips of the leaves start to turn yellow in summer, stop watering and let the plants dry out, so the bulbs will mature properly.

GARDEN USES AND PLANTING TECHNIQUES. Healthy garlic leaves add an interesting vertical element to an ornamental garden. Garlic also helps keep pests at bay. Plant it around the base of roses and other ornamental shrubs to encourage deer to move along, because they don't like the smell. If you add annuals to your perennial bed, be sure to include some garlic. Keep in mind, however, that the bulb needs room to develop. In the vegetable bed they do well in a polyculture mix with cabbage relatives, beets and chard, tomatoes, chamomile, and strawberries. Garlic is extremely useful in many cuisines, and garlic braids make wonderful gifts.

PLANT CLOVES. In the ground: Break the bulbs apart and plant individual cloves of garlic directly in the ground in October or November. Dig a wide, shallow hole or a long, shallow trench into your enriched garden soil. Put 1 cup of bone meal into the hole or trench and mix it with the soil in the bottom. Now refill the hole or trench with the good garden soil you prepared. Poke holes in the soil with your finger 1 to 2 inches deep and about 3 inches apart. Slide the garlic cloves into the holes, pointed end up. Press gently and spread mulch 3 inches deep over the area. **In containers:** Use at least a one-gallon pot for up to three individual garlic plants. If you want to plant garlic with other vegetables, use either a 5-gallon pot or a half whiskey barrel. Either one is large enough to accommodate several garlic plants, as well as the other vegetables. Whichever pot you choose, make sure there is a drainage hole. Place a small square of window screen over the hole, inside the pot, and add ½ inch of gravel. Fill the pot with the container soil mix you prepared. Follow directions for planting in the ground, except use the container soil mix when additional soil is needed. Be sure to mulch (top-dress).

PROBLEM-SOLVING. Garlic is really fun to grow and relatively pest- and disease-free. Nevertheless, there is a surprisingly long list of problems that occasionally appear. Please read the Introduction to avoid trouble in the first place. Also have a look at "Change Growing Conditions to Solve Problems" on page 192. If you encounter pests or diseases, consult the Family Problem-Solving Guide on page 175.

Green beans

Phaseolus vulgaris

Family Problem-Solving Guide, page 167

DESCRIPTION. Green beans (aka string beans, wax beans, snap beans, pole beans, bush beans, shellie beans, dry beans) are frost-sensitive, herbaceous, annual twining vines (pole beans) or low-growing bushes. Pole beans grow 8 to 10 feet tall or more and require a support to climb on. Bush beans grow less than 2 feet tall and wide and are self-supporting. It is important to choose the right cultivar for your climate and taste. For help, see the Appendix.

SEASON. A warm-season crop. Plant in late spring or early summer after all danger of frost is past.

TEMPERATURE. Beans thrive where summer daytime high temperatures average 70 to 80°F and the soil temperature is 60 to 70°F. Seeds planted in soil that is too cool generally fail to germinate and rot, so wait until the soil is warm enough before you plant. Make sure your summer planting allows enough time for plants to mature before the first frost of autumn. Read plant labels and catalog descriptions and note days to maturity. Frost kills beans.

SOIL. Start with well-drained, biologically active soil that is rich in organic matter. To learn how to create such healthy soil, see page 194. Feed with a complete, balanced organic fertilizer and compost at the beginning of each growing season. Avoid high-nitrogen fertilizers, as beans will respond with lush vegetative growth and few flowers and fruits (pods). Feed with an additional ½ cup of organic fertilizer during the growing season, gently raking the nutrients into the soil around the plants. Like all beans, green beans are shallow-rooted, so do your raking and hoeing carefully to avoid damaging their root system. Control weeds and conserve moisture by spreading mulch to a depth of 3 inches after the plants are a foot tall.

LIGHT. Beans need full sun (six to 12 hours daily) to do their best.

WATER. Beans require regular water. Give them 1 inch per week, by watering the root zone, not the foliage. The planting site must be well drained. Use raised beds or large containers if your drainage is poor or the water table is high.

GARDEN USES AND PLANTING TECHNIQUES. To grow pole beans, be sure to prepare the structure they're going to climb before you plant the seeds. You can use twine, tripods of bamboo poles, limbs of trees arranged in a teepee fashion, or you can grow them on a net or trellis. These support structures offer a shaded microhabitat on their north side. Annuals that appreciate midsummer shade will thrive there. In the polyculture garden, sow a few seeds in a small patch among plants that require similar growing conditions. Beans fix nitrogen in the soil, so they feed plants around them; they are especially useful planted around trees and shrubs that need extra nutrients. In the U.S. Southwest, Native Americans used a classic, and very successful, polyculture guild by planting beans with corn and squash.

START SEEDS. Because bean seedlings don't transplant well, the best planting technique is to sow seeds directly where you want plants to grow. Prepare the garden bed with the good soil mix you made. Or, to grow in a container, start with either a 5-gallon pot or a half whiskey barrel. Make sure there is a drainage hole. Place a small square of window screen over the hole, inside the pot, and add ½ inch of gravel. Then fill the pot with the container soil mix you made. After the last spring frost, water the soil (either in the garden or in the container) thoroughly before sowing. Be sure the soil is loose. Sow the seeds 1 to 3 inches apart and about an inch deep. In a container, plant them in a circle. Seeds should germinate in four to seven days. For bush beans, sow small amounts of seed every two or three weeks for a continuous harvest. Pole beans continue to produce through the season.

ADDITIONAL TECHNIQUES. You'll have better success with your beans if the seeds are inoculated with nitrogen-fixing bacteria. You can buy seeds that are already inoculated, or you can buy some inoculum and do it yourself, just before sowing, following instructions on the package. The bacteria and the bean plant form a symbiosis. The bacteria take nitrogen out of the air and feed it to the bean, while the bean makes carbohydrate and feeds it to the bacteria. Thus, beans make their nitrogen fertilizer out of the air.

PROBLEM-SOLVING. Beans are so prolific and easy to grow that we doubt you will encounter serious problems. Please read the Introduction to avoid trouble in the first place. Also see "Change Growing Conditions to Solve Problems" on page 192. If you encounter pests or diseases, consult the Family Problem-Solving Guide on page 167.

Kale and collard greens

Brassica oleracea Acephala Group

Family Problem-Solving Guide, page 124

DESCRIPTION. Kale and collard greens are biennials grown as annuals. Plants grow 12 to 18 inches tall and 8 to 12 inches wide or more, depending on the cultivar. For help choosing the best cultivar for your circumstances, see the Appendix.

SEASON. Both are cool-season crops. Plant in early spring. You can also plant kale and collard greens in the late summer to take advantage of the cool fall weather. Frost improves the flavor of the leaves and makes them sweeter. Where winter daytime temperatures average in the 60s, stagger plantings throughout the year to enjoy these greens year-round.

TEMPERATURE. Kale and collard greens grow best when daytime temperatures average 60 to 65°F. Excessively hot temperatures or ten or more days of cool temperatures (35 to 45°F) may cause the plants to bolt. Seeds germinate most efficiently when the ambient temperature is 45 to 95°F.

SOIL. Start with well-drained, biologically active soil that is rich in organic matter. To learn how to create such healthy soil, see page 194. Feed twice during the growing season. When you plant the seedlings, add ½ cup of balanced, organic fertilizer to the planting hole. When the plants are half grown, feed again: pull mulch away from each plant, and sprinkle ½ cup of complete, balanced organic fertilizer around it; then replace the mulch. Mulch is particularly important to kale and collard greens, both of which prefer cool soil temperatures. Best soil pH range is 6 to 7. Adding lime to raise the pH to 7.2 helps control clubroot, although kale and collard greens are less susceptible to this fungus than are other cabbage relatives.

LIGHT. Kale and collard greens need six to 12 hours of direct sun per day. Where daytime temperatures are hot (above 75°F), provide dappled/filtered shade.

WATER. These greens thrive with consistent moisture and an average of 1 inch of water per week. Do not let the soil dry out or become waterlogged, and be sure to water the soil, not the foliage.

GARDEN USES AND PLANTING TECHNIQUES. The exuberant foliage of kale and collard greens is particularly attractive in the flower garden. Interplant it among bachelor buttons, calendula, marigolds, dill, nasturtium, rosemary, sage, and thyme to attract beneficial predators. This practice saves you a lot of work. For additional polyculture benefits, sow a few seeds in a small patch among plants that require similar growing conditions; try planting them with scallions, beets, lettuce, onion, peas, and spinach. Do not put kale or collard greens in the same bed or container where they, or any relative, grew within the past three years.

START SEEDS. Begin indoors six to eight weeks before the estimated last spring frost. Once seeds have germinated, set the plantlets outdoors during the warmest part of the day and bring them in at night for two weeks before transplanting them to their permanent outdoor location. In the fall, sow seeds in the ground or container ten to 12 weeks before the estimated first fall frost.

PLANT SEEDLINGS. In the ground: Space plants about 1½ feet apart in full sun. Dig a hole 1 inch deeper than the seedling's container. Add ½ cup of balanced, organic fertilizer to the soil in the bottom of the hole, and mix well. Slide both plant and potting soil out of the container and into the hole, roots down. The top surface of the seedling's potting mix should be 1 inch lower than the ground. Do not bury any leaves. Fill the hole with the soil mix you prepared as needed, and press gently all around the plant to create a shallow basin. Place a cutworm collar around the stem. Now fill the basin with water. Once the water has drained away, spread mulch 3 inches deep around the plant and about 1 inch away from its stem. In containers: Use a 5-gallon pot with a drainage hole. Place a small square of window screen over the hole, inside the pot, and add ½ inch of gravel. Fill the pot with the container soil mix you prepared. Follow directions for planting in the ground, except use the container soil mix when additional soil is needed. Be sure to mulch (top-dress).

PROBLEM-SOLVING. Kale and collard greens are easy and should provide you with an abundant harvest for steaming and stir-frying. Happily, they suffer from fewer of the cabbage family maladies. If you meet all the nutrient requirements to keep plants growing quickly; keep the garden weeded and mulched; and do not compost roots or other tissue of cabbage relatives, you should produce a bumper crop. Also keep pests out with a row cover or other protection as soon as plants are in the ground or container. If your climate allows, it is also best to grow kale and collard greens in the fall, when there are far fewer pests. Please read the Introduction to avoid trouble in the first place. Also see "Change Growing Conditions to Solve Problems" on page 192. If you encounter pests or diseases, consult the Family Problem-Solving Guide on page 124.

Kohlrabi

Brassica oleracea var. *gongylodes*

Family Problem-Solving Guide, page 124

DESCRIPTION. A biennial grown as an annual, with plants 2 feet tall and 1½ feet wide or more, depending on the cultivar. For help choosing the right cultivar for your circumstances, see the Appendix.

SEASON. A cool-season crop. Plant in early spring, or, better yet, in late summer to take advantage of the cool fall weather. Where winter daytime temperatures average in the 60s, stagger plantings throughout the year to enjoy kohlrabi year-round.

TEMPERATURE. Kohlrabi grows best when daytime temperatures average 65 to 75°F. Excessively hot temperatures or ten or more days of cool temperatures (35 to 45°F) may cause plants to bolt. Seeds germinate most efficiently when the ambient temperature is 45 to 95°F.

SOIL. Start with well-drained, biologically active soil that is rich in organic matter. To learn how to create such healthy soil, see page 194. Feed twice during the growing season. When you plant the seedlings, add ½ cup of balanced, organic fertilizer to the planting hole. After the plants have been in the ground about a month, feed again: pull mulch away from each plant, and sprinkle ½ cup of complete, balanced organic fertilizer around it; then replace the mulch. Mulch is particularly important to kohlrabi, which prefers cool soil temperatures. Best soil pH range is 6 to 7. Adding lime to raise the pH to 7.2 helps control clubroot, although kohlrabi is less susceptible to this fungus than are other cabbage relatives.

LIGHT. Kohlrabi needs six to 12 hours of direct sun per day. Where daytime temperatures are hot (above 75°F), provide dappled/filtered shade.

WATER. Kohlrabi thrives with consistent moisture and an average of 1 inch of water per week. Do not let the soil dry out or become waterlogged, and be sure to water the soil, not the foliage.

GARDEN USES AND PLANTING TECHNIQUES. Kohlrabi, especially the red varieties, is particularly attractive in the flower garden; interplant it among bachelor buttons, calendula, dill, nasturtium, rosemary, sage, and thyme to attract beneficial predators. This practice saves you a lot of work. For additional polyculture benefits, try planting it with scallions, beets, lettuce, onion, peas, and spinach. Do not put kohlrabi in the same bed or container where it, or any relative, grew within the past three years.

START SEEDS. Begin indoors two weeks before the estimated last spring frost. Once seeds have germinated, set the plantlets outdoors during the warmest part of the day and bring them in at night for two weeks before transplanting them to their permanent outdoor location. In the fall, sow seeds in the ground or container eight weeks before the estimated first fall frost.

PLANT SEEDLINGS. In the ground: Space plants about 1½ feet apart in full sun. Dig a hole 1 inch deeper than the seedling's container. Add ½ cup of balanced, organic fertilizer to the soil in the bottom of the hole, and mix well. Slide both plant and potting soil out of the container and into the hole, roots down. The top surface of the seedling's potting mix should be 1 inch lower than the ground. Do not bury any leaves. Fill the hole with the soil mix you prepared as needed, and press gently all around the plant to create a shallow basin. Place a cutworm collar around the stem. Now fill the basin with water. Once the water has drained away, spread mulch 3 inches deep around the plant and about 1 inch away from its stem. **In containers:** Use a 5-gallon pot with a drainage hole. Place a small square of window screen over the hole, inside the pot, and add ½ inch of gravel. Fill the pot with the container soil mix you prepared. Follow directions for planting in the ground, except use the container soil mix when additional soil is needed. Be sure to mulch (top-dress).

PROBLEM-SOLVING. Kohlrabi is very easy to grow and is little troubled by cabbage family maladies. If you meet all the nutrient requirements to keep plants growing quickly; keep the garden weeded and mulched; and do not compost roots or other tissue of cabbage relatives, you should produce a bumper crop. Place row covers or other protective barriers over plants as soon as they are in the ground or in containers. If your climate allows, it is best to grow kohlrabi in the fall, when there are far fewer pests. Please read the Introduction to avoid trouble in the first place. Also refer to "Change Growing Conditions to Solve Problems" on page 192. If you encounter pests or diseases, consult the Family Problem-Solving Guide on page 124.

Leeks

Allium porrum

Family Problem-Solving Guide, page 175

DESCRIPTION. Leeks are biennials grown as annuals in the garden. They grow 18 to 24 inches tall and wide, depending on the cultivar you choose. For help with this decision, see the Appendix.

SEASON. A cool-season crop. Plant in early spring for best performance. If summers are hot where you live (regularly above 75°F) but winters are mild (highs average in the 60s), plant them in summer for a fall and winter crop.

TEMPERATURE. Leeks prefer daytime high temperatures between 55 and 75°F. They tolerate freezing down to 20°F without mulching, but if temperatures drop below that, spread straw mulch to protect the plants. Plants will resume growth in spring but are likely to flower quickly. Seed germination is fairly rapid if the ambient temperature is 70 to 75°F.

SOIL. Start with well-drained, biologically active soil that is rich in organic matter. To learn how to create such healthy soil, see page 194. Add a complete, balanced organic fertilizer, composted manure, and/or compost to the garden bed at the beginning of each growing season. Give leeks more fertilizer (½ cup per plant) halfway through the growing season. Take care to remove lumps and rocks; the soil should be loose. Spread 3 inches of mulch over the ground after you have thinned the seedlings. Best soil pH range is 6 to 7.5.

LIGHT. Plant in six to 12 hours of direct sun per day.

WATER. Leeks need consistent moisture and 1 inch of water each week. Apply water to the root zone, not the foliage.

GARDEN USES AND PLANTING TECHNIQUES.
Healthy leek leaves are an attractive element in an ornamental garden. If you add annuals to your perennial bed each year, consider leeks. They provide coarse texture and vertical form. Plant them with ornamental grasses, marigolds, nasturtiums, and strelitzia. In the vegetable bed, leeks do well in a polyculture mix with lettuce, spinach, artichokes, peas, bachelor buttons, calendula, and violas.

START SEEDS. Eight to ten weeks before the anticipated last spring frost, plant seeds ½ inch deep in shallow pots indoors. After seeds germinate, move the pot of seedlings to a cold frame or other cool location for two weeks. You can also start seeds eight to ten weeks before the anticipated first autumn frost for a fall and winter crop. Planting leeks from seed directly in the ground isn't easy. It's better to start them indoors or to plant seedlings.

PLANT SEEDLINGS. In the ground: Leek seedlings are sometimes available in shallow pots or packs containing many seedlings. Take the plants out of the pot and separate them into individual seedlings, keeping some soil around each root ball. Poke holes, using a hand tool, in the enriched garden soil you have prepared. The holes should be about 6 inches deep and 8 to 10 inches apart. Set one seedling in each hole with its topmost leaves sticking out, and then water them gently so the holes gradually fill with soil. Burying the seedlings deeply helps to blanch the stalks and make them tender and white. When the plants are actively growing again, spread mulch 3 inches deep around the plants and about 1 inch away from their stems. **In containers:** For an individual leek plant, use a 5-gallon pot. If you want to plant several leeks with other vegetables and flowers, use a half whiskey barrel. Make sure there is a drainage hole. Place a small square of window screen over the hole, inside the pot, and add ½ inch of gravel. Fill the pot with the container soil mix you prepared. Follow directions for planting in the ground, except use the container soil mix when additional soil is needed. Be sure to mulch (top-dress).

PROBLEM-SOLVING. Leeks are easy to grow and rarely have problems if you meet their basic needs. Please read the Introduction to avoid trouble in the first place. "Change Growing Conditions to Solve Problems" on page 192 will guide you through any necessary adjustments. If you encounter pests or diseases, consult the Family Problem-Solving Guide on page 175.

Lettuce

Lactuca sativa

Family Problem-Solving Guide, page 118

DESCRIPTION. Lettuce is an annual that can grow 12 to 15 inches tall and wide. Its size and shape, however, will depend greatly on the cultivar that you select. Lettuce types include tight head (iceberg, for example), loose head (Boston, for example), loose leaf (oak leaf, for example), and romaine (aka cos). For help selecting the best cultivar for your climate and taste, see the Appendix.

SEASON. A cool-season crop. Plant in early spring, or in late summer to take advantage of the cool fall weather. Where winter daytime temperatures average in the 60s, stagger plantings throughout the year to enjoy lettuce year-round.

TEMPERATURE. Lettuce grows best when daytime temperatures average 60 to 65°F. When summer temperatures exceed 75°F, plants tend to bolt. If the temperature suddenly goes below freezing, lettuce will not survive, but if temperatures drop slowly, lettuce can tolerate down to 28°F. Seeds germinate most efficiently when the ambient temperature is 40 to 80°F. Different types of lettuce (and different cultivars of those types) vary enormously as to how much heat or cold is tolerable; check the seed packet or catalog description to nail down this information.

SOIL. Start with well-drained, biologically active soil that is rich in organic matter. To learn how to create such healthy soil, see page 194. Feed twice during the growing season. When you plant seedlings, add ½ cup of balanced, organic fertilizer to the planting hole. After one month, feed again: pull mulch away from each plant, and sprinkle ½ cup of the organic fertilizer around it; then replace the mulch. Mulch is particularly important to lettuce, which prefers cool soil temperatures. Best soil pH range is 6 to 7.5.

LIGHT. Lettuce needs six to 12 hours of direct sun per day. Where daytime temperatures are hot (above 75°F), provide dappled/filtered shade.

WATER. Lettuce thrives with consistent moisture and an average of 1 inch of water per week. Do not let the soil dry out or become waterlogged, and be sure to water the soil, not the foliage.

GARDEN USES AND PLANTING TECHNIQUES. Lettuce can be an attractive addition to the flower garden and is especially suitable for containers. Every year we grow "salad bowls," which contain seed mixes of lettuces, violas, chives, scallions, and basil, and get wonderful fresh salads all season long. Interplant lettuce among dill, nasturtium, rosemary, sage, and thyme to attract beneficial predators. This practice saves you a lot of work. For additional polyculture benefits, try planting it with garlic, carrots, cucumber, onions, and beets.

START SEEDS. Indoors: Begin six to eight weeks before the estimated last spring frost. Once seeds have germinated, set the plantlets outdoors during the warmest part of the day and bring them in at night for two weeks before transplanting them to their permanent outdoor location. **Outdoors:** Sow the seeds about four weeks before the last expected spring frost. Sprinkle seeds over the prepared garden bed or in containers, and barely cover them with the soil mix you prepared. In the fall, sow seeds in the ground or container ten to 12 weeks before the estimated first fall frost. As the seedlings germinate, thin them, and eat the thinnings.

PLANT SEEDLINGS. In the ground: Choose a location in full sun. For head lettuce, space the plants about 12 inches apart; other varieties can be as close as 4 inches apart. Dig a hole 1 inch deeper than the seedling's container. Add ½ cup of balanced, or-

ganic fertilizer to the soil in the bottom of the hole, and mix well. Slide both plant and potting soil out of the container and into the hole, roots down. The top surface of the seedling's potting mix should be 1 inch lower than the ground. Do not bury any leaves. Fill the hole with the soil mix you prepared as needed, and press gently all around the plant to create a shallow basin. Place a cutworm collar around the plantlet. Now fill the basin with water. Once the water has drained away, spread mulch 3 inches deep around the plant, and about 1 inch away from its base. **In containers:** Use a wide pot that is at least 6 inches deep. Make sure there is a drainage hole. Place a small square of window screen over the hole, inside the pot, and add ½ inch of gravel. Fill the pot with the container soil mix you prepared. Follow directions for planting in the ground, except use the container soil mix when additional soil is needed. Be sure to mulch (top-dress).

PROBLEM-SOLVING. Lettuce is very easy and satisfying to grow. We have rarely encountered the potential pests and diseases listed in the Family Problem-Solving Guide for lettuce and its kin. We have, however, had problems with birds and mammals that want to share our produce: have a look at the Troublesome Wildlife Problem-Solving Guide on page 213. Other than that, our best advice is to meet all the nutrient requirements to keep plants growing quickly, and keep the garden weeded and mulched. Place protective barriers over the plants as soon as they are in the ground or containers. If your climate allows, it is also best to grow lettuce in the fall, when there are far fewer pests. Please read the Introduction to avoid trouble in the first place. "Change Growing Conditions to Solve Problems" on page 192 will guide you through any necessary adjustments. If you encounter pests or diseases, consult the Family Problem-Solving Guide on page 118.

Lima beans

Phaseolus lunatus

Family Problem-Solving Guide, page 167

DESCRIPTION. Lima beans (aka butter beans) are frost-sensitive, herbaceous, annual twining vines (pole bean types) or low-growing bushes. Pole lima beans grow 8 to 15 feet tall or more and require a support. Bush lima beans grow less than 2 feet tall and wide and are self-supporting. For help choosing the best cultivar for your circumstances, see the Appendix.

SEASON. A warm-season crop. Plant in late spring or early summer after all danger of frost is past.

TEMPERATURE. Lima beans thrive where summer daytime high temperatures average 60 to 70°F. Seeds planted in soil that is too cool generally fail to germinate and rot, so wait until the soil is warm enough to plant seeds in spring. For seed germination, the optimum soil temperature is 65 to 85°F. Make sure your summer planting allows enough time for plants to mature before the first frost of autumn. Check the days to maturity on package labels or catalog descriptions. Frost kills lima beans.

SOIL. Start with well-drained, biologically active soil that is rich in organic matter. To learn how to create such healthy soil, see page 194. Feed with a complete, balanced organic fertilizer and compost at the beginning of each growing season. Avoid high-nitrogen fertilizers, as limas will respond with lush vegetative growth and few flowers and fruits (pods). Feed them additional organic fertilizer during the growing season, gently raking the nutrients into the soil around the plants. Like all beans, limas are shallow-rooted, so do your raking and hoeing carefully to avoid damaging their root system.

Control weeds and conserve moisture by spreading mulch to a depth of 3 inches after the plants are a foot tall.

LIGHT. Lima beans need full sun (six to 12 hours daily) to do their best.

WATER. Lima beans require regular water. Give them 1 inch per week, by watering the root zone, not the foliage. The planting site must be well drained; use raised beds or large containers if your drainage is poor or the water table is high.

GARDEN USES AND PLANTING TECHNIQUES. To grow pole lima beans, be sure to prepare the structure they're going to climb before you plant the seeds. You can use twine, tripods of bamboo poles, or limbs of trees arranged in a teepee fashion; or you can grow them on a fence, net, or trellis. These support structures offer a shaded microhabitat on their north side; annuals that appreciate midsummer shade will thrive there. Use lima beans as you would common beans in a polyculture mix with corn and squash. Also interplant them with vegetables and flowers in the daisy and carrot families to attract beneficial predators. In the polyculture garden, sow a few seeds in a small patch among plants that require similar growing conditions.

START SEEDS. Because lima bean seedlings are prone to transplant shock, it is best to sow seeds directly where you want plants to grow. Prepare the garden bed with the good soil mix you made. Or, to grow in a container, start with either a 5-gallon pot or a half whiskey barrel. Make sure there is a drainage hole. Place a small square of window screen over the hole, inside the pot, and add ½ inch of gravel. Then fill the pot with the container soil mix you made. After the last spring frost, water the soil (either in the garden or in the container) thoroughly before sowing. Be sure the soil is loose. Sow the seeds about 6 inches apart and about 1½ to 2 inches deep. In a container, plant them in a circle. Seeds should germinate in four to seven days.

ADDITIONAL TECHNIQUES. You'll have better success with your lima beans if the seeds are inoculated with nitrogen-fixing bacteria. You can buy seeds that are already inoculated, or you can buy some inoculum and do it yourself, just before sowing, following instructions on the package. The bacteria and the bean plant form a symbiosis. The bacteria take nitrogen out of the air and feed it to the bean, while the bean makes carbohydrate and feeds it to the bacteria. Thus, lima beans make their own nitrogen fertilizer out of the air.

PROBLEM-SOLVING. Lima beans are easy to grow. Despite the length of the list of potential problems in the pea family guide, you should not encounter serious problems. Stroll through the garden looking for issues, and nip problems in the bud. Please read the Introduction to avoid trouble in the first place. Also refer to "Change Growing Conditions to Solve Problems" on page 192. If you encounter pests or diseases, consult the Family Problem-Solving Guide on page 167.

Melons

Cucumis melo

Family Problem-Solving Guide, page 149

DESCRIPTION. Melons, including cantaloupe, muskmelon, honeydew, casawba, crenshaw, Persian, and others, are frost-sensitive, herbaceous, annual vines with tendrils. Melon vines grow about 2 feet high and sprawl over 30 to 40 square feet; they can climb a 6-foot A-frame or trellis or crawl across the ground. Compact bush types, about 2 feet high and 3 to 4 feet across, are also available. Choose the right cultivar for your climate and taste. For help with this decision, see the Appendix. Each plant makes male (pollen-bearing) and female (fruit-bearing) flowers. The first flowers will always be male and cannot produce fruit. Be patient. As the plant gets a little older, it will make female flowers and produce a generous crop of fruit after the bees have done their job.

SEASON. A warm-season crop. Plant in late spring or early summer after all danger of frost is past.

TEMPERATURE. Melons thrive where summer daytime highs average 65 to 75°F and the soil temperature is at least 60°F. They seem to do well no matter how hot it gets, but give them some dappled shade if afternoons are very hot (over 98°F) and sunny. Seeds planted in soil that is too cool generally fail to germinate and rot, so wait till the soil has warmed up to plant. Make sure your summer planting allows enough time for the fruit to mature before the first frost of autumn. Pay attention to days to maturity on plant labels or in catalog descriptions. Frost kills melons.

SOIL. Start with well-drained, biologically active soil that is rich in organic matter. To learn how to create such healthy soil, see page 194. Feed with a complete, balanced organic fertilizer and compost at the beginning of each growing season. Feed with additional organic fertilizer during the growing season, gently raking the nutrients into the soil around the plants. Control weeds, conserve moisture, and protect fruit lying on the ground by spreading mulch to a depth of 3 inches once plants are growing well. Maintain a pH of 6 to 6.5.

LIGHT. Melons need full sun (six to 12 hours daily) to do their best.

WATER. Melons require a steady supply of moisture. Give them 1 inch of water per week, watering the root zone, not the foliage. Increase the amount of water to as much as 2 inches a week when the vines support a heavy fruit crop. The planting site must be well drained; use raised beds or large containers if your drainage is poor or the water table is high.

GARDEN USES AND PLANTING TECHNIQUES. Melons are usually grown sprawling across the ground, but smaller-fruited varieties can be grown on an A-frame or trellis, and the bush types work well in containers. To grow melons on a support, be sure to prepare the structure they're going to climb before you plant the seeds. You can use sturdy stakes, tripods of bamboo, or limbs of trees arranged in a teepee fashion; or you can grow them on a net or trellis. These support structures offer a shaded microhabitat on their north side; annuals that appreciate midsummer shade will thrive there. Their sprawling habit makes melons good companions for corn and beans. Space them well apart from each other, and interplant them with flowers that attract beneficial predators. Melons grow well with tomatoes, okra, fennel, rosemary, sunflowers, and echinacea.

START SEEDS. Because melon seedlings often suffer from transplant shock, it is best to sow seeds directly where you want the vines to grow. Prepare the garden bed with the good soil mix you made. Or, to grow in a container, select a compact variety and start with either a 5-gallon pot or a half whiskey barrel. Make sure there is a drainage hole. Place a small square of window screen over the hole, inside the pot, and add ½ inch of gravel. Then fill the pot with the container soil mix you made. After the last spring frost, water the soil (either in the garden or in the container) thoroughly before sowing. Be sure the soil is loose. Sow the seeds about 1 inch deep. Many gardeners prefer to plant melons on a little hill or mound about a foot across. Poke a hole in the soil with your finger or a stick, and put two or three seeds in the hole. Make only one planting hole in a hill or a container. In a garden bed, space the holes or mounds 4 to 8 feet apart, with 6 feet between rows. Seeds should germinate in four to seven days. Thin to one robust seedling per planting hole.

ADDITIONAL TECHNIQUES. Melons need a long, warm growing season. Heat makes the fruit sweet. When the fruits reach baseball size, put two bricks or stones, side by side, beside the fruit and place the young fruit on top of them. Keeping the fruit up off the ground helps avoid certain diseases. In addition, the stones absorb heat during the day and keep the fruit warm at night. Some gardeners like to suspend the fruit in a net sling or old nylon stocking from a support structure to keep it off the ground.

PROBLEM-SOLVING. Melons are prolific and easy to grow as long as the cultivar you choose matches the length of your growing season; check the days to maturity on the cultivar label to be sure. We doubt you will encounter serious problems, but the squash family does have a long list of potential difficulties. Close observation helps nip these in the bud. Please read the Introduction to avoid trouble in the first place. "Change Growing Conditions to Solve Problems" on page 192 will guide you through any necessary adjustments. If you encounter pests or diseases, consult the Family Problem-Solving Guide on page 149.

Mustard greens

Brassica spp.

Family Problem-Solving Guide, page 124

DESCRIPTION. Mustard greens include curly-leaved and Florida broadleaf mustards (*Brassica juncea*), tendergreen mustard (*B. rapa* Perviridis Group), and Asian greens. All are fast-growing annuals to 2 feet tall. For help selecting the best cultivar for your climate and taste, see the Appendix.

SEASON. These are cool-season crops. Plant in early spring, or in late summer to take advantage of the cool fall weather. Where winter daytime temperatures average in the 60s, grow as winter crops. Plant more seeds or seedlings every two weeks or so in order to have harvestable crops over a long season.

TEMPERATURE. Mustard grows best when daytime temperatures average 60 to 65°F. Excessively hot temperatures (above 75°F) will cause the plants to bolt. Seeds germinate most efficiently when the ambient temperature is 45 to 95°F.

SOIL. Start with well-drained, biologically active soil that is rich in organic matter. To learn how to create such healthy soil, see page 194. Feed twice during the growing season. When you plant the seedlings, add ½ cup of balanced, organic fertilizer to the planting hole. When the plants are half grown, feed again: pull mulch away from each plant, and sprinkle ½ cup of complete, balanced organic fertilizer around it; then replace the mulch. Mulch is particularly important to mustard, which prefers cool soil temperatures. Best soil pH range is 6 to 7. Adding lime to raise the pH to 7.2 helps control clubroot, although mustard is less susceptible to this fungus than are other cabbage relatives.

LIGHT. Mustard needs six to 12 hours of direct sun per day. Where daytime temperatures are hot (above 75°F), provide dappled/filtered shade.

WATER. Mustard thrives with consistent moisture and an average of 1 inch of water per week. Do not let the soil dry out or become waterlogged, and be sure to water the soil, not the foliage.

GARDEN USES AND PLANTING TECHNIQUES. Mustard, especially the red varieties, is particularly attractive in the flower garden. Interplant it among bachelor buttons, calendula, dill, nasturtium, rosemary, sage, and thyme to attract beneficial predators. You will save yourself a lot of work. For additional polyculture benefits, try planting it with beets, lettuce, onion, peas, scallions, and spinach. Do not put mustard in the same bed or container where it, or any relative, grew within the past three years.

START SEEDS. Begin indoors two weeks before the estimated last spring frost. Once seeds have germinated, set the plantlets outdoors during the warmest part of the day and bring them in at night for two weeks before transplanting them to their permanent outdoor location. In the fall, sow seeds in the ground or container five to eight weeks before the estimated first fall frost.

PLANT SEEDLINGS. In the ground: Space plants about 6 inches apart in full sun. Dig a hole 1 inch deeper than the seedling's container. Add a ½ cup of balanced, organic fertilizer to the soil in the bottom of the hole, and mix well. Slide both plant and potting soil out of the container and into the hole, roots down. The top surface of the seedling's potting mix should be 1 inch lower than the ground. Do not bury any leaves. Fill the hole with the soil mix you prepared as needed, and press gently all around the plant to create a shallow basin. Now fill the basin with water. Once the water has drained away, spread mulch 3 inches deep around the plant and about 1 inch away from its stem. **In containers:** Use a 5-gallon pot with a drainage hole. Place a small square of window screen over the hole, inside the pot, and add ½ inch of gravel. Fill the pot with the container soil mix you prepared. Follow directions for planting in the ground, except use the container soil mix when additional soil is needed. Be sure to mulch (top-dress).

PROBLEM-SOLVING. Mustard is very easy and satisfying to grow. If you meet all the nutrient requirements to keep plants growing quickly, keep the garden weeded and mulched, and do not compost roots or other tissue of cabbage relatives, you should produce a bumper crop. Place protective barriers such as row covers over the plants as soon as they are in the ground or containers. If your climate allows, it is also best to grow mustard in the fall, when there are far fewer pests. Please read the Introduction to avoid trouble in the first place. Also refer to "Change Growing Conditions to Solve Problems" on page 192. If you encounter pests or diseases, consult the Family Problem-Solving Guide on page 124.

Okra

Abelmoschus esculentus

Family Problem-Solving Guide, page 179

DESCRIPTION. Okra (aka gumbo) is a frost-sensitive tropical annual that grows 6 feet tall or more.

SEASON. A warm-season crop. Plant in late spring or early summer after all danger of frost is past. Days to maturity are 55 to 60, depending on the cultivar. To select the best cultivar for your circumstances, find help in the Appendix.

TEMPERATURE. Okra thrives where summer daytime high temperatures average 70 to 85°F and nighttime temperatures are above 55°F. For seed germination, the optimum soil temperature is 75 to 90°F. Seeds planted in soil that is too cool generally fail to germinate and rot. Make sure your summer planting allows enough time for the fruit to mature before the first frost of autumn. Pay attention to days to maturity on plant labels and catalog descriptions. Frost kills okra.

SOIL. Start with well-drained, biologically active soil that is rich in organic matter. To learn how to create such healthy soil, see page 194. Feed with a complete, balanced organic fertilizer and compost at the beginning of each growing season. Feed with additional organic fertilizer when the plants set their first pods and again when they are as high as your shoulders. Gently rake the nutrients into the soil around the plants. Okra is shallow-rooted, so do your raking and hoeing carefully to avoid damaging its root system. Control weeds and conserve moisture by spreading mulch to a depth of 3 inches when the plants are 6 inches tall. Carefully rake mulch away to apply fertilizer, and then put it back in place. Maintain a pH of 6.5 to 7.5.

LIGHT. Okra needs full sun (six to 12 hours daily) to do its best.

WATER. Okra requires regular water. Give it 1 inch per week, watering the root zone, not the foliage. The planting site must be well drained; use raised beds or large containers if your drainage is poor or the water table is high.

GARDEN USES AND PLANTING TECHNIQUES. Okra, an attractive ornamental plant with large, bold, lobed leaves and very pretty hibiscus-like flowers, is well worth including in your flower beds. Because of its large size, okra provides a shaded micro-habitat on its north side; annuals that appreciate midsummer shade will thrive there. Plant it among corn, tomatoes, pole beans, echinacea, rosemary, catmint, and fennel. In the polyculture garden, sow a few seeds in a small patch among plants that require similar growing conditions.

START SEEDS. Because okra seedlings are sensitive to root disturbance, the best planting technique is to sow seeds directly where you want plants to grow. Prepare the garden bed with the good soil mix you made. Or, to grow okra in a container, start with a half whiskey barrel. Make sure there is a drainage hole. Place a small square of window screen over the hole, inside the pot, and add ½ inch of gravel. Then fill the pot with the container soil mix you made. After the last spring frost, water the soil (either in the garden or in the container) thoroughly before sowing. Be sure the soil is loose. Soak the seeds overnight in water and select only the plump ones for sowing. Sow seeds 12 to 18 inches apart and about an inch deep. In a container, plant seeds in a circle.

ADDITIONAL TECHNIQUES. The pretty okra flowers last only a day. Three or four days later, the pods are ready to pick. Harvest them every couple of days, or the plants will stop producing. Clip pods off the plants with pruning shears. Be sure to wear gloves; many cultivars are spiny, and all will make you itch.

PROBLEM-SOLVING. Okra is prolific, easy to grow, and delicious to eat. It has few problems if you can match its climate requirements. Please read the Introduction to avoid trouble in the first place. Also refer to "Change Growing Conditions to Solve Problems" on page 192. If you encounter pests or diseases, consult the Family Problem-Solving Guide on page 179.

Onions, shallots, and scallions

Allium cepa

Family Problem-Solving Guide, page 175

DESCRIPTION. Onions are bulb-forming biennials, usually grown as annuals.

SEASON. Cool-season. Exact planting time depends on the variety and your location, due to the day-length requirements for bulb formation, but early spring is usually best.

TEMPERATURE. Onions prefer daytime highs of 55 to 75°F. Above 75°F, they stop growing, the bulbs mature, and plants go dormant. If spring temperatures dip below 50°F for three weeks, the little plants will bolt and fail to make a bulb. If you plant in summer and bulbs are fully formed by autumn, you can leave the onions in the ground and harvest all winter, but they do not tolerate temperatures below 28°F.

SOIL. Start with healthy soil (see page 194) and a pH of 6 to 7.5. At planting time, add 1 cup of bone meal to every 2 gallons of the soil mix you prepared. Add a complete, balanced organic fertilizer, composted manure, and/or compost to the garden bed at the beginning of each growing season. Do not give onions more fertilizer; it can prevent proper maturation of the bulbs. Take care to remove lumps and rocks; loose soil gives the bulbs room to develop. Spread 3 inches of mulch over the ground after you have thinned the seedlings.

LIGHT. Plants need full sun. If you grow as scallions (for their greens only), onions will tolerate light, dappled shade. Bulb formation depends on the number of hours of daylight (or darkness) the plants perceive in a 24-hour period. Intermediate ("day-neutral") varieties start to make bulbs with 13 to 14 daylight hours. "Short day" onions begin bulb formation in spring or fall, when daylight hours number 11 to 13. "Long day" onions begin bulb formation in summer, when the number of daylight hours is 14 or more. Read seed packets or plant labels carefully. How far north or south of the equator you are determines how many hours of daylight you'll get in summer.

WATER. Apply 1 inch of water weekly to the root zone. When leaf tips start to turn yellow, stop watering and let the plants dry out so the bulbs will mature properly.

GARDEN USES AND PLANTING TECHNIQUES. Healthy onion leaves make an attractive vertical element in an ornamental garden. In the vegetable bed, onions do well in a polyculture mix with spinach, chard, and lettuce.

START SEEDS. Indoors: Begin two to six weeks before the anticipated last spring frost. Plant seeds ½ inch deep in shallow pots. Air temperature of 70 to 75°F is optimal for germination. After germination, move the pot of seedlings to a cold frame or other cool location. If you do not have a cold frame, move the seedlings outdoors during the day and bring them in at night until all danger of frost is past. **Outdoors:** Plant seeds directly in the ground after the last spring frost, while temperatures are still cool, or in an outdoor container that is at least a foot deep. Scatter the seeds and cover with ½ inch of your prepared soil mix. Thin seedlings when they are 2 to 3 inches tall, so that the strong healthy ones remain 3 to 4 inches apart. Enjoy the tender, edible thinnings. When seedlings are 6 to 10 inches tall, spread at least 2 inches of mulch around them to control weeds. You can also plant seeds four to eight weeks before the anticipated first fall frost, using the techniques just described.

PLANT SEEDLINGS. In the ground: Onion seedlings are usually available in shallow pots containing many seedlings. Take the plants out of the pot and separate them into individual seedlings, keeping some soil around the root ball. Dig a wide, shallow hole or a long, shallow trench, the same depth as the plant's container, in the enriched garden soil

you have prepared. Put 1 cup of bone meal into the hole and mix it with the soil in the bottom. Now refill the hole or trench with your good garden soil. Poke holes in the soil with your finger; make them as deep as the container in which your onion seedlings were growing and about 3 inches apart. Slide the little plants into the holes, and position the roots in the bottom of the hole. The plant should sit in its new location at the same depth as in the container from which it came. Do not bury any leaves. Press gently all around the plant to create a shallow basin, and fill it with water. Once the water has drained away, spread mulch 3 inches deep around the plant and about 1 inch away from its stem. **In containers:** For an individual onion plant, use a one-gallon pot. If you want to plant several onions with other vegetables, use a 5-gallon pot or half whiskey barrel. Whichever pot you choose, make sure there is a drainage hole. Place a small square of window screen over the hole, inside the pot, and add ½ inch of gravel. Fill the pot with the container soil mix you prepared. Follow directions for planting in the ground, except use the container soil mix when additional soil is needed. Be sure to mulch (top-dress).

PLANT SETS. Onion sets are tiny bulbs that will sprout and grow to make full-size bulbs. Plant them later in the spring, when the weather is warmer. Prepare beds or pots with soil enriched with bone meal, as just noted for seeds and seedlings, and plant the little bulbs about an inch deep. If temperatures dip below 50°F right after the sets have sprouted, they'll bolt and fail to make a bulb.

PROBLEM-SOLVING. Read the Introduction to avoid trouble in the first place. Also refer to "Change Growing Conditions to Solve Problems" on page 192. Use row covers or other barriers as soon as you plant onions to prevent thrips (a common problem), and pay attention to their particular needs as to temperature and daylength. If you encounter pests or diseases, consult the Family Problem-Solving Guide on page 175.

Parsnips

Pastinaca sativa

Family Problem-Solving Guide, page 139

DESCRIPTION. Parsnips are biennials grown as annuals in the garden. For help choosing the right cultivar for your circumstances, see the Appendix.

SEASON. A cool-season crop. Time the planting so that it matures about the same time as your first fall frost.

TEMPERATURE. Parsnips thrive when the daytime high temperatures are between 60 and 70°F.

SOIL. Start with well-drained, biologically active soil that is rich in organic matter. To learn how to create such healthy soil, see page 194. Rocks or other obstructions cause parsnips to distort; soil should be light and loose to avoid this problem. At planting time, add an organic fertilizer or compost with an N-P-K ratio of 1-2-2 to the garden bed or container. These nutrients should last the entire season and will be most accessible if the soil pH is 6 to 6.8.

LIGHT. Parsnips do best in full sun (six to 12 hours daily) but appreciate dappled shade if temperatures average above 75°F.

WATER. This is one of the most important aspects of growing parsnips successfully. They want an average of 1 inch of water per week, but if they dry out between waterings they become tough and somewhat bitter. If the soil is waterlogged, they can crack or fork. Vigilance and mulch help ensure consistent moisture, a key to parsnip happiness.

GARDEN USES AND PLANTING TECHNIQUES. The foliage of parsnips complements many flowers and herbs. Parsnips are an especially good choice for raised beds and mixed containers, because it is much easier to create the kind of loose soil they like in these circumstances. Plant radishes with the parsnips because radishes germinate more quickly and will keep the soil from crusting over. Violas, calendula, bachelor buttons, California poppies, peas, and leeks make good companions in the polyculture garden.

START SEEDS. Prepare the garden bed with the good soil mix you made. Or, to grow in a container, start with either a 5-gallon pot or a half whiskey barrel. Make sure there is a drainage hole. Place a small square of window screen over the hole, inside the pot, and add ½ inch of gravel. Then fill the pot with the container soil mix you made. Add an organic fertilizer or compost with an N-P-K ratio of 1-2-2 to the garden bed or container. Parsnips seeds are very small, and the easiest way to sow the seeds is to mix them with a light potting soil, vermiculite, or sifted compost. Sprinkle the seeds where you want them to grow, then cover with ¾ inch of the light soil mix. If you decide to grow radishes with the parsnips, mix the radish seeds into the seed mix as well. Do not tamp down the soil, but water very gently, taking care not to wash the seeds away. Parsnip seeds take three weeks to germinate, so keep an eye out and be patient. Keep the soil moist to encourage germination. This may require daily watering. Harvest the radishes as they germinate to give the parsnips room to grow. When the parsnips are 1 to 2 inches tall, thin the plantlets so that the strongest shoots are about 2 inches apart. Two weeks later, thin them again, to about 8 inches apart, depending on the mature size of the cultivar you selected. Spread at least 3 inches of organic mulch to keep weeds from growing and to maintain consistent soil moisture. Do not transplant parsnips.

PROBLEM-SOLVING. Like carrots, parsnips are somewhat finicky about their need for loose soil and consistent moisture, but they are otherwise easy to grow. If you've followed these guidelines, you should have few problems. Place barriers, such as row covers, over the plants to avoid pests and diseases. Read the Introduction to avoid trouble in the first place. "Change Growing Conditions to Solve Problems" on page 192 will guide you through any necessary adjustments. If you encounter pests or diseases, consult the Family Problem-Solving Guide on page 139.

Peas

Pisum sativum

Family Problem-Solving Guide, page 167

DESCRIPTION. Peas (aka English peas, snow peas, snap peas) are frost-sensitive, herbaceous, annual vines with tendrils. They grow 4 to 6 feet tall and 2 to 4 feet wide. Compact, low-growing, bushy cultivars are also available. For help selecting the cultivar that works best for you, see the Appendix.

SEASON. A cool-season crop. Plant in early spring as soon as the soil can be worked, or in late summer for a fall crop. If you live where winters are mild (daytime highs average 60°F), peas are a good winter crop. The crop matures in 55 to 70 days, depending on the cultivar.

TEMPERATURE. Peas thrive where daytime high temperatures average 60 to 65°F. They languish and stop producing when days get hotter than 75°F. Make sure your summer planting allows enough time for plants to mature before the first frost of autumn. However, peas can tolerate frost and light freezes.

SOIL. Start with well-drained, biologically active soil that is rich in organic matter. To learn how to create such healthy soil, see page 194. Feed with a complete, balanced organic fertilizer and compost at the beginning of each growing season. Avoid high-nitrogen fertilizers. Feed with additional organic fertilizer during the growing season, gently raking the nutrients into the soil around the plants. Like all beans, peas are shallow-rooted, so do your raking and hoeing carefully to avoid damaging their root system. Control weeds and conserve moisture by spreading mulch to a depth of 3 inches once plants are growing well. Best soil pH range is 6 to 7.5.

LIGHT. Peas need full sun (six to 12 hours daily) to do their best.

WATER. Peas require regular water. Give them 1 inch per week, watering the root zone, not the foliage. The planting site must be well drained; use raised beds or large containers if your drainage is poor or the water table is high.

GARDEN USES AND PLANTING TECHNIQUES. Dwarf varieties don't need a support to climb on, but the tall vining types do. Be sure to prepare your stakes, A-frames, or trellises before you plant your seeds. Pea flowers are very pretty, and the plants look nice on trellises or garden fences. In the polyculture garden, sow a few seeds in a small patch among plants that require similar growing conditions. These shallow-rooted plants do well with deep-rooted vegetables, such as carrots and beets. They also do well with cool-season plants such as spinach, cabbage, broccoli, lettuce, scallions, violas, cornflowers, and calendula.

START SEEDS. Pea seedlings have fragile roots, which makes them prone to transplant shock, so the best planting technique is to sow seeds directly where you want plants to grow. Prepare the garden bed with the good soil mix you made. Or, to grow in a container, start with either a 5-gallon pot or a half whiskey barrel. Make sure there is a drainage hole. Place a small square of window screen over the hole, inside the pot, and add ½ inch of gravel. Then fill the pot with the container soil mix you made. Water the soil (either in the garden or in the container) thoroughly before sowing. Be sure the soil is loose. Sow the seeds 1 to 2 inches apart and about 1 inch deep. Thin seedlings to 2 to 4 inches apart. In a container, plant them in a circle. Seeds should germinate in one to two weeks. Make successive sowings every two weeks until mid-spring for continuous harvest until summertime heat curtails production.

ADDITIONAL TECHNIQUES. You'll have better success with your peas if the seeds are inoculated with nitrogen-fixing bacteria. You can buy seeds that are already inoculated, or you can buy some inoculum and do it yourself, just before sowing, following instructions on the package. The bacteria and the pea plants form a symbiosis. The bacteria take nitrogen out of the air and feed it to the pea, while the pea makes carbohydrate and feeds it to the bacteria. Thus, peas make their own nitrogen fertilizer from the air.

PROBLEM-SOLVING. Peas are prolific, easy to grow, and really like cool weather. Our best advice is to plant them in early spring or late summer to give them the temperatures they like and to avoid the peak populations of insect pests. Please read the Introduction to avoid trouble in the first place. Also refer to "Change Growing Conditions to Solve Problems" on page 192. If you encounter pests or diseases, consult the Family Problem-Solving Guide on page 167.

Peppers

Capsicum annuum

Family Problem-Solving Guide, page 157

DESCRIPTION. Peppers, including bell, chili, and paprika, are annuals that are usually grown as freestanding small bushes, 2 to 3 feet tall and 2 feet wide. For help choosing the right cultivar for your climate and taste, see the Appendix.

SEASON. A warm-season crop. Plant in late spring or early summer after all danger of frost is past.

TEMPERATURE. Peppers thrive where daytime high temperatures average 70 to 85°F and the soil temperature is at least 65°F. Seeds germinate most efficiently when the ambient temperature is 65 to 95°F. Seeds planted in soil that is too cool generally fail to germinate and rot, so wait until the soil is warm enough to plant. The fiery taste of chili peppers increases when grown hot and dry. Make sure your summer planting allows enough time for the peppers to mature before the first frost of autumn. Check the days to maturity on the plant labels or catalog descriptions to be sure. Frost kills peppers.

SOIL. Start with well-drained, biologically active soil that is rich in organic matter. To learn how to create such healthy soil, see page 194. Feed with a complete, balanced organic fertilizer and compost at the beginning of each growing season. Feed with additional organic fertilizer during the growing season, gently raking the nutrients into the soil around the plants. Control weeds, conserve moisture, and protect fruit close to the ground by spreading mulch to a depth of 3 inches once plants are growing well. Best soil pH range is 5.5 to 7.

LIGHT. Peppers need full sun (six to 12 hours daily) to do their best.

WATER. Give peppers 1 inch of water per week, watering the root zone, not the foliage. Bell peppers require a steady supply of moisture, not too dry and not too wet, to maintain their sweet, mild flavor. Chili peppers become hotter when grown on the dry side. Avoid irregular watering, where conditions bounce back and forth between extremely dry and extremely wet. The planting site must be well drained; use raised beds or large containers if your drainage is poor or the water table is high.

GARDEN USES AND PLANTING TECHNIQUES. Peppers are a good medium-size bush for a polyculture garden; sow a few seeds in a small patch among plants that require similar growing conditions. As the peppers ripen from green to red, yellow, or orange, they add a very attractive note to the mixed border. They grow well with beans, squash, and corn in the vegetable bed. Interplant them with flowers in the daisy, carrot, and mint families to attract beneficial predators. Do not put peppers in the same bed or container where they, or any relative, grew within the past three years.

START SEEDS. Indoors: Begin six to eight weeks before the estimated last spring frost. Set the plantlets outdoors during the warmest part of the day and bring them in at night for two weeks before transplanting them to their permanent outdoor location. Plant them outdoors after all danger of frost is past. **Outdoors:** Prepare the garden bed with the good soil mix you made. Or, to grow in a container, select a compact variety and start with either a 5-gallon pot or a half whiskey barrel. Make sure there is a drainage hole. Place a small square of window screen over the hole, inside the pot, and add ½ inch of gravel. Then fill the pot with the container soil mix you made. After the last spring frost, water the soil (either in the garden or in the container) thoroughly before sowing. Be sure the soil is loose. Sow the seeds about ¼ inch deep. Poke a hole in the soil with your finger or a stick, and put two or three seeds in the hole. In a garden bed, space your planting holes 1 to 2 feet apart, with 2 to 3 feet between rows. Seeds should germinate in five to ten days in warm soil. Thin to one robust seedling per planting hole.

PLANT SEEDLINGS. Prepare the garden bed or container following the instructions for starting seeds. Peppers don't generally need a support. Choose a location in full sun. Space the plants 1 to 2 feet apart, with 2 to 3 feet between rows. Dig a hole 1 inch deeper than the seedling's container. Add ½ cup of balanced, organic fertilizer to the soil in the bottom of the hole, and mix well. Slide both plant and potting soil out of the container and into the hole, roots down. The top surface of the seedling's potting mix should be 1 inch lower than the ground. Do not bury any leaves. Fill the hole with the soil mix you prepared as needed, and press gently all around the plant to create a shallow basin. Place a cutworm collar around the stem. Now fill the basin with water. Once the water has drained away, spread mulch 3 inches deep around the plant and about 1 inch away from its stem.

PROBLEM-SOLVING. All peppers are prolific and easy to grow, suffering from far fewer problems than their cousin the tomato. Please read the Introduction to avoid trouble in the first place. Also refer to "Change Growing Conditions to Solve Problems" on page 192. If you encounter pests or diseases, consult the Family Problem-Solving Guide on page 157.

Potatoes

Solanum tuberosum

Family Problem-Solving Guide, page 157

DESCRIPTION. Plants are bushy, herbaceous perennials that are grown as annuals. They grow 2 to 2 ½ feet tall and 2 feet wide. For help choosing the right cultivar for your circumstances, see the Appendix.

SEASON. A cool-season crop. Plant in early spring about three weeks before the anticipated last spring frost. If you live where winter daytime temperatures average in the 60s, you can also plant potatoes in the late summer to take advantage of the cool fall weather.

TEMPERATURE. Potatoes thrive where daytime high temperatures average 60 to 65°F and the soil temperature is at least 65°F. If you plant in summer for a fall crop, make sure you allow enough time for the tubers to mature before the first frost of autumn. Check the days to maturity on the plant label to be sure. Frost kills the above-ground portion of potato plants.

SOIL. Start with well-drained, biologically active soil that is rich in organic matter. To learn how to create such healthy soil, see page 194. Feed with a complete, balanced organic fertilizer and compost at the beginning of each growing season. Feed with additional organic fertilizer one time during the growing season, gently raking the nutrients into the soil around the plants. Control weeds and conserve moisture by spreading mulch to a depth of 3 inches once plants are growing well. Maintain an acid soil pH of 5 to 6.

LIGHT. Potatoes need full sun (six to 12 hours daily) to do their best.

WATER. Potatoes require a steady supply of moisture, not too dry and not too wet, to maintain their shape. Give them 1 inch of water per week, watering the root zone, not the foliage. Avoid irregular watering, where conditions bounce back and forth between extremely dry and extremely wet: it causes the tubers to develop weird shapes. The planting site must be well drained; use raised beds or large containers if your drainage is poor or the water table is high.

GARDEN USES AND PLANTING TECHNIQUES. Freestanding, bushy potato plants play nicely with beets, onions, carrots, and any of the cabbage family crops. Interplant them with marigolds and some of the larger members of the daisy, mint, and carrot families for an attractive polyculture bed. Do not put potatoes in the same bed or container where they, or any relative, grew within the past three years.

PLANT SEED POTATOES. Seed potatoes are specially grown, certified disease-free, small potato tubers. Cut the seed potatoes into chunks following the directions on the label. Each chunk must have an "eye" (a dormant bud in a node) that will sprout and grow into a stem. If a seed potato is smaller than an egg don't cut it up, just plant it whole. Prepare the garden bed with the good soil mix you made. Add ½ cup of balanced, organic fertilizer to the native garden soil for each plant, and mix well. To grow potatoes in a container, select a compact variety with small tubers and grow in a half whiskey barrel. Make sure there is a drainage hole. Place a small square of window screen over the hole, inside the pot, and add ½ inch of gravel. Then fill two-thirds of the pot with the container soil mix you made.

Add ½ cup of balanced, organic fertilizer to each pot and mix well. Three weeks before the last anticipated spring frost, plant your seed potatoes 3 or 4 inches deep. Poke a hole in the soil with a stick or trowel and put one seed potato chunk in the hole. In a garden bed, space your planting holes a foot apart, with 2 feet between rows. In containers, plant only one seed potato per pot. As the plants grow, add 2 to 4 more inches of soil to the containers and, in the garden, rake soil up around the plants into little hills. You need to do this once or twice as the plants grow. This "hilling" helps to avoid injury and protects tubers from certain insects and diseases and from turning green due to too much light. When you're satisfied with the "hills" around your plants, add a layer of mulch to control weeds and conserve moisture.

PROBLEM-SOLVING. There are dozens of potato cultivars. They come in many sizes and shapes, and in a rainbow assortment of skin and flesh colors. They are all prolific and relatively easy to grow. Pests in the soil pose the greatest threat. Excluding pests from the garden and maintaining healthy soil will help keep problems from becoming serious. Please read the Introduction to avoid trouble in the first place. Also refer to "Change Growing Conditions to Solve Problems" on page 192. If you encounter pests or diseases, consult the Family Problem-Solving Guide on page 157.

Pumpkins and other winter squash

Cucurbita spp.

Family Problem-Solving Guide, page 149

DESCRIPTION. Winter squash includes butternut (*Cucurbita moschata*), hubbard (*C. maxima*), delicata and acorn (*C. pepo*), cushaw (*C. mixta*), and pumpkins (developed from several squash species). Plants are frost-sensitive, herbaceous, annual vines with tendrils. For help choosing the best cultivar for your circumstances, see the Appendix. Winter squash vines grow big, sprawling over 25 square feet; they can climb a 6-foot trellis or crawl across the ground. Compact bush types, better suited for containers, are also available. Each plant makes male (pollen-bearing) and female (fruit-bearing) flowers. The first flowers will always be male and cannot produce fruit. Be patient. As the plant gets a little older, it will make female flowers and produce a generous crop of fruit after the bees have done their job.

SEASON. These are warm-season crops. Plant in late spring or early summer after all danger of frost is past. Unlike summer squash, from which we harvest immature fruit all season long, we must wait for winter squash to mature before we can harvest them. Check the days to maturity on the label of the cultivar you select to make sure your growing season is long enough.

TEMPERATURE. Squash thrives where daytime high temperatures average 65 to 75°F and the soil temperature is at least 60°F. Seeds planted in soil that is too cool generally fail to germinate and rot, so wait until the soil is warm enough to plant. Frost kills squash.

SOIL. Start with well-drained, biologically active soil that is rich in organic matter. To learn how to create such healthy soil, see page 194. Feed the soil with high-nitrogen organic fertilizer and compost at the beginning of each growing season. Feed with additional organic fertilizer during the growing season, gently raking the nutrients into the soil around the plants. Control weeds, conserve moisture, and protect fruit lying on the ground by mulching to a depth of 3 inches once plants are growing well. Place extra mulch under developing fruit to protect it from soil-borne pests and diseases. Best soil pH range is 6 to 7.5.

LIGHT. Squash needs full sun (six to 12 hours daily) to do its best.

WATER. Squash requires regular water. Give plants 1 inch per week, watering the root zone, not the foliage. Increase the amount of water to as much as 2 inches a week when the vines support a heavy fruit crop. The planting site must be well drained; use raised beds or large containers if your drainage is poor or the water table is high.

GARDEN USES AND PLANTING TECHNIQUES. A smaller-fruited, vine-type winter squash can be grown on a support structure to conserve space and hold the fruit off the ground. Be sure to prepare the structure before you plant the seeds. You can use sturdy stakes, tripods of bamboo, or limbs of trees arranged in a teepee fashion; or you can grow plants on a net or trellis. The support structure provides a shaded microhabitat on its north side; annuals that appreciate midsummer shade will thrive there. Do not attempt to grow a large-fruited variety of winter squash, such as a big Halloween pumpkin, on a support structure: the plant's stems will break under the weight of the fruit. Bush-type winter squash and pumpkins need no support. As with summer squash, the indigenous peoples of Mesoamerica planted winter squash in guilds with beans and corn. All three plants require similar growing conditions and grow well together. Fennel, dill, okra, tomatoes, sunflowers, gaillardia, echinacea, and marigolds are other good polyculture companions for winter squash.

START SEEDS. All winter squash seedlings are susceptible to transplant shock, so it is best to sow seeds directly where you want the vines to grow. Prepare the garden bed with the good soil mix you made. Or, to grow in a container, start with either a 5-gallon pot or a half whiskey barrel. Make sure there is a drainage hole. Place a small square of window screen over the hole, inside the pot, and add ½ inch of gravel. Then fill the pot with the container soil mix you made. After the last spring frost, water the soil (either in the garden or in the container) thoroughly before sowing. Be sure the soil is loose. Sow the seeds about 1 inch deep. Many gardeners prefer to plant squash on a little hill or mound about a foot across. Poke a hole in the soil with your finger or a stick, and put two or three seeds in each hole. In a container, make only one planting hole and be sure to select a compact cultivar. In a garden bed, space the planting holes 4 to 6 feet apart. Seeds should germinate in four to seven days. Thin to one robust seedling per planting hole.

PROBLEM-SOLVING. As long as your climate will support the long growing season of most winter squash, and you meet their basic needs, you should have few problems with them. Please read the Introduction to avoid trouble in the first place. Also refer to "Change Growing Conditions to Solve Problems" on page 192. If you encounter pests or diseases, consult the Family Problem-Solving Guide on page 149.

Radishes

Raphanus sativus

Family Problem-Solving Guide, page 124

DESCRIPTION. Radishes, including daikon, are biennials grown as annuals. Plants grow 6 to 12 inches tall and 12 inches wide. Root shape varies from spherical to cylindrical, size varies from small to large, and color may be red, pink, white, black, or purple—all depending on the cultivar. For help choosing the right cultivar for your climate and taste, see the Appendix.

SEASON. A cool-season crop. Plant in early spring for a spring through early summer harvest, or in late summer for a fall harvest. Most cultivars do not succeed in the hottest days of summer (they bolt), but some heat-resistant varieties are available. All grow fast, maturing in 40 to 60 days.

TEMPERATURE. Radishes do best when daytime high temperatures are between 40 and 60°F. When daytime highs average above 80°F, plants do not thrive. They often bolt, roots become bitter, and the leaf tips may burn. Seeds germinate best when the ambient temperature is 50 to 80°F.

SOIL. Start with well-drained, biologically active soil that is rich in organic matter. To learn how to create such healthy soil, see page 194. At the beginning of the growing season, add organic compost or fertilizer that is slightly higher in nitrogen (N) than it is in phosphorus (P) or potassium (K). Use a fertilizer with a ratio of 10-7-7 or something similar, or add extra nitrogen (in the form of chicken manure, for instance) to a balanced fertilizer or compost. The higher nitrogen helps plants grow quickly and produce tastier roots. Add a dose of this fertilizer (scatter ½ cup over about 2 square feet) again after you thin the seedlings. Best soil pH range is 6 to 7.5.

LIGHT. When temperatures are moderate, as radishes prefer, they need six to 12 hours of direct sun per day. Where daytime temperatures are hot (above 70°F), provide dappled/filtered shade.

WATER. Radishes like consistent moisture and an average of 1 inch of water per week. Do not let the soil dry out or become waterlogged. These plants develop strong, hot flavors and get woody when grown dry. Keep them moist, and they'll stay mild and tender.

GARDEN USES AND PLANTING TECHNIQUES. The relatively nondescript foliage of radishes can be scattered through an ornamental garden of low- to medium-growing flowers and spring bulbs. Sow a small amount of seed in a small patch among plants that require similar growing conditions. Radishes work especially well in a container mix of annual flowers, scallions, and herbs. For polyculture benefits, mix radish seeds with those of carrot and parsnip. Radishes germinate quickly, keeping the soil from forming a crust, which helps carrots and parsnips stay healthy. Do not put radishes in the same bed or container where they, or any relative, grew within the last three years.

START SEEDS. Because radishes are susceptible to transplant shock, it is best to sow seeds directly where you want plants to grow. Prepare the garden bed with the good soil mix you made. Or, to grow in a container, start with a one-gallon pot for the smaller kinds of radish; for big radishes, like daikon, use a 5-gallon pot. Whichever pot you choose, make sure there is a drainage hole. Place a small square of window screen over the hole, inside the pot, and add ½ inch of gravel. Then fill the pot with the container soil mix you made. In early spring, about a month before the last expected spring frost, sow radish seeds (either in the garden or in the container) about 1 inch apart and about ½ inch deep. Water immediately and keep the soil moist but not soggy until the seeds germinate, which should occur in four to seven days. As the seedlings appear, thin them to 4 to 8 inches apart, further if you chose a large cultivar. After thinning, scatter ½ cup high-nitrogen organic fertilizer, and then spread mulch 1 to 3 inches deep, depending on the size of the plants. Mulch controls weeds and retains consistent soil moisture. Sow small quantities of seeds every two weeks to extend your harvest season, but time your crops so that they mature before the heat of summer.

PROBLEM-SOLVING. Radishes are quite easy to grow; they are quick and trouble-free, so long as you pay attention to their moisture and temperature requirements. Please read the Introduction to avoid trouble in the first place. Also refer to "Change Growing Conditions to Solve Problems" on page 192. For difficulties with diseases and pests, see the Family Problem-Solving Guide on page 124.

Rhubarb

Rheum rhabarbarum

Family Problem-Solving Guide, page 183

DESCRIPTION. Rhubarb is a hardy perennial; it dies down to the ground in winter and resumes growth in spring, to 3 feet tall and 6 feet wide. For help choosing the best cultivar for your circumstances, see the Appendix.

SEASON. A cool-season crop. Plant in early spring.

TEMPERATURE. Rhubarb does best with daytime high temperatures of 60 to 65°F. When daytime highs average above 75°F, plants will go dormant. They resprout when temperatures get cooler in the autumn. Rhubarb tolerates frost and freezing. It requires a cold period at 40°F in order to break dormancy. Grow rhubarb as an annual if you live where you do not get this cold period.

SOIL. Start with well-drained, biologically active soil that is rich in organic matter. To learn how to create such healthy soil, see page 194. At the beginning of the growing season, add organic compost or complete, balanced, organic fertilizer to your soil mix.

LIGHT. When temperatures are moderate, as rhubarb prefers, it needs six to 12 hours of direct sun per day. Where daytime temperatures are hot (above 70°F), provide dappled/filtered shade.

WATER. Rhubarb likes consistent moisture and an average of 1 inch of water per week.

GARDEN USES AND PLANTING TECHNIQUES. Rhubarb has very attractive, large, tropical-looking foliage and bright red stalks. Never harvest all the stems at once; remove only a few at a time. This veggie is a welcome addition to an ornamental garden or a large mixed container of perennial flowers and grasses. Create a polyculture by planting it with other medium-growing flowers and spring bulbs.

PLANT DORMANT ROOTS. In the ground: Dig a hole about 2 feet wide and 1 foot deep. Fill the hole with the in-ground soil mix you prepared. Use a trowel, or your hands, to make a hole the same size as the root, and insert the root into this hole with its vegetative buds up. Make sure all these buds are 1 inch below soil level. Press down on the soil mix gently to form a shallow basin, and fill it with water. Once the water has drained away, spread mulch 3 inches deep. **In containers:** Use a 5-gallon pot or a half whiskey barrel. Make sure there is a drainage hole. Place a small square of window screen over the hole, inside the pot, and add ½ inch of gravel. Fill the container with the container soil mix you prepared. Follow the steps for planting dormant roots in the ground, except use the container soil mix to fill the hole. Be sure to mulch (top-dress).

PROBLEM-SOLVING. Except in the hottest days of summer, rhubarb is quite easy to grow. You should rarely encounter problems. Please read the Introduction to avoid trouble in the first place. Also refer to "Change Growing Conditions to Solve Problems" on page 192. If you encounter pests or diseases, consult the Family Problem-Solving Guide on page 183.

Sorrel

Rumex spp.

Family Problem-Solving Guide, page 183

DESCRIPTION. Sorrel is a hardy perennial that is often grown as an annual. Common sorrel (*Rumex acetosa*) grows 3 feet tall, French sorrel (*R. scutatus*) only half as high. For help choosing the best cultivar for your circumstances, see the Appendix.

SEASON. A cool-season crop. Plant in early spring. Days to maturity are about 60.

TEMPERATURE. Sorrel does best with daytime high temperatures of 60 to 65°F. When daytime highs average above 80°F, plants may try to flower and set seed. To keep the tasty leaves coming, cut the flowers off the plants and don't let them make seeds. Common sorrel tolerates frost and light freezing. Spread mulch over the plants in winter, and they will resume growth in spring. French sorrel is slightly less cold tolerant. Seeds germinate best when the ambient temperature is 45 to 75°F.

SOIL. Start with well-drained, biologically active soil that is rich in organic matter. To learn how to create such healthy soil, see page 194. At the beginning of the growing season, add organic compost or complete, balanced, organic fertilizer to your soil mix. Best soil pH range is 6 to 7.5.

LIGHT. When temperatures are moderate, as sorrel prefers, it needs six to 12 hours of direct sun per day. Where daytime temperatures are hot (above 70°F), provide dappled/filtered shade.

WATER. Sorrel likes consistent moisture and an average of 1 inch of water per week. French sorrel is a bit more tolerant of drought than common sorrel.

GARDEN USES AND PLANTING TECHNIQUES. Sorrel's very attractive arrowhead-shaped foliage is a welcome addition to an ornamental garden or large mixed container of medium-growing spring bulbs, perennial flowers and grasses. It also grows well with cool-season flowers like calendula, violas, and bachelor buttons. In the polyculture vegetable garden, sow a few seeds in a small patch among plants that require similar growing conditions, such as cabbage relatives, onions, and peas.

START SEEDS. Sow seeds directly where you want plants to grow. Prepare the garden bed with the good soil mix you made. Or, to grow in a container, use a 5-gallon pot for both kinds of sorrel. To grow sorrel with other vegetables and flowers use a wider container, such as a half whiskey barrel. Whichever pot you choose, make sure there is a drainage hole. Place a small square of window screen over the hole, inside the pot, and add ½ inch of gravel. Then fill the pot with the container soil mix you made. In early spring, three weeks to a month before the estimated last spring frost, sow seeds (either in the garden or in the container) about 2 inches apart and about ½ inch deep. Water immediately and keep the soil moist but not soggy until the seeds germinate, which should occur in a week or two. As the seedlings appear, thin them to 4 to 8 inches apart, and enjoy the edible thinnings. After thinning, add a dose of fertilizer, then spread mulch 1 to 3 inches deep, depending on the size of the plants, to control weeds and to retain soil moisture.

PROBLEM-SOLVING. Sorrel does not like extreme heat, so this is likely to be the primary problem you'll face. Please read the Introduction to avoid trouble in the first place. Also refer to "Change Growing Conditions to Solve Problems" on page 192. If you encounter pests or diseases, consult the Family Problem-Solving Guide on page 183.

Soybeans

Glycine max

Family Problem-Solving Guide, page 167

DESCRIPTION. Soybeans (aka edamame) are frost-sensitive, herbaceous annuals. Plants grow 2 feet tall and wide and are self-supporting. For help choosing the best cultivar for your climate, see the Appendix.

SEASON. A warm-season crop. Plant in spring after all danger of frost is past.

TEMPERATURE. Soybeans thrive where daytime high temperatures average 68 to 86°F and humidity is high. For seed germination, the optimum soil temperature is 60 to 70°F. Seeds planted in soil that is too cool generally fail to germinate and rot, so wait until the soil is warm enough before planting. Frost kills soybeans.

SOIL. Start with well-drained, biologically active soil that is rich in organic matter. To learn how to create such healthy soil, see page 194. Feed with a complete, balanced organic fertilizer and compost at the beginning of each growing season. Avoid high-nitrogen fertilizers, as soybeans will respond with lush vegetative growth and few flowers and fruits (pods). Feed with an additional ½ cup of organic fertilizer during the growing season, gently raking the nutrients into the soil around the plants. Like all beans, soybeans are shallow-rooted, so do your raking and hoeing carefully to avoid damaging their root system. Control weeds and conserve moisture by spreading mulch to a depth of 3 inches after the plants are about 6 inches tall.

LIGHT. Soybeans need full sun (six to 12 hours daily) to do their best. Some soybean varieties are daylength-sensitive, which means flowering and fruiting is triggered by a specific number of hours of daylight. For an easier time growing soybeans, choose cultivars that are not daylength-sensitive. Read seed package labels and catalog descriptions carefully.

WATER. Soybeans require regular water. They produce poorly in dry environments. Give them 1 inch of water per week, watering the root zone, not the foliage. The planting site must be well drained; use raised beds or large containers if your drainage is poor or the water table is high.

GARDEN USES AND PLANTING TECHNIQUES. Soybeans fix nitrogen in the soil, feeding plants around them, so they are especially useful planted around trees and shrubs that need extra nutrients. Even though soybeans are native to Asia, you can use them as you would common beans in a classic polyculture mix with corn and squash. Interplant them with warm-season vegetables and flowers in the daisy and carrot families to attract beneficial predators. Harvest when the seeds are still green, and you have fresh edamame.

START SEEDS. Because soybean seedlings are prone to transplant shock, it is best to sow seeds directly where you want plants to grow. Prepare the garden bed with the good soil mix you made. Or, to grow in a container, start with either a 5-gallon pot or a half whiskey barrel. Make sure there is a drainage hole. Place a small square of window screen over the hole, inside the pot, and add ½ inch of gravel. Then fill the pot with the container soil mix you made. After the last spring frost, water the soil (either in the garden or in the container) thoroughly before sowing. Be sure the soil is loose. Sow the seeds about 3 inches apart and about 1 inch deep. In a container, plant them in a circle. Seeds should

germinate in four to seven days. Soybean pods ripen all at once, so sow small amounts of seed every two or three weeks for a continuous harvest.

ADDITIONAL TECHNIQUES. You'll have better success with your soybeans if the seeds are inoculated with nitrogen-fixing bacteria. You can buy seeds that are already inoculated, or you can buy some inoculum and do it yourself, just before sowing, following instructions on the package. Be sure you obtain inoculum specifically for soybeans. Inoculum for other beans will not work on them. The bacteria and the bean plant form a symbiosis. The bacteria take nitrogen out of the air and feed it to the bean, the bean makes carbohydrate and feeds it to the bacteria. Thus, soybeans can make their own nitrogen fertilizer out of the air.

PROBLEM-SOLVING. Like most beans, soybeans are pretty easy to grow, but sometimes, despite your best efforts, challenges arise. Please read the Introduction to avoid trouble in the first place. Also refer to "Change Growing Conditions to Solve Problems" on page 192. If you encounter pests or diseases, consult the Family Problem-Solving Guide on page 167.

Spinach

Spinacia oleracea

Family Problem-Solving Guide, page 134

DESCRIPTION. A biennial grown as an annual. Plants grow 4 to 6 inches tall and 6 to 8 inches wide, depending on the cultivar. For help choosing the best cultivar for your circumstances, see the Appendix.

SEASON. A cool-season crop. Plant in early spring for harvests from spring through early summer, or in late summer for a fall harvest. Most cultivars do not succeed in the hottest days of summer (they bolt), but some heat-resistant varieties are available. If you live where winters are warm, with daytime highs averaging in the 60s, spinach is a great winter vegetable. Days to maturity are 40 to 50.

TEMPERATURE. Spinach does best when daytime high temperatures are 60 to 65°F. When daytime highs average above 80°F, plants do not thrive. In the long days of summer, spinach often bolts, and the leaf tips may burn in the heat. Spinach tolerates frost and light freezing, but severe cold may kill it. Cover plants with mulch in winter to protect them from severe freezing, and they will resume growth in spring. Seeds germinate best when the ambient temperature is 45 to 75°F.

SOIL. Start with well-drained, biologically active soil that is rich in organic matter. To learn how to create such healthy soil, see page 194. At the beginning of the growing season add organic compost or fertilizer that is higher in nitrogen (N) than it is in phosphorus (P) or potassium (K). Use a fertilizer with a ratio of 10-7-7 or something similar, or add extra nitrogen (in the form of chicken manure, for instance) to a balanced fertilizer or compost. The higher nitrogen helps plants grow quickly and produce tastier leaves. Add a dose of this fertilizer again about two weeks after sowing, at the time you thin seedlings. Best soil pH range is 6 to 7.5.

LIGHT. When temperatures are moderate, as spinach prefers, it needs six to 12 hours of direct sun per day. Where daytime temperatures are hot (above 70°F), provide dappled/filtered shade.

WATER. Spinach likes consistent moisture and an average of 1 inch of water per week. Do not let the soil dry out or become waterlogged. These plants will bolt if grown dry and hot. Keep them moist, and they'll stay mild and tender.

GARDEN USES AND PLANTING TECHNIQUES. The attractive foliage of spinach can be scattered through an ornamental garden or in a container mix of annual flowers. Grow spinach in a polyculture mix that includes other low- to medium-growing spring bulbs, cool-season flowers like calendula, violas, and bachelor buttons, and vegetables like peas, cabbage relatives, onions, and leeks.

START SEEDS. The best way to get spinach going is to sow the seeds directly where you want plants to grow. Prepare the garden bed with the good soil mix you made. Or, to grow in a container, use a one-gallon pot for most kinds of spinach. To grow spinach with other vegetables and flowers, use a 5-gallon pot, or select a container that is wide and shallow. Whichever pot you choose, make sure there is a drainage hole. Place a small square of window screen over the hole, inside the pot, and add ½ inch of gravel. Then fill the pot with the container soil mix you made. In early spring, three weeks to a month before the estimated last spring frost, sow spinach seeds (either in the garden or in the container) about 2 inches apart and about ½ inch deep. Water immediately and keep the soil moist but not soggy until the seeds germinate, which should occur in a week or two. As the seedlings appear, thin them to 4 to 8 inches apart, further if you chose a large cultivar. Enjoy the edible thinnings. After thinning, spread mulch 1 to 3 inches deep, depending on the size of the plants, to control weeds and to retain consistent soil moisture. Sow small quantities of seeds every two weeks to extend your harvest season, but time your crops so that they mature before or after the heat of summer.

PROBLEM-SOLVING. Except in the hottest days of summer, spinach is quite easy to grow. You should rarely encounter problems. Please read the Introduction to avoid trouble in the first place. Also refer to "Change Growing Conditions to Solve Problems" on page 192. If you encounter pests or diseases, consult the Family Problem-Solving Guide on page 134.

Sweet potatoes

Ipomoea batatas

Family Problem-Solving Guide, page 185

DESCRIPTION. Sweet potatoes are annual vines that grow 12 to 18 inches tall and trail along the ground for 4 to 8 feet or more. Sweet potatoes with deep orange roots are often mistakenly called yams, and the pale ones are called sweet potatoes. True yams, very different from sweet potatoes, are in the family Dioscoreaceae and are not covered in this book. For help selecting the best cultivar for your climate and taste, see the Appendix.

SEASON. A warm-season crop. Plant in late spring or early summer after all danger of frost is past. Days to maturity are 100 to 150, depending on the cultivar—in other words, a long, warm growing season is required.

TEMPERATURE. Sweet potatoes grow best where daytime high temperatures average 70 to 85°F. When you plant rooted cuttings of sweet potato, the soil temperature should be 60 to 85°F. Sweet potato rooted cuttings that are planted in cool soil generally fail to grow and just rot. Make sure your summer planting allows enough time for the tuberous roots to mature before the first frost of autumn. Frost kills sweet potatoes.

SOIL. Start with well-drained, biologically active soil that is rich in organic matter. To learn how to create such healthy soil, see page 194. Feed with ½ cup of a complete, balanced organic fertilizer, bone meal, and compost at the beginning of each growing season. Gently rake the nutrients into the soil around the plants. Keep the soil loose. Sweet potatoes are shallow-rooted, so do your raking and hoeing carefully to avoid damaging their root system. Control weeds and conserve moisture by spreading mulch to a depth of 3 inches when the plants are firmly rooted and after applying fertilizer. An acid soil pH of 5 to 6 is best.

LIGHT. Sweet potatoes need full sun (six to 12 hours daily) to do their best.

WATER. Sweet potatoes require regular water. Give them 1 inch per week, watering the root zone, not the foliage. Allow the soil to dry out a bit between waterings. Plant your sweet potatoes in raised beds or large containers if your drainage is poor or the water table is high.

GARDEN USES AND PLANTING TECHNIQUES. Sweet potato vines have beautiful foliage and flowers, and are very attractive in flower beds and containers. Reap the benefits of the polyculture approach by planting them with other warm-season, low-growing plants such as peppers, eggplant, tomatillos, marigolds, gaillardia, catmint, and thyme.

PLANT SLIPS. Purchase certified disease-free slips, as the rooted cuttings of sweet potatoes are known, from a garden center or mail-order nursery. Order the slips for delivery after the last anticipated spring frost in your area. It's also easy to grow your own slips from tuberous roots, but you have no guarantee that your propagation material is free of disease. To make your own slips, put a sweet potato root with its stem end up, root end down, in a jar with enough water to cover the bottom inch of the root. Sprouts will begin to grow out of the top of the sweet potato. When sprouts are about 6 inches long, they will develop roots at their bases. Twist off each sprout with its roots intact. Prepare the garden bed with the good soil mix you made. Or, to grow sweet

potatoes in a container, start with a half whiskey barrel. Make sure there is a drainage hole. Place a small square of window screen over the hole, inside the pot, and add ½ inch of gravel. Then fill the pot with the container soil mix you made. After the last spring frost, water the soil (either in the garden or in the container) thoroughly before planting the slips. Plant slips about 12 inches apart and 2 to 4 inches deep in loose soil. In a container, plant them in a circle. Spread mulch over the ground or potting media to a depth of 3 inches.

PROBLEM-SOLVING. Sweet potatoes are easy to grow in the right climate, one that has a long, warm growing season. Please read the Introduction to avoid trouble in the first place. Also refer to "Change Growing Conditions to Solve Problems" on page 192. If you encounter pests or diseases, consult the Family Problem-Solving Guide on page 185.

Tomatillos

Physalis ixocarpa

Family Problem-Solving Guide, page 157

DESCRIPTION. Tomatillos (aka husk tomatoes) are bushy annuals that grow 3 to 4 feet tall and wide. For help choosing the best cultivar for your circumstances, see the Appendix.

SEASON. A warm-season crop. Plant in late spring or early summer after all danger of frost is past.

TEMPERATURE. Tomatillos thrive where daytime high temperatures average 70 to 75°F and the soil temperature is at least 60°F. Seeds germinate most efficiently when the ambient temperature is 60 to 85°F. Seeds planted in soil that is too cool generally fail to germinate and rot, so wait to plant until the soil is warm enough. Make sure your summer planting allows enough time for the fruit to mature before the first frost of autumn; check the days to maturity on the cultivar label to be sure. Frost kills tomatillos.

SOIL. Start with well-drained, biologically active soil that is rich in organic matter. To learn how to create such healthy soil, see page 194. Feed with a complete, balanced organic fertilizer and compost at the beginning of each growing season. Feed with additional organic fertilizer during the growing season, gently raking the nutrients into the soil around the plants. Avoid high-nitrogen fertilizers, as tomatillos will respond with lush vegetative growth and few flowers and fruits. Control weeds and conserve moisture by spreading mulch to a depth of 3 inches once plants are growing well. Best soil pH range is 5.8 to 7.

LIGHT. Tomatillos need full sun (six to 12 hours daily) to do their best.

WATER. Tomatillos require a steady supply of moisture, not too dry and not too wet. Give them 1 inch of water per week, watering the root zone, not the foliage. Avoid irregular watering, where conditions bounce back and forth between extremely dry and extremely wet. The planting site must be well drained; use raised beds or large containers if your drainage is poor or the water table is high.

GARDEN USES AND PLANTING TECHNIQUES. Tomatillos, a staple in Mexican cuisine, are becoming more popular and widely known in home gardens. Their husks resemble those of the related Chinese lanterns (*Physalis alkekengi*), making these plants a lovely freestanding addition to perennial beds. They usually don't need a support, but if you'd like to contain their sprawling habit a bit, use wire tomato cages. Interplant tomatillos with rosemary, cilantro, onions, and beans, and, to attract beneficial predators, with flowers in the carrot, daisy, and mint families. Do not put tomatillos in the same bed or container where they, or any relative, grew within the past three years.

START SEEDS. Indoors: Begin six to eight weeks before the estimated last spring frost. Set the plantlets outdoors during the warmest part of the day and bring them in at night for two weeks before transplanting them to their permanent outdoor location. Plant them outdoors after all danger of frost is past. **Outdoors:** Prepare the garden bed with the good soil mix you made. Or, to grow in a container, select a compact variety and start with either a 5-gallon pot or a half whiskey barrel. Make sure there is a drainage hole. Place a small square of window screen over the hole, inside the pot, and add ½ inch of gravel. Then fill the pot with the container soil mix you made. After the last spring frost, water the soil (either in the garden or in the container) thoroughly before sowing. Be sure the soil is loose. Sow the seeds about ½ inch deep. Poke a hole in the soil with your finger or a stick, and put two or three seeds in the hole. In a garden bed, space your planting holes 2 to 3 feet apart, with 3 to 6 feet between rows. Seeds should germinate in five days in warm soil. Thin to one robust seedling per planting hole.

PLANT SEEDLINGS. Prepare the garden bed or container following the instructions for starting seeds. Choose a location in full sun. Space the plants 2 to 3 feet apart, with 3 to 6 feet between rows. Dig a hole 1 inch deeper than the seedling's container. Add ½ cup of balanced, organic fertilizer to the soil in the bottom of the hole, and mix well. Slide both plant and potting soil out of the container and into the hole, roots down. The top surface of the seedling's potting mix should be 1 inch lower than the ground. Do not bury any leaves. Fill the hole with the soil mix you prepared as needed, and press gently all around the plant to create a shallow basin. Place a cutworm collar around the stem. Now fill the basin with water. Once the water has drained away, spread mulch 3 inches deep around the plant and about 1 inch away from its stem.

PROBLEM-SOLVING. Tomatillos are prolific and easy to grow, suffering from fewer problems than their relative, the tomato. Please read the Introduction to avoid trouble in the first place. Also refer to "Change Growing Conditions to Solve Problems" on page 192. If you encounter pests or diseases, consult the Family Problem-Solving Guide on page 157.

Tomatoes

Solanum spp.

Family Problem-Solving Guide, page 157

DESCRIPTION. Tomatoes (*Solanum lycopersicum*), cherry tomatoes (*S. lycopersicum* var. *cerasiforme*), and currant tomatoes (*S. pimpinellifolium*) are frost-sensitive, herbaceous perennial vines grown as annuals. Determinate tomatoes grow 4 feet tall or less; indeterminate plants reach 7 to 15 feet. Both grow 2 to 3 feet wide. Compact types, about 2 feet high and wide, are perfect for containers. Choose a cultivar that suits your climate, space, and taste.

SEASON. A warm-season crop, tomatoes will grow year-round if days are above 70°F and nights above 55°F. Otherwise, plant in late spring or early summer when all danger of frost is past.

TEMPERATURE. Germination is best at ambient temperatures of 60 to 85°F. If soil is too cool (under 60°F), seeds fail to germinate and rot. Check the days to maturity on the cultivar label to be sure any summer planting allows enough time for fruit to mature. Tomatoes thrive in daytime highs of 70 to 75°F. Frost kills them.

SOIL. Start with healthy soil (see page 194) with a pH of 5.8 to 7. Feed with a complete, balanced organic fertilizer and compost at the beginning of each growing season. Gently rake additional organic fertilizer into the soil around the plants all season. Avoid high-nitrogen fertilizers, as tomatoes will respond with lush vegetative growth and few flowers and fruits. Spread mulch to a depth of 3 inches once plants are growing well.

LIGHT. Tomatoes need full sun (six to 12 hours daily) to do their best.

WATER. Steady, consistent watering, 1 inch per week, helps control blossom-end rot and cracking of the fruit. Water the root zone, not the foliage. Avoid irregular watering. Use raised beds or large containers if your drainage is poor or the water table is high.

GARDEN USES AND PLANTING TECHNIQUES. Tomatoes are generally grown tied to wooden stakes, wire cages, or on a trellis or teepee support. The vines can be left to sprawl across the ground, but any fruit in contact with the soil attracts slugs, snails, and other pests, and runs the risk of infection by fungal and bacterial pathogens. Be sure to prepare the structure they're going to climb before you plant tomato seedlings. Combine smaller (determinate) tomato plants with flowers such as cosmos, gaillardia, rudbeckia, coreopsis, and marigolds; include herbs such as rosemary, basil, and cilantro. Larger vines play well with corn, beans, okra, and sunflowers. Do not put tomatoes in the same bed or container where they, or any relative, grew within the past three years.

START SEEDS. **Indoors:** Begin six to ten weeks before the estimated last spring frost. Set plantlets outdoors during the warmest part of the day and bring them in at night for two weeks before transplanting them to their permanent outdoor location, when all danger of frost is past. **Outdoors:** Prepare the garden bed with the good soil mix you made. Or, to grow in a container, select a compact variety and start with either a 5-gallon pot or a half whiskey barrel. Make sure there is a drainage hole. Place a small square of window screen over the hole, inside the pot, and add ½ inch of gravel. Then fill the pot with the container soil mix you made. After the last expected spring frost, loosen the soil and water thoroughly. Poke a ½-inch-deep hole in the soil with your finger or a stick, and put two or three seeds in the hole. In a garden bed, space your planting holes 2 to 3 feet apart, with 3 to 6 feet between rows. Seeds should germinate in seven to 14 days. Thin to one robust seedling per planting hole.

PLANT SEEDLINGS. Prepare the garden bed or container following the instructions for starting seeds outdoors. Space the plants 1 to 2 feet apart, with 2 to 3 feet between rows, in full sun. Dig a hole 1 inch deeper than the seedling's container. Pour a ½ cup of balanced, organic fertilizer into the hole and mix well with surrounding soil. Slide both plant and potting soil out of the container and into the hole, roots down. The top surface of the seedling's potting mix should be 1 inch lower than the ground. Do not bury any leaves. Fill the hole with the soil mix you prepared as needed, and press gently all around the plant to create a shallow basin. Place a cutworm collar around the stem. Now fill the basin with water. Once the water has drained away, spread mulch 3 inches deep around the plant and about 1 inch away from its stem.

ADDITIONAL TECHNIQUES. Tomato plants produce large numbers of side shoots, or suckers. If you let these grow, you will harvest a larger number of smaller tomatoes. If you prune away the side shoots, you will harvest a smaller number of larger fruits. If your goal is big fruit, then prune. Otherwise, don't bother. If you live where summer nights are warm and humid, you have hundreds of cultivars from which to choose. Where summer nights are dry and cool (as in much of western North America), choices will be limited to those with shorter days to maturity.

PROBLEM-SOLVING. Tasty homegrown tomatoes beat storebought any day and are well worth the effort you make to keep them healthy. Fungal infections are the most serious challenges you may face. Our best advice is to use a polyculture approach, make sure there is adequate air movement, rotate your crops, and water the soil, not the foliage. Please read the Introduction to avoid trouble in the first place. Also refer to "Change Growing Conditions to Solve Problems" on page 192. If you encounter pests or diseases, consult the Family Problem-Solving Guide on page 157.

Turnips and rutabagas

Brassica spp.

Family Problem-Solving Guide, page 124

DESCRIPTION. Both turnips (*Brassica rapa* var. *rapa*) and rutabagas (*B. napus* var. *napobrassica*) are biennials grown as annuals. Plants are 1 to 2 feet tall and 1 foot wide, depending on the cultivar. For help selecting the best cultivar for your climate and taste, see the Appendix.

SEASON. Both are cool-season crops. Plant in early spring for an early summer harvest, or in early fall for an early winter harvest. These plants do not succeed in the hottest days of summer (they bolt). If you live where winter daytime temperatures average in the 60s, turnips and rutabagas are great winter vegetables.

TEMPERATURE. Turnips and rutabagas do best when daytime high temperatures are between 40 and 60°F. When daytime highs average above 75°F, plants often bolt, and the leaf tips may burn. Seeds germinate best when the ambient temperature is 50 to 80°F.

SOIL. Start with well-drained, biologically active soil that is rich in organic matter. To learn how to create such healthy soil, see page 194. At the beginning of the growing season, add organic compost or fertilizer that is slightly higher in nitrogen (N) than it is in phosphorus (P) or potassium (K). Use a fertilizer with a ratio of 10-7-7 or something similar, or add extra nitrogen (in the form of chicken manure, for instance) to a balanced fertilizer or compost. The higher nitrogen helps plants grow quickly and produce tastier roots. Add a dose (½ cup over 2 square feet) of this fertilizer again about two to three weeks after sowing, at the time you thin the seedlings. Best soil pH range is 6 to 7.5.

LIGHT. When temperatures are moderate, as they prefer, turnips and rutabagas need six to 12 hours of direct sun per day. Where daytime temperatures are hot (above 75°F), provide dappled/filtered shade.

WATER. Turnips and rutabagas like consistent moisture and an average of 1 inch of water per week. Do not let the soil dry out or become waterlogged. These plants develop strong flavors and get woody when grown dry. Keep them moist, and they'll stay mild and tender.

GARDEN USES AND PLANTING TECHNIQUES. The relatively nondescript foliage of turnips and rutabagas can be scattered through an ornamental garden or in a container mix of annual flowers. They are easily paired with other low- to medium-growing flowers and spring bulbs, and lend themselves particularly well to a polyculture approach in the garden. Plant them with other cool-season flowers and vegetables such as peas, violas, sweet alyssum, carrots, lettuce, and scallions. Do not put turnips or rutabagas in the same bed or container where they, or any relative, grew within the last three years.

START SEEDS. Because these plants can suffer from transplant shock, it is best to sow seeds directly where you want plants to grow. Prepare the garden bed with the good soil mix you made. Or, to grow in a container, start with a one-gallon pot with a drainage hole. Place a small square of window screen over the hole, inside the pot, and add ½ inch of gravel. Then fill the pot with the container soil mix you made. About a month before the last expected spring frost, sow turnip seeds about 1 inch apart and about ¼ to ½ inch deep. Sow rutabaga seeds 2 to 4 inches apart and at the same depth

as turnip seeds. Water immediately and keep the soil moist but not soggy until the seeds germinate, which should occur in four to seven days. As the seedlings appear, thin them to 4 to 8 inches apart, further if you chose a large cultivar. After thinning, scatter ½ cup of organic fertilizer over the soil. Then spread mulch 1 to 3 inches deep, depending on the size of the plants, to control weeds and to retain consistent soil moisture. Sow small quantities of seeds every two to three weeks to extend your harvest season, but time your crops so that they mature before the heat of summer.

PROBLEM-SOLVING. Except for their moisture requirements, turnips and rutabagas are easy to grow. However, they are vulnerable to the many problems that plague the cabbage family. Close observation will help nip problems in the bud, so be sure, as always, to spend time in your vegetable garden. Please read the Introduction to avoid trouble in the first place. Also refer to "Change Growing Conditions to Solve Problems" on page 192. If you encounter pests or diseases, consult the Family Problem-Solving Guide on page 124.

Watermelon

Citrullus lanatus

Family Problem-Solving Guide, page 149

DESCRIPTION. Watermelons are frost-sensitive, herbaceous, annual vines with tendrils. Standard large-fruited watermelon vines grow 2 to 3 feet high and sprawl over 64 square feet; they can climb a 6-foot A-frame or trellis, or crawl across the ground. Small-fruited, compact types, about 2 feet high and 3 to 4 feet across, are also available. Each plant makes male (pollen-bearing) and female (fruit-bearing) flowers. The first flowers will always be male and cannot produce fruit. Be patient. As the plant gets a little older, it will make female flowers and produce a generous crop of fruit after the bees have done their job. For help choosing the best cultivar for your garden, see the Appendix.

SEASON. A warm-season crop. Plant in late spring or early summer after all danger of frost is past.

TEMPERATURE. Watermelons thrive where daytime high temperatures average 70 to 80°F and the soil temperature is at least 70°F. Seeds planted in soil that is too cool generally fail to germinate and rot, so wait to plant until the soil is warm enough. Make sure your summer planting allows enough time for the fruit to mature before the first frost of autumn. Frost kills watermelons.

SOIL. Start with well-drained, biologically active soil that is rich in organic matter. To learn how to create such healthy soil, see page 194. Feed with a complete, balanced organic fertilizer and compost at the beginning of each growing season. Feed with additional organic fertilizer during the growing season, gently raking the nutrients into the soil around the plants. Control weeds, conserve moisture, and protect fruit lying on the ground by spreading mulch to a depth of 3 inches once plants are growing well. Maintain a soil pH of 6 to 6.5.

LIGHT. Watermelons need full sun (six to 12 hours daily) to do their best.

WATER. Watermelons require a steady supply of moisture. Give them 1 inch of water per week, watering the root zone, not the foliage. Increase the amount of water to as much as 2 inches a week when the vines support a heavy fruit crop. The planting site must be well drained; use raised beds or large containers if your drainage is poor or the water table is high.

GARDEN USES AND PLANTING TECHNIQUES. Watermelons are usually grown sprawling across the ground; smaller-fruited compact varieties do well in containers and can be grown on an A-frame or trellis. To grow watermelons on a support, be sure to prepare the structure they're going to climb before you plant the seeds. You can use sturdy stakes, tripods of bamboo, or limbs of trees arranged in a teepee fashion; or you can grow them on a net or trellis. These support structures offer a shaded microhabitat on their north side; annuals that appreciate midsummer shade will thrive there. Be sure to support the heavy fruit in slings made from cloth, or it will break the vines. Plant watermelons with other warm-season vegetables and flowers, such as corn, beans, tomatoes, coreopsis, echinacea, rudbeckia, and gaillardia.

START SEEDS. Because watermelon seedlings are susceptible to transplant shock, it is best to sow seeds directly where you want the vines to grow. Prepare the garden bed with the good soil mix you made. Or, to grow in a container, select a compact variety and use a half whiskey barrel. Make sure there is a drainage hole. Place a small square of window screen over the hole, inside the pot, and add ½ inch of gravel. Then fill the pot with the container soil mix you made. After the last spring frost, water the soil (either in the garden or in the container) thoroughly before sowing. Be sure the soil is loose. Sow the seeds about 1 inch deep. Many gardeners prefer to plant watermelons on a little hill or mound about a foot across. Poke a hole in the soil with your finger or a stick, and put two or three seeds in the hole. Make only one planting hole in a hill or a container. In a garden bed, space your planting holes or mounds 4 to 8 feet apart, with 6 feet between rows, depending on the size of the cultivars you choose. Seeds should germinate in four to seven days. Thin to one robust seedling per planting hole.

ADDITIONAL TECHNIQUES. Watermelons need a long, warm growing season. Heat makes the fruit sweet. When the fruits reach baseball size, put two bricks or stones, side by side, beside the fruit and place the young fruit on top of them. Keeping the fruit up off the ground helps avoid certain diseases; in addition, the stones absorb heat during the day and keep the fruit warm at night. Some gardeners like to suspend the fruit in a net sling or old nylon stocking from a support structure to keep it off the ground.

PROBLEM-SOLVING. Watermelons are easy to grow, but you must select your cultivar with care. Many need a very long, warm growing season, and you will be unhappy with the result if you don't choose the right plant for your climate. Please read the Introduction to avoid trouble in the first place. Also refer to "Change Growing Conditions to Solve Problems" on page 192. If you encounter pests or diseases, consult the Family Problem-Solving Guide on page 149.

Zucchini and other summer squash

Cucurbita pepo

Family Problem-Solving Guide, page 149

DESCRIPTION. Summer squash, including zucchini, pattypan, and yellow crookneck, are frost-sensitive, herbaceous, annual vines with tendrils. Vines can trail for 4 feet and grow 3 feet high. Compact bush types, 2 feet across and 3 feet high, are also available. For help choosing the right cultivar for your circumstances, see the Appendix. Each plant makes male (pollen-bearing) and female (fruit-bearing) flowers. The first flowers will always be male and cannot produce fruit. Be patient. As the plant gets a little older, it will make female flowers and produce a generous crop of fruit after the bees have done their job.

SEASON. A warm-season crop. Plant in late spring or early summer after all danger of frost is past.

TEMPERATURE. Squash thrives where daytime high temperatures average 65 to 75°F and the soil temperature is at least 60°F. Seeds planted in soil that is too cool generally fail to germinate and rot, so wait to plant until the soil is warm enough. Check the days to maturity on the cultivar label to make sure your summer planting allows enough time for the plants to produce fruit before the first frost of autumn. Squash is killed by frost.

SOIL. Start with well-drained, biologically active soil that is rich in organic matter. To learn how to create such healthy soil, see page 194. Feed the soil with high-nitrogen organic fertilizer and compost at the beginning of each growing season. Feed with additional organic fertilizer during the growing season, gently raking the nutrients into the soil around the plants. Control weeds, conserve moisture, and protect fruit lying on the ground by spreading mulch to a depth of 3 inches once plants are growing well. Best soil pH range is 6 to 7.5.

LIGHT. Squash needs full sun (six to 12 hours daily) to do its best.

WATER. Squash requires regular water. Give plants 1 inch per week, watering the root zone, not the foliage. Increase the amount of water to as much as 2 inches a week when the vines support a heavy fruit crop. The planting site must be well drained; use raised beds or large containers if your drainage is poor or the water table is high.

GARDEN USES AND PLANTING TECHNIQUES. A vine-type summer squash can be grown on a support structure to conserve space and hold fruit off the ground. Be sure to prepare the structure it's going to climb before you plant the seeds. You can use sturdy stakes, tripods of bamboo, or limbs of trees arranged in a teepee fashion; or you can grow them on a net or trellis. These support structures offer a shaded microhabitat on their north side; annuals that appreciate midsummer shade will thrive there. The bush types need no such support and work well in containers. A classic polyculture use of squash was developed by the indigenous people of Mesoamerica; they always planted squash with corn and beans. Squash also plays well with tomatoes, fennel, dill, sunflowers, gaillardia, echinacea, and marigolds.

START SEEDS. Because squash seedlings do not transplant well, it is best to sow seeds directly where you want the vines to grow. Prepare the garden bed with the good soil mix you made. Or, to grow in a container, start with either a 5-gallon pot or a half whiskey barrel. Make sure there is a drainage hole. Place a small square of window screen over the hole, inside the pot, and add ½ inch of gravel. Then fill the pot with the container soil mix you made. After the last spring frost, water the soil (either in the garden or in the container) thoroughly before sowing. Be sure the soil is loose. Sow the seeds about 1 inch deep. Many gardeners prefer to plant squash on a little hill or mound about a foot across. Poke a hole in the soil with your finger or a stick, and put two or three seeds in the hole. Make only one planting hole in a hill or a container. In a garden bed, space the planting holes 2 feet apart. Seeds should germinate in four to seven days. Thin to one robust seedling per planting hole.

PROBLEM-SOLVING. Prolific and easy to grow, zucchini and other summer squash are nevertheless susceptible to several insect pests and diseases. Please read the Introduction to avoid trouble in the first place. Also refer to "Change Growing Conditions to Solve Problems" on page 192. If you encounter pests or diseases, consult the Family Problem-Solving Guide on page 149.

Family Problem-Solving Guides

Throughout these guides, the most toxic remedies for a particular diagnosis are always listed last and should be turned to only if all else fails.

Artichokes, Chicory, Endive, Escarole, Lettuce, Radicchio

Symptom	Diagnosis	Solution
Tiny gray, pink, or green, soft-bodied, pear-shaped insects, with two tubes on their rear ends, gather on the undersides of leaves. A clear, sticky substance coats the upper surfaces of leaves. A black coating that easily rubs off (sooty mold) may occur on lower leaves.	Aphids	Row covers, page 214 Blast with hose, page 217 Encourage beneficials, page 208 Beneficial predators, page 218 Insecticidal soap, page 221 Neem, page 223 Horticultural oil, page 223 Sulfur, page 224 Pyrethrin, page 224
Whitish trails loop across the leaf. Insect larvae (maggots) are inside the leaf. Adults are flies.	Leafminers	Row covers, page 214 Plant polycultures, page 205 Rotate your crops, page 207 Weed, page 210 Encourage beneficials, page 208 Beneficial predators, page 218 Neem, page 223 Horticultural oil, page 223 Sulfur, page 224 Pyrethrin, page 224
Holes appear in the leaves and flower buds of artichokes. Serpentine brown trails on flower buds confirm the diagnosis.	Caterpillars: plume moth larvae	Row covers, page 214 Plant polycultures, page 205 Weed, page 210 Sanitize, page 210 Hand-pick pests, page 217 Resistant cultivars, page 227 Encourage beneficials, page 208 Beneficial predators, page 218 Insecticidal soap, page 221 BTK, page 221 Neem, page 223 Horticultural oil, page 223 Sulfur, page 224 Pyrethrin, page 224

Symptom	Diagnosis	Solution
 Brown or green caterpillars hide in the soil and curl into a C shape when disturbed. They come out at night and mow down seedlings and plants just above the soil line.	**Caterpillars: cutworms**	Row covers, page 214 Plant polycultures, page 205 Rotate your crops, page 207 Cutworm collars, page 214 Beneficial nematodes, page 220
 Large irregular holes appear on the edges and sometimes in the middle of leaves. Look for small, black pellets of excrement. The soft tissue on the undersides of leaves may be eaten away. You may also find the pest, but it is hard to see.	**Caterpillars: cabbage loopers, alfalfa loopers, armyworms, corn earworms**	Row covers, page 214 Weed, page 210 Sanitize, page 210 Hand-pick pests, page 217 Resistant cultivars, page 227 Encourage beneficials, page 208 Beneficial predators, page 218 Insecticidal soap, page 221 BTK, page 221 Neem, page 223 Horticultural oil, page 223 Sulfur, page 224 Pyrethrin, page 224
 Leaves are stippled with whitish dots. You may see very tiny, wedge-shaped, fast-flying insects. Photo shows an extreme close-up of this colorful pest.	**Leafhoppers**	Row covers, page 214 Weed, page 210 Sanitize, page 210 Kaolin spray, page 217 Insecticidal soap, page 221 *Beauveria bassiana*, page 223 Neem, page 223 Horticultural oil, page 223 Pyrethrin, page 224

Symptom	Diagnosis	Solution
Small, bright-white insects fly away when disturbed. Large colonies gather on the undersides of leaves. A clear, sticky substance may coat the upper surfaces of leaves. A black coating that easily rubs off (sooty mold) may occur on lower leaves.	Whitefly	Row covers, page 214 Blast with hose, page 217 Vacuum, page 217 Move the air, page 210 Traps, page 218 Encourage beneficials, page 208 Beneficial predators, page 220 Insecticidal soap, page 221 Neem, page 223 Horticultural oil, page 223 Sulfur, page 224 Pyrethrin, page 224
Large holes appear on the edges and in the middle of leaves. Grasshoppers jump and fly about the garden.	Grasshoppers	Row covers, page 214 Plant polycultures, page 205 Rotate your crops, page 207 Weed, page 210 Encourage beneficials, page 208 Beneficial predators, page 218 Nosema spore, page 221 Neem, page 223 Horticultural oil, page 223 Pyrethrin, page 224
Holes appear in tender new leaves. Small, brown and black insects with two pincers on their rear ends hide during the day and come out at night.	Earwigs	Row covers, page 214 Traps, page 218 Diatomaceous earth, page 222 Spinosad, page 223
Large, irregular holes appear in the middle of leaves. Look for slime trails, slugs, or snails nearby. They hide during the day and come out at night to raid your garden.	Slugs or snails	Row covers, page 214 Hand-pick pests, page 217 Copper tape, page 217 Traps, page 218 Iron phosphate, page 222 Diatomaceous earth, page 222

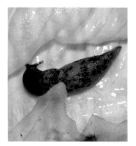

Symptom	Diagnosis	Solution
Leaves curl up, turn brown, and die. Look for a white, powdery coating on the upper surfaces of older leaves.	**Powdery mildew**	Sanitize, page 210 Resistant cultivars, page 227 Move the air, page 210 Plant polycultures, page 205 Weed, page 210 Mulch, page 210 Baking soda, page 225 *Bacillus subtilis*, page 225 Neem, page 226 Sulfur, page 226 Copper, page 226
Heads of leafy vegetables become brown and slimy, and then rot. Before that can happen, keep an eye out for rust-colored, sunken, oozing spots on lower (older) leaves.	**Bottom rot**	Sanitize, page 210 Manage water, page 199 Resistant cultivars, page 227 Improve drainage, page 205 Move the air, page 210 Plant polycultures, page 205 Rotate your crops, page 207 Weed, page 210 Mulch, page 210 Create healthy soil, page 194 Solarize the soil, page 199
Small, dark spots with yellow halos develop on leaves. Spots grow bigger, become angular, and dry up. Centers of spots may fall out, leaving holes. Leaves may be killed.	**Anthracnose leaf-spot fungus**	Sanitize, page 210 Manage water, page 199 Resistant cultivars, page 227 Improve drainage, page 205 Move the air, page 210 Plant polycultures, page 205 Rotate your crops, page 207 Weed, page 210 Mulch, page 210 Create healthy soil, page 194 Baking soda, page 225 *Bacillus subtilis*, page 225 Sulfur, page 226 Copper, page 226

Symptom	Diagnosis	Solution
Stem and lower leaves rot. Look for gray-brown, fuzzy mold growing on the rotting areas.	Gray mold, botrytis	Sanitize, page 210 Manage water, page 199 Resistant cultivars, page 227 Improve drainage, page 205 Move the air, page 210 Plant polycultures, page 205 Rotate your crops, page 207 Weed, page 210 Mulch, page 210 Create healthy soil, page 194 Baking soda, page 225 *Bacillus subtilis*, page 225 Neem, page 226 Sulfur, page 226 Copper, page 226
Fluffy, white, cottony mold develops from water-soaked spots on leaves and stems. Sometimes black seed-like pellets appear within the mold.	White mold, stem canker, soft rot, crown rot, lettuce drop	Sanitize, page 210 Manage water, page 199 Resistant cultivars, page 227 Improve drainage, page 205 Move the air, page 210 Plant polycultures, page 205 Rotate your crops, page 207 Weed, page 210 Mulch, page 210 Create healthy soil, page 194 Solarize the soil, page 199
Seeds fail to germinate and rot. Seedlings fall over and die.	Damping off	Sanitize, page 210 Manage water, page 199 Resistant cultivars, page 227 Improve drainage, page 205 Move the air, page 210 Plant polycultures, page 205 Rotate your crops, page 207 Weed, page 210 Mulch, page 210 Create healthy soil, page 194 Baking soda, page 225 *Bacillus subtilis*, page 225 *Trichoderma harzianum*, page 226 Copper, page 226

Symptom	Diagnosis	Solution
Leaves are wilted. Plants are stunted and yellow. Dead patches appear on leaf edges. Cut the stem and root in half lengthwise and look for brown veins to confirm the diagnosis.	Verticillium wilt	Sanitize, page 210 Manage water, page 199 Resistant cultivars, page 227 Improve drainage, page 205 Move the air, page 210 Plant polycultures, page 205 Rotate your crops, page 207 Weed, page 210 Mulch, page 210 Create healthy soil, page 194 Solarize the soil, page 199
Large areas on the leaves turn black, and the plant collapses. Before this occurs, look for small, water-soaked, angular spots on older leaves. Spots rapidly turn black and coalesce into the damage you see here.	Bacterial spot	Sanitize, page 210 Manage water, page 199 Resistant cultivars, page 227 Improve drainage, page 205 Move the air, page 210 Plant polycultures, page 205 Rotate your crops, page 207 Weed, page 210 Mulch, page 210 Create healthy soil, page 194 Copper, page 226
Mottled yellow marks appear on leaves. Plants become stunted. Photo shows mosaic virus on cabbage. Aphids spread this disease.	Mosaic viruses: lettuce mosaic, turnip mosaic, beet western yellows, beet yellow stunt	Sanitize, page 210 Resistant cultivars, page 227 Weed, page 210 Mulch, page 210 See aphid solutions, page 118
Plants are severely stunted, and leaves are distorted and have dark spots of dead tissue. Leafhoppers spread this disease.	Curly dwarf virus	Sanitize, page 210 Resistant cultivars, page 227 Weed, page 210 Mulch, page 210 See leafhopper solutions, page 119

Arugula, Bok Choy, Broccoli, Brussels Sprouts, Cabbage, Cauliflower, Chinese Cabbage, Collard Greens, Kale, Kohlrabi, Mustard Greens, Radishes, Rutabagas, Turnips

	Symptom	Diagnosis	Solution
	Tiny gray or green, soft-bodied, pear-shaped insects, with two tubes on their rear ends, cluster on the undersides of leaves. A clear, sticky substance coats the upper surfaces of leaves. A black coating that easily rubs off (sooty mold) may occur on lower leaves.	Aphids	Row covers, page 214 Blast with hose, page 217 Encourage beneficials, page 208 Beneficial predators, page 218 Insecticidal soap, page 221 Neem, page 223 Horticultural oil, page 223 Sulfur, page 224 Pyrethrin, page 224
	Small, bright-white in-sects fly away when dis-turbed. Large colonies on the undersides of leaves deposit patches of white residue. A clear, sticky substance coats the up-per surfaces of leaves. A black coating that easily rubs off (sooty mold) may occur on lower leaves.	Whitefly	Row covers, page 214 Blast with hose, page 217 Vacuum, page 217 Move the air, page 210 Traps, page 218 Encourage beneficials, page 208 Beneficial predators, page 218 Insecticidal soap, page 221 Neem, page 223 Horticultural oil, page 223 Sulfur, page 224 Pyrethrin, page 224

Symptom	Diagnosis	Solution
Large, irregular holes appear in the middle and on the edges of leaves. You may also see tunnels in the heads of broccoli, Brussels sprouts, cabbage, and cauliflower. Leaves may be skeletonized (soft tissue is eaten away, tough veins remain). Look for caterpillars to confirm your diagnosis.	**Caterpillars: cabbage loopers, imported cabbage worms, cross-striped cabbage worm, diamondback moth larvae, beet armyworms**	Row covers, page 214 Plant polycultures, page 205 Weed, page 210 Sanitize, page 210 Hand-pick pests, page 217 Resistant cultivars, page 227 Encourage beneficials, page 208 Beneficial predators, page 218 Insecticidal soap, page 221 BTK, page 221 Neem, page 223 Horticultural oil, page 223 Sulfur, page 224 Pyrethrin, page 224
Brown or green caterpillars hide in the soil and curl into a C shape when disturbed. They come out at night and mow down seedlings and plants just above the soil line.	**Caterpillars: cutworms**	Row covers, page 214 Plant polycultures, page 205 Rotate your crops, page 207 Cutworm collars, page 214 Beneficial nematodes, page 220
Many very small, round holes appear in leaves. You may also see tiny black beetles that jump like fleas.	**Flea beetles**	Row covers, page 214 Plant polycultures, page 205 Encourage beneficials, page 208 Insecticidal soap, page 221 *Beauveria bassiana*, page 223 Spinosad, page 223 Neem, page 223 Horticultural oil, page 223 Sulfur, page 224 Pyrethrin, page 224

Symptom	Diagnosis	Solution
When you see adult flea beetles on plants, or you see the damage they do, you can be sure their larvae are in the soil, eating the roots.	Flea beetle larvae	Plant polycultures, page 205 Rotate your crops, page 207 Beneficial nematodes, page 220
Plants are stunted. Leaves turn yellow and purplish, and are prone to wilting. Roots are riddled with tunnels that have maggots inside. Turnips and radishes frequently show this damage.	Cabbage maggots	Row covers, page 214 Plant polycultures, page 205 Rotate your crops, page 207 Weed, page 210 Tar paper, page 214 Encourage beneficials, page 208 Beneficial nematodes, page 220 Neem, page 223 Horticultural oil, page 223 Sulfur, page 224 Pyrethrin, page 224
Shield-shaped bugs on the plant pierce leaves and flower buds with their needle-like mouthparts. Leaves become spotted and twisted, then wilt and turn brown. Broccoli flower buds turn black.	Harlequin bugs, stink bugs, tarnished plant bugs, lygus bugs	Row covers, page 214 Plant polycultures, page 205 Hand-pick pests, page 217 Weed, page 210 Sanitize, page 210 Encourage beneficials, page 208 Beneficial predators, page 218 Kaolin spray, page 217 Garlic spray, page 220 Insecticidal soap, page 221 *Beauveria bassiana*, page 223 Neem, page 223 Horticultural oil, page 223 Pyrethrin, page 224

Symptom	Diagnosis	Solution
Large holes appear on the edges and in the middle of leaves. Grasshoppers jump and fly about the garden.	**Grasshoppers**	Row covers, page 214 Plant polycultures, page 205 Rotate your crops, page 207 Weed, page 210 Encourage beneficials, page 208 Beneficial predators, page 218 Nosema spore, page 221 Neem, page 223 Horticultural oil, page 223 Sulfur, page 224 Pyrethrin, page 224
Large, irregular holes appear in the middle of leaves. Look for slime trails, slugs, or snails nearby. They hide during the day and come out at night to raid your garden.	**Slugs or snails**	Row covers, page 214 Hand-pick pests, page 217 Copper tape, page 217 Traps, page 218 Iron phosphate, page 222 Diatomaceous earth, page 222
Leaves turn yellow, and dark pits develop within the yellow areas. A thin, white coating appears on the undersides of discolored leaves.	**Downy mildew**	Sanitize, page 210 Manage water, page 199 Resistant cultivars, page 227 Improve drainage, page 205 Move the air, page 210 Plant polycultures, page 205 Rotate your crops, page 207 Weed, page 210 Mulch, page 210 Create healthy soil, page 194 Baking soda, page 225 *Bacillus subtilis*, page 225 Neem, page 226 Copper, page 226

Symptom	Diagnosis	Solution
 Large yellow areas develop on leaves, which then wilt, turn brown, and drop off. Often, leaves on only one side of the plant will show symptoms.	**Cabbage yellows, fusarium wilt**	Sanitize, page 210 Manage water, page 199 Resistant cultivars, page 227 Improve drainage, page 205 Move the air, page 210 Plant polycultures, page 205 Rotate your crops, page 207 Weed, page 210 Mulch, page 210 Create healthy soil, page 194 Solarize the soil, page 199
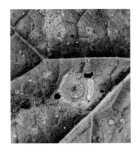 Fluffy, white, cottony mold develops from water-soaked spots on leaves and stems. Sometimes black seed-like pellets appear within the mold.	**White mold, stem canker, soft rot, crown rot**	Sanitize, page 210 Manage water, page 199 Resistant cultivars, page 227 Improve drainage, page 205 Move the air, page 210 Plant polycultures, page 205 Rotate your crops, page 207 Weed, page 210 Mulch, page 210 Create healthy soil, page 194 Solarize the soil, page 199
Dark spots or blotches with target-like concentric rings appear on mature leaves.	**Alternaria blight**	Sanitize, page 210 Manage water, page 199 Resistant cultivars, page 227 Improve drainage, page 205 Move the air, page 210 Plant polycultures, page 205 Rotate your crops, page 207 Weed, page 210 Mulch, page 210 Create healthy soil, page 194 Baking soda, page 225 *Bacillus subtilis*, page 225 Sulfur, page 226 Copper, page 226

Symptom	Diagnosis	Solution
Plants wilt easily, and become stunted. Leaves have large yellow splotches that turn brown. Thick, club-like roots confirm the diagnosis.	Clubroot	Sanitize, page 210 Manage water, page 199 Resistant cultivars, page 227 Improve drainage, page 205 Move the air, page 210 Plant polycultures, page 205 Rotate your crops, page 207 Weed, page 210 Mulch, page 210 Create healthy soil, page 194 Measure and modify pH, page 199
Seeds fail to germinate and rot. Seedlings fall over and die.	Damping off	Sanitize, page 210 Manage water, page 199 Resistant cultivars, page 227 Improve drainage, page 205 Move the air, page 210 Plant polycultures, page 205 Rotate your crops, page 207 Weed, page 210 Mulch, page 210 Create healthy soil, page 194 Baking soda, page 225 *Bacillus subtilis*, page 225 *Trichoderma harzianum*, page 226 Copper, page 226
You see V-shaped, yellow spots that turn brown on leaves.	Black rot	Sanitize, page 210 Manage water, page 199 Resistant cultivars, page 227 Improve drainage, page 205 Move the air, page 210 Plant polycultures, page 205 Rotate your crops, page 207 Weed, page 210 Mulch, page 210 Create healthy soil, page 194 Copper, page 226

Symptom	Diagnosis	Solution
Heads or leaves turn brown or black, then rot.	**Bacterial soft rot**	Sanitize, page 210 Manage water, page 199 Resistant cultivars, page 227 Improve drainage, page 205 Move the air, page 210 Plant polycultures, page 205 Rotate your crops, page 207 Weed, page 210 Mulch, page 210 Create healthy soil, page 194 Copper, page 226
Mottled yellow marks appear on leaves. Plants become stunted. Aphids spread this disease.	**Mosaic viruses: lettuce mosaic, turnip mosaic, beet western yellows, beet yellow stunt**	Sanitize, page 210 Resistant cultivars, page 227 Weed, page 210 Mulch, page 210 See aphid solutions, page 124

Asparagus

Symptom	Diagnosis	Solution
Dark grubs on the plant destroy the foliage.	**Asparagus beetle larvae**	Row covers, page 214 Plant polycultures, page 205 Hand-pick pests, page 217 Encourage beneficials, page 208 Insecticidal soap, page 221 BTSD, page 222 *Beauveria bassiana*, page 223 Spinosad, page 223 Neem, page 223 Horticultural oil, page 223 Sulfur, page 224 Pyrethrin, page 224
Brown scars on stems cause them to curl into a shepherd's crook. Beetles and larvae feeding on foliage can cause significant defoliation.	**Common asparagus beetles, spotted asparagus beetles**	Row covers, page 214 Plant polycultures, page 205 Hand-pick pests, page 217 Encourage beneficials, page 208 Insecticidal soap, page 221 BTSD, page 222 *Beauveria bassiana*, page 223 Spinosad, page 223 Neem, page 223 Horticultural oil, page 223 Sulfur, page 224 Pyrethrin, page 224
You see beetles on the plant. They are destroying foliage, flowers, and fruits.	**Japanese beetles, spotted cucumber beetles, spotted asparagus beetles**	Row covers, page 214 Plant polycultures, page 205 Hand-pick pests, page 217 Encourage beneficials, page 208 Insecticidal soap, page 221 BTSD, page 222 *Beauveria bassiana*, page 223 Spinosad, page 223 Neem, page 223 Horticultural oil, page 223 Sulfur, page 224 Pyrethrin, page 224

Symptom	Diagnosis	Solution
You find light-colored grubs in the soil.	**Larvae of Japanese beetles, spotted cucumber beetles**	Plant polycultures, page 205 Rotate your crops, page 207 Beneficial nematodes, page 220 Milky spore, page 222
Slime trails, slugs, or snails are in the garden, and new spears are damaged. These pests hide during the day and come out at night to raid your garden.	**Slugs or snails**	Row covers, page 214 Hand-pick pests, page 217 Copper tape, page 217 Traps, page 218 Iron phosphate, page 222 Diatomaceous earth, page 222
Light green, oval-shaped spots appear on the stalks in spring. The spots turn tan, becoming black/brown streaks in summer.	**Rust**	Sanitize, page 210 Manage water, page 199 Resistant cultivars, page 227 Improve drainage, page 205 Move the air, page 210 Plant polycultures, page 205 Rotate your crops, page 207 Weed, page 210 Mulch, page 210 Create healthy soil, page 194 Baking soda, page 225 *Bacillus subtilis*, page 225 Sulfur, page 226 Copper, page 226

Symptom	Diagnosis	Solution
Some stems turn yellow and wilt. Plants become stunted, declining gradually. Reddish brown discoloration appears at the base of stems.	**Fusarium wilt**	Sanitize, page 210 Manage water, page 199 Resistant cultivars, page 227 Improve drainage, page 205 Move the air, page 210 Plant polycultures, page 205 Rotate your crops, page 207 Weed, page 210 Mulch, page 210 Create healthy soil, page 194 Solarize soil, page 199

Beets, Chard, Spinach

Symptom	Diagnosis	Solution
Tightly curled and crinkled leaves hide tiny black or gray, soft-bodied, pear-shaped insects, with two tubes on their rear ends.	Aphids	Row covers, page 214 Blast with hose, page 217 Encourage beneficials, page 208 Beneficial predators, page 218 Insecticidal soap, page 221 Neem, page 223 Horticultural oil, page 223 Sulfur, page 224 Pyrethrin, page 224
Caterpillars eat large irregular holes on the edges and sometimes in the middle of leaves. You may see small black pellets of excrement.	Caterpillars: cabbage loopers, alfalfa loopers, armyworms, corn earworms	Row covers, page 214 Plant polycultures, page 205 Weed, page 210 Sanitize, page 210 Hand-pick pests, page 217 Resistant cultivars, page 227 Encourage beneficials, page 208 Beneficial predators, page 218 Insecticidal soap, page 221 BTK, page 221 Neem, page 223 Horticultural oil, page 223 Sulfur, page 224 Pyrethrin, page 224
Large blotches appear on leaves. Maggots hide inside these blotches and eat the inside of the leaf. The adult insect is a fly.	Leafminers	Row covers, page 214 Plant polycultures, page 205 Rotate your crops, page 207 Weed, page 210 Encourage beneficials, page 208 Beneficial predators, page 218 Neem, page 223 Horticultural oil, page 223 Sulfur, page 224 Pyrethrin, page 224

Symptom	Diagnosis	Solution
Brown or green caterpillars hide in the soil and curl into a C shape when disturbed. They come out at night and mow down seedlings and plants just above the soil line.	Caterpillars: cutworms	Row covers, page 214 Plant polycultures, page 205 Rotate your crops, page 207 Cutworm collars, page 214 Beneficial nematodes, page 220
Many very small, round holes appear in leaves. You may also see tiny beetles that jump like fleas.	Flea beetles	Row covers, page 214 Encourage beneficials, page 208 Insecticidal soap, page 221 *Beauveria bassiana*, page 223 Spinosad, page 223 Neem, page 223 Horticultural oil, page 223 Sulfur, page 224 Pyrethrin, page 224
Tiny white or pink specks stipple leaves. You may see small, wedge-shaped, fast-flying insects.	Leafhoppers	Row covers, page 214 Weed, page 210 Sanitize, page 210 Kaolin spray, page 217 Insecticidal soap, page 221 *Beauveria bassiana*, page 223 Neem, page 223 Horticultural oil, page 223 Pyrethrin, page 224
Large holes appear on the edges and in the middle of leaves. Grasshoppers jump and fly about the garden. Photo shows a katydid, a close relative of grasshoppers.	Grasshoppers	Row covers, page 214 Plant polycultures, page 205 Rotate your crops, page 207 Weed, page 210 Encourage beneficials, page 208 Beneficial predators, page 218 Nosema spore, page 221 Neem, page 223 Horticultural oil, page 223 Pyrethrin, page 224

Symptom	Diagnosis	Solution
Holes appear in tender new leaves. Look for small brown and black insects with two pincers on their rear ends to confirm your diagnosis.	Earwigs	Row covers, page 214 Traps, page 218 Diatomaceous earth, page 222 Spinosad, page 223
Large, irregular holes appear in the middle of leaves. Look for slime trails, slugs, or snails nearby. They hide during the day and come out at night to raid your garden.	Slugs or snails	Row covers, page 214 Hand-pick pests, page 217 Copper tape, page 217 Traps, page 218 Iron phosphate, page 222 Diatomaceous earth, page 222
Leaves turn yellow and wilt. Roots have odd, knot-like swellings.	Root-knot nematodes	Plant polycultures, page 205 Rotate your crops, page 207 Create healthy soil, page 194 Resistant cultivars, page 227 Solarize the soil, page 199

Symptom	Diagnosis	Solution
Leaves have yellow patches that turn brown. White or gray fuzz appears on the undersides of leaves. Leaves die. Beets often have rough, cracked skin.	Downy mildew	Sanitize, page 210 Manage water, page 199 Resistant cultivars, page 227 Improve drainage, page 205 Move the air, page 210 Plant polycultures, page 205 Rotate your crops, page 207 Weed, page 210 Mulch, page 210 Create healthy soil, page 194 Baking soda, page 225 *Bacillus subtilis*, page 225 Neem, page 226 Copper, page 226
Seeds fail to germinate and rot. Seedlings fall over and die.	Damping off	Sanitize, page 210 Manage water, page 199 Resistant cultivars, page 227 Improve drainage, page 205 Move the air, page 210 Plant polycultures, page 205 Rotate your crops, page 207 Weed, page 210 Mulch, page 210 Create healthy soil, page 194 Baking soda, page 225 *Bacillus subtilis*, page 225 *Trichoderma harzianum*, page 226 Copper, page 226
Plants wilt, turn yellow, and die. Roots appear water-soaked, mushy, brown-black, and dead.	Root rot, fusarium wilt	Sanitize, page 210 Manage water, page 199 Resistant cultivars, page 227 Improve drainage, page 205 Move the air, page 210 Plant polycultures, page 205 Rotate your crops, page 207 Weed, page 210 Mulch, page 210 Create healthy soil, page 194 Solarize the soil, page 199

Symptom	Diagnosis	Solution
 Small, dark-colored spots develop on leaves, and the center of the spots falls out, leaving holes. Leaves may be killed. Plants may be stunted.	Anthracnose leaf-spot fungus	Sanitize, page 210 Manage water, page 199 Resistant cultivars, page 227 Improve drainage, page 205 Move the air, page 210 Plant polycultures, page 205 Rotate your crops, page 207 Weed, page 210 Mulch, page 210 Create healthy soil, page 194 Baking soda, page 225 *Bacillus subtilis*, page 225 Sulfur, page 226 Copper, page 226
Leaves curl and roll up. Plants are stunted and turn yellow. Photo shows identical symptoms on a tomato. Aphids spread this disease.	Curly top virus	Sanitize, page 210 Resistant cultivars, page 227 Weed, page 210 Mulch, page 210 See aphid solutions, page 134

PESTS AND DISEASES OF
Carrots, Parsnips

Symptom	Diagnosis	Solution
The main root (carrot or parsnip) has rust-colored tunnels eaten into it. Yellowish white maggots may be present. Plants are stunted, and turn yellow and die. Small feeder roots are eaten away.	**Carrot rust fly, carrot maggots**	Row covers, page 214 Plant polycultures, page 205 Rotate your crops, page 207 Weed, page 210 Tar paper, page 214 Encourage beneficials, page 208 Beneficial nematodes, page 220 Neem, page 223 Horticultural oil, page 223 Sulfur, page 224 Pyrethrin, page 224
Brown or green caterpillars hide in the soil and curl into a C shape when disturbed. They come out at night and mow down seedlings and plants just above the soil line.	**Caterpillars: cutworm**	Row covers, page 214 Plant polycultures, page 205 Rotate your crops, page 207 Cutworm collars, page 214 Beneficial nematodes, page 220
Large greenish white caterpillars with black rings and yellow spots devour leaves.	**Caterpillars: parsley worm**	These are the larvae of the black swallowtail butterfly. Take them out of your garden and place them on a wild member of the carrot family, such as Queen Anne's lace.

Symptom	Diagnosis	Solution
Tiny white specks stipple the leaves. You may see small, wedge-shaped, fast-flying insects.	**Leafhoppers**	Row covers, page 214 Weed, page 210 Sanitize, page 210 Kaolin spray, page 217 Insecticidal soap, page 221 *Beauveria bassiana*, page 223 Neem, page 223 Horticultural oil, page 223 Pyrethrin, page 224
Leaves develop brown blotches where maggots feed inside leaf tissue. The adult insect is a fly.	**Leafminers**	Row covers, page 214 Plant polycultures, page 205 Rotate your crops, page 207 Weed, page 210 Encourage beneficials, page 208 Beneficial predators, page 218 Neem, page 223 Horticultural oil, page 223 Sulfur, page 224 Pyrethrin, page 224
Small black holes appear in the main root (carrot or parsnip). Look for yellow-brown, segmented, hard-shelled "worms" in the soil.	**Wireworms**	Plant polycultures, page 205 Rotate your crops, page 207 Beneficial nematodes, page 220
Large holes appear in leaves and on the main root. Look for slime trails, slugs, or snails nearby. They hide during the day and come out at night to raid your garden.	**Slugs or snails**	Row covers, page 214 Hand-pick pests, page 217 Copper tape, page 217 Traps, page 218 Iron phosphate, page 222 Diatomaceous earth, page 222

Symptom	Diagnosis	Solution
Leaves develop brown areas, then shrivel and die.	**Leaf-spot fungi or bacteria**	Sanitize, page 210 Manage water, page 199 Resistant cultivars, page 227 Improve drainage, page 205 Move the air, page 210 Plant polycultures, page 205 Rotate your crops, page 207 Weed, page 210 Mulch, page 210 Create healthy soil, page 194 Sulfur, page 226 Copper, page 226
Seeds germinate poorly, or fail to germinate and rot. Seedlings fall over and die.	**Damping off**	Sanitize, page 210 Manage water, page 199 Resistant cultivars, page 227 Improve drainage, page 205 Move the air, page 210 Plant polycultures, page 205 Rotate your crops, page 207 Weed, page 210 Mulch, page 210 Create healthy soil, page 194 Baking soda, page 225 *Bacillus subtilis*, page 225 *Trichoderma harzianum*, page 226 Copper, page 226
Plants wilt. Leaves, stems, and roots become brown, black, and rotten. Fluffy, white mold grows on the rotted plant parts.	**Root rot, white mold, southern blight**	Sanitize, page 210 Manage water, page 199 Resistant cultivars, page 227 Improve drainage, page 205 Move the air, page 210 Plant polycultures, page 205 Rotate your crops, page 207 Weed, page 210 Mulch, page 210 Create healthy soil, page 194 Solarize the soil, page 199

Symptom	Diagnosis	Solution
Soft, watery, slimy, brown decay develops on the main root (which may also smell bad). Plants turn yellow, wilt, and collapse.	**Bacterial soft rot**	Sanitize, page 210 Manage water, page 199 Resistant cultivars, page 227 Improve drainage, page 205 Move the air, page 210 Plant polycultures, page 205 Rotate your crops, page 207 Weed, page 210 Mulch, page 210 Create healthy soil, page 194 Copper, page 226
Plants are stunted, and foliage turns yellow. Lots of very thin, hairy feeder roots grow from the main root. Leafhoppers spread this disease.	**Aster yellows, carrot yellows**	Sanitize, page 210 Resistant cultivars, page 227 Weed, page 210 Mulch, page 210 See leafhopper solutions, page 140

Corn

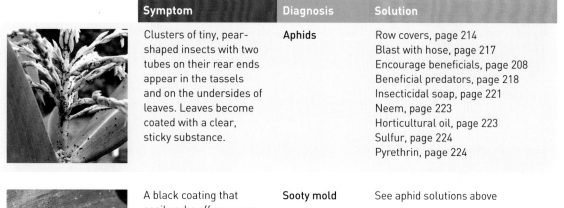

Symptom	Diagnosis	Solution
 Clusters of tiny, pear-shaped insects with two tubes on their rear ends appear in the tassels and on the undersides of leaves. Leaves become coated with a clear, sticky substance.	Aphids	Row covers, page 214 Blast with hose, page 217 Encourage beneficials, page 208 Beneficial predators, page 218 Insecticidal soap, page 221 Neem, page 223 Horticultural oil, page 223 Sulfur, page 224 Pyrethrin, page 224
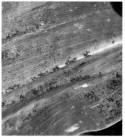 A black coating that easily rubs off grows on leaves. Plants are infested with aphids.	Sooty mold	See aphid solutions above
Leaves are skeletonized (soft tissue is eaten away, tough veins remain). Beetles are often present on the plants. Silks may be chewed and are sometimes completely gone.	Japanese beetles, cucumber beetles	Row covers, page 214 Hand-pick pests, page 217 Encourage beneficials, page 208 Insecticidal soap, page 221 BTSD, page 222 *Beauveria bassiana*, page 223 Spinosad, page 223 Neem, page 223 Horticultural oil, page 223 Sulfur, page 224 Pyrethrin, page 224

Symptom	Diagnosis	Solution
The tips of the ears have damaged kernels. Look for small black beetles with yellow spots to confirm your diagnosis.	Sap beetles	Row covers, page 214 Hand-pick pests, page 217 Encourage beneficials, page 208 Insecticidal soap, page 221 BTSD, page 222 *Beauveria bassiana*, page 223 Spinosad, page 223 Neem, page 223 Horticultural oil, page 223 Sulfur, page 224 Pyrethrin, page 224
White grubs with brown heads live in the soil and eat the roots. Plants may become stunted.	Corn rootworms, corn flea beetles, Japanese beetles	Plant polycultures, page 205 Rotate your crops, page 207 Beneficial nematodes, page 220 Milky spore, page 222
Large, irregular holes appear on leaf edges. Plants can be defoliated. Look for caterpillars to confirm your diagnosis.	Caterpillars: corn earworms, armyworms	Row covers, page 214 Plant polycultures, page 205 Weed, page 210 Sanitize, page 210 Hand-pick pests, page 217 Resistant cultivars, page 227 Encourage beneficials, page 208 Beneficial predators, page 218 Insecticidal soap, page 221 BTK, page 221 Neem, page 223 Horticultural oil, page 223 Sulfur, page 224 Pyrethrin, page 224

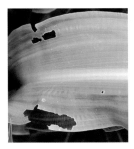

Symptom	Diagnosis	Solution
You find green or brown caterpillars inside the ears. Kernels and silks are chewed.	**Caterpillars: corn ear- worms, fall armyworms**	Row covers, page 214 Plant polycultures, page 205 Weed, page 210 Sanitize, page 210 Hand-pick pests, page 217 Resistant cultivars, page 227 Encourage beneficials, page 208 Beneficial predators, page 218 Insecticidal soap, page 221 BTK, page 221 Neem, page 223 Horticultural oil, page 223 Sulfur, page 224 Pyrethrin, page 224
Large holes appear on the edges and in the middle of leaves. Grass-hoppers jump and fly about the garden.	**Grasshoppers**	Row covers, page 214 Plant polycultures, page 205 Rotate your crops, page 207 Weed, page 210 Encourage beneficials, page 208 Beneficial predators, page 218 Nosema spore, page 221 Neem, page 223 Horticultural oil, page 223 Sulfur, page 224 Pyrethrin, page 224
Small, brown and black insects with two pincers on their rear ends hide during the day and come out at night to eat holes in tender new leaves. They munch on corn silk, too, resulting in poorly filled ears.	**Earwigs**	Row covers, page 214 Traps, page 218 Diatomaceous earth, page 222 Spinosad, page 223

Symptom	Diagnosis	Solution
 Small holes appear in corn stalks. Stalks may topple over. Caterpillars may bore through shucks and be inside or on the ears. Tassels may break off where caterpillars are feeding.	**Caterpillars: European corn borers**	Row covers, page 214 Plant polycultures, page 205 Weed, page 210 Sanitize, page 210 Hand-pick pests, page 217 Resistant cultivars, page 227 Encourage beneficials, page 208 Beneficial predators, page 218 Insecticidal soap, page 221 BTK, page 221 Neem, page 223 Horticultural oil, page 223 Sulfur, page 224 Pyrethrin, page 224
 Brown or green caterpillars hide in the soil and curl into a C shape when disturbed. They come out at night and mow down seedlings and plants just above the soil line.	**Caterpillars: cutworms**	Row covers, page 214 Plant polycultures, page 205 Rotate your crops, page 207 Cutworm collars, page 214 Beneficial nematodes, page 220
 Seeds fail to sprout, or few seedlings emerge. Seedlings may be damaged. Small yellowish maggots are in the soil and inside seeds.	**Seedcorn maggots**	Row covers, page 214 Plant polycultures, page 205 Rotate your crops, page 207 Weed, page 210 Encourage beneficials, page 208 Beneficial nematodes, page 220 Neem, page 223 Horticultural oil, page 223 Sulfur, page 224 Pyrethrin, page 224

Symptom	Diagnosis	Solution
 Seedlings are stunted, grow poorly, and fail to thrive. Look for yellow-brown, segmented, hard-shelled "worms" in the soil to confirm your diagnosis.	**Wireworms (adult is a click beetle)**	Plant polycultures, page 205 Rotate your crops, page 207 Beneficial nematodes, page 220
 Large, irregular holes appear in the middle of leaves. Look for slime trails, slugs, or snails nearby. They hide during the day and come out at night to raid your garden.	**Slugs or snails**	Row covers, page 214 Hand-pick pests, page 217 Copper tape, page 217 Traps, page 218 Iron phosphate, page 222 Diatomaceous earth, page 222
Some ears develop seeds that are greatly enlarged, swollen, and turn white. Later they become blue-gray and full of black powdery spores. This fungus is a delicacy, known as huitlacoche, in Mexican cuisine. Consider harvesting and eating it.	**Smut**	Sanitize, page 210 Manage water, page 199 Resistant cultivars, page 227 Improve drainage, page 205 Move the air, page 210 Plant polycultures, page 205 Rotate your crops, page 207 Weed, page 210 Mulch, page 210 Create healthy soil, page 194 Baking soda, page 225 *Bacillus subtilis*, page 225 Sulfur, page 226 Copper, page 226

Symptom	Diagnosis	Solution
Leaves develop raised blisters of orange-brown spots that have rust-colored, powdery spores.	Rust	Sanitize, page 210 Manage water, page 199 Resistant cultivars, page 227 Improve drainage, page 205 Move the air, page 210 Plant polycultures, page 205 Rotate your crops, page 207 Weed, page 210 Mulch, page 210 Create healthy soil, page 194 Baking soda, page 225 *Bacillus subtilis*, page 225 Sulfur, page 226 Copper, page 226
Yellow, tan, or gray spots or blotches appear on leaves.	Corn leaf-spot fungus	Sanitize, page 210 Manage water, page 199 Resistant cultivars, page 227 Improve drainage, page 205 Move the air, page 210 Plant polycultures, page 205 Rotate your crops, page 207 Weed, page 210 Mulch, page 210 Create healthy soil, page 194 Baking soda, page 225 *Bacillus subtilis*, page 225 Sulfur, page 226 Copper, page 226
Leaves have lengthwise yellow stripes. Plants wilt and are stunted. Cut the stem in half near the base of the plant, and yellow bacterial slime oozes from the cuts.	Wilt, bacterial wilt	Sanitize, page 210 Manage water, page 199 Resistant cultivars, page 227 Improve drainage, page 205 Move the air, page 210 Plant polycultures, page 205 Rotate your crops, page 207 Weed, page 210 Mulch, page 210 Create healthy soil, page 194 Copper, page 226

Cucumbers, Melons, Pumpkins, Summer Squash, Winter Squash, Watermelon, Zucchini

Symptom	Diagnosis	Solution
Tiny black, gray, or green insects cluster on the undersides of leaves. Insects are pear-shaped, with two tubes on their rear ends. A black coating that easily rubs off (sooty mold) may occur on lower leaves.	Aphids	Row covers, page 214 Blast with hose, page 217 Encourage beneficials, page 208 Beneficial predators, page 218 Insecticidal soap, page 221 Neem, page 223 Horticultural oil, page 223 Sulfur, page 224 Pyrethrin, page 224
You see small, yellow or dull orange beetles with black spots or stripes. They skeletonize leaves (eat the soft tissue, leave the tough veins). Large holes may also appear in leaves. Seedlings can be killed outright.	Cucumber beetles, Mexican bean beetles	Row covers, page 214 Hand-pick pests, page 217 Encourage beneficials, page 208 Insecticidal soap, page 221 BTSD, page 222 *Beauveria bassiana*, page 223 Spinosad, page 223 Neem, page 223 Horticultural oil, page 223 Sulfur, page 224 Pyrethrin, page 224
Tiny black beetles that jump like fleas rasp away tender leaf tissue and eat small holes in leaves.	Flea beetles	Row covers, page 214 Encourage beneficials, page 208 Insecticidal soap, page 221 *Beauveria bassiana*, page 223 Spinosad, page 223 Neem, page 223 Horticultural oil, page 223 Sulfur, page 224 Pyrethrin, page 224

Symptom	Diagnosis	Solution
You see small, brownish insects on plants. These are true bugs, not beetles. They suck sap out of the stems and leaves.	Tarnished plant bugs, lygus bugs	Row covers, page 214 Plant polycultures, page 205 Hand-pick pests, page 217 Weed, page 210 Sanitize, page 210 Encourage beneficials, page 208 Beneficial predators, page 218 Kaolin spray, page 217 Garlic spray, page 220 Insecticidal soap, page 221 *Beauveria bassiana*, page 223 Neem, page 223 Horticultural oil, page 223 Pyrethrin, page 224

Symptom	Diagnosis	Solution
Tan and black true bugs congregate on plants. They suck nutrients out of stems and leaves. Damaged leaves develop pale green to yellow flecks where bugs have fed. Young plants can be killed; vines may wilt; fruit can be pitted and scarred. Photo shows tan and black adults and silvery gray nymphs.	Squash bugs	Row covers, page 214 Plant polycultures, page 205 Hand-pick pests, page 217 Weed, page 210 Sanitize, page 210 Encourage beneficials, page 208 Beneficial predators, page 218 Kaolin spray, page 217 Garlic spray, page 220 Insecticidal soap, page 221 *Beauveria bassiana*, page 223 Neem, page 223 Horticultural oil, page 223 Pyrethrin, page 224

Symptom	Diagnosis	Solution
Large, irregular holes appear on the edges and sometimes in the middle of leaves. You may see small black pellets of excrement. Plants can be defoliated. Photo shows a cabbage looper on lettuce.	Caterpillars: armyworms, cabbage loopers, tobacco budworms, melonworms, corn earworms	Row covers, page 214 Plant polycultures, page 205 Weed, page 210 Sanitize, page 210 Hand-pick pests, page 217 Resistant cultivars, page 227 Encourage beneficials, page 208 Beneficial predators, page 218 Insecticidal soap, page 221 BTK, page 221 Neem, page 223 Horticultural oil, page 223 Sulfur, page 224 Pyrethrin, page 224

Symptom	Diagnosis	Solution
Brown or green caterpillars hide in the soil and curl into a C shape when disturbed. They come out at night and mow down seedlings and plants just above the soil line.	Caterpillars: cutworms	Row covers, page 214 Plant polycultures, page 205 Rotate your crops, page 207 Cutworm collars, page 214 Beneficial nematodes, page 220
The stem has a hole, and you see material that looks like yellowish sawdust around its opening. A caterpillar inside the stem eats the tissue and interrupts the flow of water to the foliage, flowers, and fruit, causing vines to suddenly wilt.	Caterpillars: squash vine borers	Row covers, page 214 Plant polycultures, page 205 Weed, page 210 Sanitize, page 210 Resistant cultivars, page 227 Encourage beneficials, page 208 Beneficial nematodes (inject), page 220 Insecticidal soap, page 221 BTK (inject), page 221 Neem, page 223 Horticultural oil, page 223 Sulfur, page 224 Pyrethrin, page 224
You see small, fast-moving, green insects on the undersides of leaves. They are much larger than aphids, and they hop and fly when disturbed. Severe infestations cause the leaves to curl and their tips and edges to turn brown.	Potato leafhopper, beet leafhopper	Row covers, page 214 Weed, page 210 Sanitize, page 210 Kaolin spray, page 217 Insecticidal soap, page 221 *Beauveria bassiana*, page 223 Neem, page 223 Horticultural oil, page 223 Pyrethrin, page 224

Symptom	Diagnosis	Solution
Silvery gray trails loop through the leaves. The trails start small and get bigger toward the end. Maggots inside the leaf create the tunnels as they eat the interior tissue. The adult insect is a fly.	Leafminers	Row covers, page 214 Plant polycultures, page 205 Rotate your crops, page 207 Weed, page 210 Encourage beneficials, page 208 Beneficial predators, page 218 Neem, page 223 Horticultural oil, page 223 Sulfur, page 224 Pyrethrin, page 224
Large colonies of small, bright-white insects form on the undersides of leaves. A clear, sticky substance coats the upper surfaces of leaves. A black coating that easily rubs off (sooty mold) may develop.	Whitefly	Blast with hose, page 217 Row covers, page 214 Vacuum, page 217 Move the air, page 210 Traps, page 218 Encourage beneficials, page 208 Beneficial predators, page 218 Insecticidal soap, page 221 Neem, page 223 Horticultural oil, page 223 Sulfur, page 224 Pyrethrin, page 224
Leaves have large holes. Grasshoppers jump and fly about the garden.	Grasshoppers	Row covers, page 214 Plant polycultures, page 205 Rotate your crops, page 207 Weed, page 210 Encourage beneficials, page 208 Beneficial predators, page 218 Nosema spore, page 221 Neem, page 223 Horticultural oil, page 223 Sulfur, page 224 Pyrethrin, page 224
Large ragged holes appear in leaves and on fruits. Look for slime trails, slugs, or snails nearby. They hide during the day and come out at night to raid your garden.	Slugs or snails	Row covers, page 214 Hand-pick pests, page 217 Copper tape, page 217 Traps, page 218 Iron phosphate, page 222 Diatomaceous earth, page 222

Symptom	Diagnosis	Solution
Dark spots or blotches with target-like concentric rings appear on mature leaves.	Alternaria blight	Sanitize, page 210 Manage water, page 199 Resistant cultivars, page 227 Improve drainage, page 205 Move the air, page 210 Plant polycultures, page 205 Rotate your crops, page 207 Weed, page 210 Mulch, page 210 Create healthy soil, page 194 Baking soda, page 225 *Bacillus subtilis*, page 225 Sulfur, page 226 Copper, page 226
Stems are girdled with black lesions, and fruits shrivel and hang on the plant. Plants wilt and die. Before that happens, look for leaves that show dark green spots that become bleached out, and fruits that have dark water-soaked patches that develop white spores.	Phytophthora blight, root rot	Sanitize, page 210 Manage water, page 199 Resistant cultivars, page 227 Improve drainage, page 205 Move the air, page 210 Plant polycultures, page 205 Rotate your crops, page 207 Weed, page 210 Mulch, page 210 Create healthy soil, page 194 Baking soda, page 225 *Bacillus subtilis*, page 225 Copper, page 226
Young fruits turn black and rot. Look for early stages of infection when fruits show bronzed irregular patches. The fruits might also show red-brown spots with black dots or bumps in the middle of the spots.	Black rot	Sanitize, page 210 Manage water, page 199 Resistant cultivars, page 227 Improve drainage, page 205 Move the air, page 210 Plant polycultures, page 205 Rotate your crops, page 207 Weed, page 210 Mulch, page 210 Create healthy soil, page 194 Baking soda, page 225 *Bacillus subtilis*, page 225 Copper, page 226

Symptom	Diagnosis	Solution
Fruits have sunken, wet-looking, circular spots. Spots have darker structures in the middle. Salmon-pink spores may develop.	**Fruit spot, anthracnose**	Sanitize, page 210 Manage water, page 199 Resistant cultivars, page 227 Improve drainage, page 205 Move the air, page 210 Plant polycultures, page 205 Rotate your crops, page 207 Weed, page 210 Mulch, page 210 Create healthy soil, page 194 Baking soda, page 225 *Bacillus subtilis*, page 225 Sulfur, page 226 Copper, page 226
Large brown blotches with yellow halos are confined between the veins on leaves. The brown tissue becomes crisp, and falls away, leaving holes in leaves. White spots appear on fruits, and the fruit may rot.	**Angular leaf-spot**	Sanitize, page 210 Manage water, page 199 Resistant cultivars, page 227 Improve drainage, page 205 Move the air, page 210 Plant polycultures, page 205 Rotate your crops, page 207 Weed, page 210 Mulch, page 210 Create healthy soil, page 194 Copper, page 226
Large yellow blotches appear on leaves. The blotches enlarge and turn brown. Purplish mold develops on the undersides of leaves. The blotches have no yellow halo, and the infection is not confined by the veins, as in angular leaf-spot.	**Downy mildew**	Sanitize, page 210 Manage water, page 199 Resistant cultivars, page 227 Improve drainage, page 205 Move the air, page 210 Plant polycultures, page 205 Rotate your crops, page 207 Weed, page 210 Mulch, page 210 Create healthy soil, page 194 Baking soda, page 225 *Bacillus subtilis*, page 225 Neem, page 226 Copper, page 226

Symptom	Diagnosis	Solution
Thin, white or grayish white patches develop on the upper surfaces of leaves. Leaves slowly turn brown and die.	Powdery mildew	Sanitize, page 210 Resistant cultivars, page 227 Move the air, page 210 Plant polycultures, page 205 Weed, page 210 Mulch, page 210 Baking soda, page 225 *Bacillus subtilis*, page 225 Neem, sulfur, page 226 Copper, page 226
Raised, scab-like, tan bumps develop on winter squash fruit. Earlier in the season look for pale green water-soaked spots on leaves and stems. These spots may have yellow halos. Leaves turn brown and die.	Scab	Sanitize, page 210 Manage water, page 199 Resistant cultivars, page 227 Improve drainage, page 205 Move the air, page 210 Plant polycultures, page 205 Rotate your crops, page 207 Weed, page 210 Mulch, page 210 Create healthy soil, page 194 Copper, page 226
Fluffy, white mold growing on fruits can spread to stems and leaf stalks. Brown or black seed-like pellets form inside the mold. Soon, the leaves turn yellow, and the plants wilt and die.	Southern blight, white mold, stem canker, soft rot, crown rot	Sanitize, page 210 Manage water, page 199 Resistant cultivars, page 227 Improve drainage, page 205 Move the air, page 210 Plant polycultures, page 205 Rotate your crops, page 207 Weed, page 210 Mulch, page 210 Create healthy soil, page 194 Solarize the soil, page 199
All leaves on one side of the plant wilt, curl up, and die. Slit a stem open; dark streaks inside confirm the diagnosis.	Fusarium wilt	Sanitize, page 210 Manage water, page 199 Resistant cultivars, page 227 Improve drainage, page 205 Move the air, page 210 Plant polycultures, page 205 Rotate your crops, page 207 Weed, page 210 Mulch, page 210 Create healthy soil, page 194 Solarize the soil, page 199

Symptom	Diagnosis	Solution
Brown blotches appear on leaves of seedlings that are stunted and growing poorly. Roots are mushy, gray or black, and dead.	Root rot	Sanitize, page 210 Manage water, page 199 Resistant cultivars, page 227 Improve drainage, page 205 Move the air, page 210 Plant polycultures, page 205 Rotate your crops, page 207 Weed, page 210 Mulch, page 210 Create healthy soil, page 194
Leaves turn yellow, starting with the oldest and moving to the youngest. To confirm the diagnosis, cut the stem in half, crosswise, near the base of the plant. Look for brown discoloration and slime oozing from the cuts.	Bacterial wilt	Sanitize, page 210 Manage water, page 199 Resistant cultivars, page 227 Improve drainage, page 205 Move the air, page 210 Plant polycultures, page 205 Rotate your crops, page 207 Weed, page 210 Mulch, page 210 Create healthy soil, page 194 Copper, page 226
Fruits become mottled with creamy white patches. Leaves are mottled or streaked with a mosaic of small, white, angular patches. Plants are stunted but don't die. Aphids spread this disease.	Cucumber mosaic virus	Sanitize, page 210 Resistant cultivars, page 227 Weed, page 210 Mulch, page 210 See aphid solutions, page 149

Eggplant, Peppers, Potatoes, Tomatillos, Tomatoes

Symptom	Diagnosis	Solution
Clusters of tiny green or pinkish insects appear on the undersides of leaves. Insects are pear-shaped, with two tubes on their rear ends. A black coating that easily rubs off (sooty mold) may occur on lower leaves.	**Aphids**	Row covers, page 214 Blast with hose, page 217 Encourage beneficials, page 208 Beneficial predators, page 218 Insecticidal soap, page 221 Neem, page 223 Horticultural oil, page 223 Sulfur, page 224 Pyrethrin, page 224
Beetles crawl over your plants. Large areas of leaves are eaten completely away. Photo shows adult Colorado potato beetle on the left and larva on the right.	**Colorado potato beetles, blister beetles**	Row covers, page 214 Hand-pick pests, page 217 Encourage beneficials, page 208 Insecticidal soap, page 221 BTSD, page 222 *Beauveria bassiana*, page 223 Spinosad, page 223 Neem, page 223 Horticultural oil, page 223 Sulfur, page 224 Pyrethrin, page 224
White grubs with brown heads feed on potato tubers, and on the roots of other plants in the ground. They make large shallow holes in potato tubers.	**Beetle grubs, flea beetle larvae**	Plant polycultures, page 205 Rotate your crops, page 207 Beneficial nematodes, page 220

Symptom	Diagnosis	Solution
You see tiny black beetles that jump like fleas on leaves. Small, round holes or pits appear in leaves.	Flea beetles	Row covers, page 214 Encourage beneficials, page 208 Insecticidal soap, page 221 *Beauveria bassiana*, page 223 Spinosad, page 223 Neem, page 223 Horticultural oil, page 223 Sulfur, page 224 Pyrethrin, page 224
Shield-shaped insects crawl over your plants. They stick their little beaks into the fruit. Fruits develop cloudy yellow spots, and the flesh below the spots may be hard and white.	Harlequin bugs, stink bugs, tarnished plant bugs	Row covers, page 214 Plant polycultures, page 205 Hand-pick pests, page 217 Weed, page 210 Sanitize, page 210 Encourage beneficials, page 208 Beneficial predators, page 218 Kaolin spray, page 217 Garlic spray, page 220 Insecticidal soap, page 221 *Beauveria bassiana*, page 223 Neem, page 223 Horticultural oil, page 223 Pyrethrin, page 224
Grasshoppers are active in the garden. Leaves have large holes.	Grasshoppers	Row covers, page 214 Plant polycultures, page 205 Rotate your crops, page 207 Weed, page 210 Encourage beneficials, page 208 Beneficial predators, page 218 Nosema spore, page 221 Neem, page 223 Horticultural oil, page 223 Sulfur, page 224 Pyrethrin, page 224

Symptom	Diagnosis	Solution
 Large striped caterpillars with a horn on the tail end eat holes on the edges of leaves. Plants can be defoliated.	Caterpillars: tomato hornworms	Row covers, page 214 Plant polycultures, page 205 Weed, page 210 Sanitize, page 210 Hand-pick pests, page 217 Resistant cultivars, page 227 Encourage beneficials, page 208 Beneficial predators, page 218 Insecticidal soap, page 221 BTK, page 221 Neem, page 223 Horticultural oil, page 223 Sulfur, page 224 Pyrethrin, page 224
 Brown or green striped caterpillars eat holes in leaves and bore small holes in fruit. These worms are sometimes inside the fruits.	Caterpillars: tomato fruitworms, corn earworms, European corn borers, armyworms	Row covers, page 214 Plant polycultures, page 205 Weed, page 210 Sanitize, page 210 Hand-pick pests, page 217 Resistant cultivars, page 227 Encourage beneficials, page 208 Beneficial predators, page 218 Insecticidal soap, page 221 BTK, page 221 Neem, page 223 Horticultural oil, page 223 Sulfur, page 224 Pyrethrin, page 224
 Brown or green caterpillars hide in the soil and curl into a C shape when disturbed. They come out at night and mow down seedlings and plants just above the soil line.	Caterpillars: cutworms	Row covers, page 214 Plant polycultures, page 205 Rotate your crops, page 207 Cutworm collars, page 214 Beneficial nematodes, page 220

Symptom	Diagnosis	Solution
Potato tubers have tunnels.	**Caterpillars: potato tuberworms**	Row covers, page 214 Plant polycultures, page 205 Weed, page 210 Sanitize, page 210 Hand-pick pests, page 217 Resistant cultivars, page 227 Encourage beneficials, page 208 Beneficial predators, page 218 Insecticidal soap, page 221 BTK, page 221 Neem, page 223 Horticultural oil, page 223 Sulfur, page 224 Pyrethrin, page 224

Symptom	Diagnosis	Solution
Large colonies of small, bright-white insects form on the undersides of leaves. A clear, sticky substance coats the upper surfaces of leaves. A black coating that easily rubs off (sooty mold) may develop.	**Whitefly**	Row covers, page 214 Blast with hose, page 217 Vacuum, page 217 Move the air, page 210 Traps, page 218 Encourage beneficials, page 208 Beneficial predators, page 218 Insecticidal soap, page 221 Neem, page 223 Horticultural oil, page 223 Sulfur, page 224 Pyrethrin, page 224

Symptom	Diagnosis	Solution
Small white specks freckle leaves. Leaf edges turn brown. You may see tiny wedge-shaped insects.	**Leafhoppers**	Row covers, page 214 Weed, page 210 Sanitize, page 210 Kaolin spray, page 217 Insecticidal soap, page 221 *Beauveria bassiana*, page 223 Neem, page 223 Horticultural oil, page 223 Pyrethrin, page 224

Symptom	Diagnosis	Solution
Silvery gray trails loop through the leaves. Headless, legless, whitish maggots are inside the leaf. The adult insect is a fly.	Leafminers	Row covers, page 214 Plant polycultures, page 205 Rotate your crops, page 207 Weed, page 210 Encourage beneficials, page 208 Beneficial predators, page 218 Neem, page 223 Horticultural oil, page 223 Sulfur, page 224 Pyrethrin, page 224
Holes appear in fruit, and fruit ripens prematurely and rots. Extensive internal tunnels in the fruit confirm the diagnosis. You may also find yellowish maggots inside the fruit.	Pepper maggots	Row covers, page 214 Plant polycultures, page 205 Rotate your crops, page 207 Weed, page 210 Encourage beneficials, page 208 Beneficial predators, page 218 Neem, page 223 Horticultural oil, page 223 Sulfur, page 224 Pyrethrin, page 224
You see small, brownish gray insects with long snouts on your plants. Small holes appear in leaves, flowers, and fruit. You may find insect larvae (legless, whitish grubs with brown heads) inside fruits or buds. Flower buds and fruits drop off. Fruit rots.	Pepper weevils	Row covers, page 214 Plant polycultures, page 205 Rotate your crops, page 207 Weed, page 210 Encourage beneficials, page 208 Insecticidal soap, page 221 Diatomaceous earth, page 222 *Beauveria bassiana*, page 223 Spinosad, page 223 Neem, page 223 Horticultural oil, page 223 Sulfur, page 224 Pyrethrin, page 224
Small black holes and tunnels appear in potato tubers. Look for yellow-brown, segmented, hard-shelled "worms" in the soil.	Wireworms	Plant polycultures, page 205 Rotate your crops, page 207 Beneficial nematodes, page 220

Symptom	Diagnosis	Solution
Leaves and ripe fruit have large, irregular holes. Look for slime trails, slugs, or snails nearby. They hide during the day and come out at night to raid your garden.	**Slugs or snails**	Row covers, page 214 Hand-pick pests, page 217 Copper tape, page 217 Traps, page 218 Iron phosphate, page 222 Diatomaceous earth, page 222
Brown spots with target-like concentric rings appear on leaves. The spots have yellow halos. Tomato fruit rots, starting at the stem end.	**Alternaria blight, early blight**	Sanitize, page 210 Manage water, page 199 Resistant cultivars, page 227 Improve drainage, page 205 Move the air, page 210 Plant polycultures, page 205 Rotate your crops, page 207 Weed, page 210 Mulch, page 210 Create healthy soil, page 194 Baking soda, page 225 *Bacillus subtilis*, page 225 Sulfur, page 226 Copper, page 226
Large, dark blotches with no yellow halos appear on the leaves. The blotches grow white fuzz on the undersides of the leaves. Brown spots with white fuzz develop on stems, and fruits have large greasy brown spots.	**Late blight**	Sanitize, page 210 Manage water, page 199 Resistant cultivars, page 227 Improve drainage, page 205 Move the air, page 210 Plant polycultures, page 205 Rotate your crops, page 207 Weed, page 210 Mulch, page 210 Create healthy soil, page 194 Baking soda, page 225 *Bacillus subtilis*, page 225 Sulfur, page 226 Copper, page 226

Symptom	Diagnosis	Solution
Seeds fail to germinate and rot. Seedlings fall over and die.	**Damping off**	Sanitize, page 210 Manage water, page 199 Resistant cultivars, page 227 Improve drainage, page 205 Move the air, page 210 Plant polycultures, page 205 Rotate your crops, page 207 Weed, page 210 Mulch, page 210 Create healthy soil, page 194 Baking soda, page 225 *Bacillus subtilis*, page 225 *Trichoderma harzianum*, page 226 Copper, page 226
Fruits develop wet-looking, circular depressions. These will develop darker structures in the middle, and will sometimes produce salmon-pink spores.	**Fruit spot, anthracnose**	Sanitize, page 210 Manage water, page 199 Resistant cultivars, page 227 Improve drainage, page 205 Move the air, page 210 Plant polycultures, page 205 Rotate your crops, page 207 Weed, page 210 Mulch, page 210 Create healthy soil, page 194 Baking soda, page 225 *Bacillus subtilis*, page 225 Sulfur, page 226 Copper, page 226
Leaves have brown, black, or gray spots or blotches. The spots or blotches are not confined by leaf veins (so they are not angular in shape). Look for tiny, dark bumps in the center of the spots or blotches.	**Leaf-spot fungus**	Sanitize, page 210 Manage water, page 199 Resistant cultivars, page 227 Improve drainage, page 205 Move the air, page 210 Plant polycultures, page 205 Rotate your crops, page 207 Weed, page 210 Mulch, page 210 Create healthy soil, page 194 Baking soda, page 225 *Bacillus subtilis*, page 225 Sulfur, page 226 Copper, page 226

Symptom	Diagnosis	Solution
Thin, white or grayish white patches develop on the upper surfaces of leaves.	**Powdery mildew**	Sanitize, page 210 Resistant cultivars, page 227 Move the air, page 210 Plant polycultures, page 205 Weed, page 210 Mulch, page 210 Baking soda, page 225 *Bacillus subtilis*, page 225 Neem, page 226 Sulfur, page 226 Copper, page 226
Plants wilt and die. Look for mushy, gray or black, dead roots.	**Root rot**	Sanitize, page 210 Manage water, page 199 Resistant cultivars, page 227 Improve drainage, page 205 Move the air, page 210 Plant polycultures, page 205 Rotate your crops, page 207 Weed, page 210 Mulch, page 210 Create healthy soil, page 194
Brown, corky tissue appears on the surface of potato tubers. This is unsightly but does not affect the potato's edibility or taste.	**Scab**	Sanitize, page 210 Manage water, page 199 Resistant cultivars, page 227 Improve drainage, page 205 Move the air, page 210 Plant polycultures, page 205 Rotate your crops, page 207 Weed, page 210 Mulch, page 210 Create healthy soil, page 194 Measure and modify pH, page 199

Symptom	Diagnosis	Solution
Lower leaves turn yellow and develop brown blotches on their tips. Often, this symptom appears on only one side of the plant. Leaves curl up and die. The plant's growth slows. Look for black spots on the stems near the soil line. Slit a stem open lengthwise. Dark streaks inside confirm the diagnosis.	Fusarium wilt, verticillium wilt	Sanitize, page 210 Manage water, page 199 Resistant cultivars, page 227 Improve drainage, page 205 Move the air, page 210 Plant polycultures, page 205 Rotate your crops, page 207 Weed, page 210 Mulch, page 210 Create healthy soil, page 194 Solarize the soil, page 199
Plants wilt. Leaves turn brown and die, and stems are girdled with black lesions. Fruits may have dark, water-soaked patches that develop white spores. Fruits shrivel and hang onto the plant.	Phytophthora blight	Sanitize, page 210 Manage water, page 199 Resistant cultivars, page 227 Improve drainage, page 205 Move the air, page 210 Plant polycultures, page 205 Rotate your crops, page 207 Weed, page 210 Mulch, page 210 Create healthy soil, page 194 Baking soda, page 225 *Bacillus subtilis*, page 225 Sulfur, page 226 Copper, page 226
Fluffy, white mold develops on fruit that touches the ground. Before this, you may have noticed dark, water-soaked spots on the stems at the soil line. Stems also rot and develop mold. Leaves turn yellow, and plants wilt and die as the disease progresses. Black or brown seed-like pellets form inside the mold.	Southern blight, white mold, stem canker, soft rot, crown rot	Sanitize, page 210 Manage water, page 199 Resistant cultivars, page 227 Improve drainage, page 205 Move the air, page 210 Plant polycultures, page 205 Rotate your crops, page 207 Weed, page 210 Mulch, page 210 Create healthy soil, page 194 Solarize the soil, page 199

Symptom	Diagnosis	Solution
Potato tubers are discolored and rotted in a ring under the skin.	**Bacterial ring rot**	Sanitize, page 210 Manage water, page 199 Resistant cultivars, page 227 Improve drainage, page 205 Plant polycultures, page 205 Rotate your crops, page 207 Weed, page 210 Mulch, page 210 Create healthy soil, page 194 Copper, page 226
You see small, black, rough, scab-like spots surrounded by a yellow halo on leaves. Black spots also occur on the fruit.	**Leaf-spot, bacterial spot**	Sanitize, page 210 Manage water, page 199 Resistant cultivars, page 227 Improve drainage, page 205 Move the air, page 210 Plant polycultures, page 205 Rotate your crops, page 207 Weed, page 210 Mulch, page 210 Create healthy soil, page 194 Copper, page 226
Plants are stunted, and leaves roll up, becoming stiff and yellow. Veins on the undersides of leaves turn purple. Aphids spread this disease.	**Curly top virus**	Sanitize, page 210 Resistant cultivars, page 227 Weed, page 210 Mulch, page 210 See aphid solutions, page 157

Fava Beans, Green Beans, Lima Beans, Peas, Soybeans

Symptom	Diagnosis	Solution
Germination is sparse or has failed. Seedlings are deformed, chewed, or missing leaves as they emerge from the soil.	Seedcorn maggots	Row covers, page 214 Plant polycultures, page 205 Rotate your crops, page 207 Weed, page 210 Encourage beneficials, page 208 Beneficial nematodes, page 220 Neem, page 223 Horticultural oil, page 223 Sulfur, page 224 Pyrethrin, page 224
You find shield-shaped bugs on your plant. Whitish spots appear on leaves. Flowers drop off, and the plant stops producing pods.	Harlequin bugs, stink bugs, tarnished plant bugs	Row covers, page 214 Plant polycultures, page 205 Hand-pick pests, page 217 Weed, page 210 Sanitize, page 210 Encourage beneficials, page 208 Beneficial predators, page 218 Kaolin spray, page 217 Garlic spray, page 220 Insecticidal soap, page 221 *Beauveria bassiana*, page 223 Neem, page 223 Horticultural oil, page 223 Pyrethrin, page 224
Brown or green caterpillars hide in the soil and curl into a C shape when disturbed. They come out at night to mow down seedlings and chew large holes in plants.	Caterpillars: cutworms	Row covers, page 214 Plant polycultures, page 205 Rotate your crops, page 207 Cutworm collars, page 214 Beneficial nematodes, page 220

Symptom	Diagnosis	Solution
Plants are stunted, grow poorly, and fail to thrive. Look for yellow-brown, segmented, hard-shelled "worms" in the soil.	Wireworms	Plant polycultures, page 205 Rotate your crops, page 207 Beneficial nematodes, page 220
Seeds have small, round holes. You see material that looks like sawdust coming out of the holes. You may also find small, brown beetle-like insects. Photo shows identical symptom on corn.	Bean weevils	Row covers, page 214 Plant polycultures, page 205 Rotate your crops, page 207 Weed, page 210 Encourage beneficials, page 208 Insecticidal soap, page 221 Diatomaceous earth, page 222 *Beauveria bassiana*, page 223 Spinosad, page 223 Neem, page 223 Horticultural oil, page 223 Sulfur, page 224 Pyrethrin, page 224
White grubs in the soil eat roots. Seedlings are stunted, grow poorly, and fail to thrive.	Larvae of bean leaf beetles, cucumber beetles, Japanese beetles, flea beetles	Plant polycultures, page 205 Rotate your crops, page 207 Beneficial nematodes, page 220 Milky spore, page 222
Beetles on plants eat large holes in the middle of leaves. Beneficial beetles, such as ladybird beetles (aka ladybugs), do not eat leaves.	Bean leaf beetles, cucumber beetles	Row covers, page 214 Hand-pick pests, page 217 Encourage beneficials, page 208 Insecticidal soap, page 221 BTSD, page 222 *Beauveria bassiana*, page 223 Spinosad, page 223 Neem, page 223 Horticultural oil, page 223 Sulfur, page 224 Pyrethrin, page 224

	Symptom	Diagnosis	Solution
	Caterpillars on plants eat large holes in leaf edges.	**Caterpillars**	Row covers, page 214 Plant polycultures, page 205 Weed, page 210 Sanitize, page 210 Hand-pick pests, page 217 Resistant cultivars, page 227 Encourage beneficials, page 208 Beneficial predators, page 218 Insecticidal soap, page 221 BTK, page 221 Neem, page 223 Horticultural oil, page 223 Sulfur, page 224 Pyrethrin, page 224
	Beetles on plants skel-etonize leaves, rendering them lace-like. Beneficial beetles, such as ladybird beetles (aka ladybugs), do not eat leaves.	**Mexican bean beetle adults and larvae, Japanese beetle adults**	Row covers, page 214 Hand-pick pests, page 217 Encourage beneficials, page 208 Insecticidal soap, page 221 BTSD, page 222 *Beauveria bassiana*, page 223 Spinosad, page 223 Neem, page 223 Horticultural oil, page 223 Sulfur, page 224 Pyrethrin, page 224
	Many very small, round holes appear in leaves. You may also see tiny black beetles that jump like fleas.	**Flea beetles**	Row covers, page 214 Encourage beneficials, page 208 Insecticidal soap, page 221 *Beauveria bassiana*, page 223 Spinosad, page 223 Neem, page 223 Horticultural oil, page 223 Sulfur, page 224 Pyrethrin, page 224

Symptom	Diagnosis	Solution
Small, pear-shaped, soft-bodied insects gather on the undersides of leaves and stem tips. Leaves turn yellow and then shrivel. Ants may be present.	**Aphids**	Blast with hose, page 217 Row covers, page 214 Encourage beneficials, page 208 Beneficial predators, page 218 Insecticidal soap, page 221 Neem, page 223 Horticultural oil, page 223 Sulfur, page 224 Pyrethrin, page 224
Tiny, white specks stipple the leaves. Leaf edges turn yellow and curl. You may see small, wedge-shaped, fast-flying insects.	**Leafhoppers**	Row covers, page 214 Weed, page 210 Sanitize, page 210 Kaolin spray, page 217 Insecticidal soap, page 221 *Beauveria bassiana*, page 223 Neem, page 223 Horticultural oil, page 223 Pyrethrin, page 224
Silvery gray trails loop through the leaf.	**Leafminers**	Row covers, page 214 Plant polycultures, page 205 Rotate your crops, page 207 Weed, page 210 Encourage beneficials, page 208 Beneficial predators, page 218 Neem, page 223 Horticultural oil, page 223 Sulfur, page 224 Pyrethrin, page 224
Grasshoppers jump and fly about the garden. Large holes appear on the edges and in the middle of leaves.	**Grasshoppers**	Row covers, page 214 Plant polycultures, page 205 Rotate your crops, page 207 Weed, page 210 Encourage beneficials, page 208 Beneficial predators, page 218 Nosema spore, page 221 Neem, page 223 Horticultural oil, page 223 Sulfur, page 224 Pyrethrin, page 224

Symptom	Diagnosis	Solution
Leaves turn a rusty bronze color. Tiny white specks appear on leaves. You see fine webbing on the undersides of leaves.	Mites	Blast with hose, page 217 Garlic spray, page 220 Pepper spray, page 221 Encourage beneficials, page 208 Beneficial predators, page 218 Insecticidal soap, page 221 Neem, page 223 Sulfur, page 224
Plants are stunted, grow poorly, and fail to thrive. Odd, knot-like swellings on the roots confirm the diagnosis.	Root-knot nematodes	Plant polycultures, page 205 Rotate your crops, page 207 Create healthy soil, page 194 Resistant cultivars, page 227 Solarize soil, page 199
Fuzzy, charcoal gray/brown mold develops on leaves and pods.	Gray mold, botrytis	Sanitize, page 210 Manage water, page 199 Resistant cultivars, page 227 Improve drainage, page 205 Move the air, page 210 Plant polycultures, page 205 Rotate your crops, page 207 Weed, page 210 Mulch, page 210 Create healthy soil, page 194 Baking soda, page 225 *Bacillus subtilis*, page 225 Neem, sulfur, page 226 Copper, page 226
Thin, white or grayish white patches develop on the upper surfaces of leaves.	Powdery mildew	Sanitize, page 210 Resistant cultivars, page 227 Move the air, page 210 Plant polycultures, page 205 Weed, page 210 Mulch, page 210 Baking soda, page 225 *Bacillus subtilis*, page 225 Neem, sulfur, page 226 Copper, page 226

Symptom	Diagnosis	Solution
Young shoots and flowers develop thin, whitish mold. This disease occurs only on lima beans.	Downy mildew	Sanitize, page 210 Manage water, page 199 Resistant cultivars, page 227 Improve drainage, page 205 Move the air, page 210 Plant polycultures, page 205 Rotate your crops, page 207 Weed, page 210 Mulch, page 210 Create healthy soil, page 194 Baking soda, page 225 *Bacillus subtilis*, page 225 Neem, page 226 Copper, page 226
Fluffy, white, cottony mold develops from water-soaked spots on leaves and stems. Sometimes black seed-like pellets appear within the mold. Photo shows identical symptom on sorrel.	White mold, stem canker, soft rot, crown rot	Sanitize, page 210 Manage water, page 199 Resistant cultivars, page 227 Improve drainage, page 205 Move the air, page 210 Plant polycultures, page 205 Rotate your crops, page 207 Weed, page 210 Mulch, page 210 Create healthy soil, page 194 Solarize the soil, page 199
Orange-red bumps or blisters appear on the undersides of leaves and sometimes on pods.	Rust	Sanitize, page 210 Manage water, page 199 Resistant cultivars, page 227 Improve drainage, page 205 Move the air, page 210 Plant polycultures, page 205 Rotate your crops, page 207 Weed, page 210 Mulch, page 210 Create healthy soil, page 194 Baking soda, page 225 *Bacillus subtilis*, page 225 Sulfur, page 226 Copper, page 226

Symptom	Diagnosis	Solution
 Dark, reddish, black spots appear on leaves and pods. Masses of pink spores may develop.	Anthracnose	Sanitize, page 210 Manage water, page 199 Resistant cultivars, page 227 Improve drainage, page 205 Move the air, page 210 Plant polycultures, page 205 Rotate your crops, page 207 Weed, page 210 Mulch, page 210 Create healthy soil, page 194 Baking soda, page 225 *Bacillus subtilis*, page 225 Sulfur, page 226 Copper, page 226
 Plants wilt, grow poorly, and fail to thrive. Roots are mushy, gray or black, and dead.	Root rot	Sanitize, page 210 Manage water, page 199 Resistant cultivars, page 227 Improve drainage, page 205 Move the air, page 210 Plant polycultures, page 205 Rotate your crops, page 207 Weed, page 210 Mulch, page 210 Create healthy soil, page 194
White, fuzzy mold grows at the base of seedlings. Stems are frequently dark and appear water-soaked. The seedling will collapse and die.	Damping off	Sanitize, page 210 Manage water, page 199 Resistant cultivars, page 227 Improve drainage, page 205 Move the air, page 210 Plant polycultures, page 205 Rotate your crops, page 207 Weed, page 210 Mulch, page 210 Create healthy soil, page 194 Baking soda, page 225 *Bacillus subtilis*, page 225 *Trichoderma harzianum*, page 226 Copper, page 226

Symptom	Diagnosis	Solution
 Water-soaked spots become dry and red-dish brown, and develop yellow halos. Spots are angular (confined by main veins). No white mold develops.	**Bacterial blight, common blight, halo blight**	Sanitize, page 210 Manage water, page 199 Resistant cultivars, page 227 Improve drainage, page 205 Move the air, page 210 Plant polycultures, page 205 Rotate your crops, page 207 Weed, page 210 Mulch, page 210 Create healthy soil, page 194 Copper, page 226
 Leaves and pods develop a mosaic of small, white and yellow, angular patches. Aphids spread this disease.	**Mosaic virus**	Sanitize, page 210 Resistant cultivars, page 227 Weed, page 210 Mulch, page 210 See aphid solutions, page 170
Brownish purple streaks show up on stems. Pods turn a brownish purple, and may be deformed. Leaves turn yellow. Aphids spread this dis-ease.	**Pea streak virus**	Sanitize, page 210 Resistant cultivars, page 227 Weed, page 210 Mulch, page 210 See aphid solutions, page 170

Garlic, Leeks, Onions, Scallions, Shallots

Symptom	Diagnosis	Solution
Tiny black, soft-bodied, pear-shaped insects, with two tubes on their rear ends, cluster on the base of leaves (on the bottom of the stalk).	Aphids	Row covers, page 214 Blast with hose, page 217 Encourage beneficials, page 208 Beneficial predators, page 218 Insecticidal soap, page 221 Neem, page 223 Horticultural oil, page 223 Sulfur, page 224 Pyrethrin, page 224
Large bronze and green beetles appear on your plants. Leaves have large holes in the middle or on the edges. Seedlings can be killed outright. Photo shows Japanese beetles on a dahlia.	Japanese beetles	Row covers, page 214 Hand-pick pests, page 217 Encourage beneficials, page 208 Insecticidal soap, page 221 BTSD, page 222 *Beauveria bassiana*, page 223 Spinosad, page 223 Neem, page 223 Horticultural oil, page 223 Sulfur, page 224 Pyrethrin, page 224
White grubs with brown heads live in the soil and eat the roots of your plants.	Japanese beetle larvae	Plant polycultures, page 205 Rotate your crops, page 207 Beneficial nematodes, page 220 Milky spore, page 222
Brown or green caterpillars hide in the soil and curl into a C shape when disturbed. They come out at night to mow down sets and seedlings just above the soil line.	Caterpillars: cutworms	Row covers, page 214 Plant polycultures, page 205 Rotate your crops, page 207 Cutworm collars, page 214 Beneficial nematodes, page 220

Symptom	Diagnosis	Solution
Roots are missing, and plants are stunted. Look for headless, legless, whitish maggots in the soil. Photo shows plant on the left with healthy roots. The plant on the right is missing most of its roots.	**Onion maggots**	Row covers, page 214 Plant polycultures, page 205 Rotate your crops, page 207 Weed, page 210 Tar paper, page 214 Encourage beneficials, page 208 Beneficial nematodes, page 218 Neem, page 223 Horticultural oil, page 223 Sulfur, page 224 Pyrethrin, page 224
Seedlings are very different sizes. Seed germination occurs at different times, or seeds fail to germinate, and/or seedlings are stunted. Find headless, legless, whitish maggots in the soil, eating the roots and seeds.	**Seedcorn maggots**	Row covers, page 214 Plant polycultures, page 205 Rotate your crops, page 207 Weed, page 210 Encourage beneficials, page 208 Beneficial nematodes, page 218 Neem, page 223 Horticultural oil, page 223 Sulfur, page 224 Pyrethrin, page 224
Leaves develop silvery streaks. Tiny insects rasp away soft tissue of leaves.	**Thrips**	Row covers, page 214 Weed, page 210 Sanitize, page 210 Encourage beneficials, page 208 Pepper spray, page 221 Insecticidal soap, page 221 *Beauveria bassiana*, page 223 Spinosad, page 223 Neem, page 223 Horticultural oil, page 223 Pyrethrin, page 224
Bulbs become soft, mushy, and black. Tiny white mites infest bulbs. Plants become stunted.	**Bulb mites**	Plant polycultures, page 205 Rotate your crops, page 207 Create healthy soil, page 194

Symptom	Diagnosis	Solution
Large, irregular holes appear in the middle of leaves. Look for slime trails, slugs, or snails nearby. They hide during the day and come out at night to raid your garden.	**Slugs or snails**	Row covers, page 214 Hand-pick pests, page 217 Copper tape, page 217 Traps, page 218 Iron phosphate, page 222 Diatomaceous earth, page 222
Bulbs develop dark brown to black patches on the outer scales. Seedlings develop blisters filled with dusty black or dark brown spores near the soil line.	**Onion smut**	Sanitize, page 210 Manage water, page 199 Resistant cultivars, page 227 Improve drainage, page 205 Move the air, page 210 Plant polycultures, page 205 Rotate your crops, page 207 Weed, page 210 Mulch, page 210 Create healthy soil, page 194 Baking soda, page 225 *Bacillus subtilis*, page 225 Copper, page 226
Outer bulb scales appear water-soaked, then dry and shrivel. Masses of black spores develop between the scales.	**Black mold**	Sanitize, page 210 Manage water, page 199 Resistant cultivars, page 227 Improve drainage, page 205 Move the air, page 210 Plant polycultures, page 205 Rotate your crops, page 207 Weed, page 210 Mulch, page 210 Create healthy soil, page 194 Baking soda, page 225 *Bacillus subtilis*, page 225 Copper, page 226

Symptom	Diagnosis	Solution
 Leaves (beginning with the older ones) turn yellow, wilt, and die. Leaves and bulb scales at the soil line have dark, water-soaked spots. Roots rot. Fluffy, white mold develops around the base of the bulb. Small black seed-like lumps form inside the mold.	White rot, white mold	Sanitize, page 210 Manage water, page 199 Resistant cultivars, page 227 Improve drainage, page 205 Move the air, page 210 Plant polycultures, page 205 Rotate your crops, page 207 Weed, page 210 Mulch, page 210 Create healthy soil, page 194 Solarize the soil, page 199
 Leaves turn yellow from the tips and die back. Roots are dark brown to dark pink. Cut bulbs in half vertically and look for brown discoloration of the stem at the base of the bulb to confirm the diagnosis. This fungus develops in hot weather.	Fusarium basal rot	Sanitize, page 210 Manage water, page 199 Resistant cultivars, page 227 Cool- and warm-season crops, page 192 Improve drainage, page 205 Move the air, page 210 Plant polycultures, page 205 Rotate your crops, page 207 Weed, page 210 Mulch, page 210 Create healthy soil, page 194 Solarize the soil, page 199
Small rusty-red bumps appear on the foliage. The bumps produce orange-red, dust-like spores. Leaves turn yellow and collapse. Bulbs are stunted.	Rust	Sanitize, page 210 Manage water, page 199 Resistant cultivars, page 227 Improve drainage, page 205 Move the air, page 210 Plant polycultures, page 205 Rotate your crops, page 207 Weed, page 210 Mulch, page 210 Create healthy soil, page 194 Baking soda, page 225 *Bacillus subtilis*, page 225 Sulfur, page 226 Copper, page 226

Okra

Symptom	Diagnosis	Solution
Clusters of tiny insects, attended by ants, gather on the stems and undersides of leaves. The insects are pear-shaped, with two tubes on their rear ends. A black coating that easily rubs off (sooty mold) may occur on lower leaves.	Aphids	Row covers, page 214 Blast with hose, page 217 Encourage beneficials, page 208 Beneficial predators, page 218 Insecticidal soap, page 221 Neem, page 223 Horticultural oil, page 223 Sulfur, page 224 Pyrethrin, page 224
Several species of ants raise and protect aphids, which they bring to your plants. Control ants to control aphids.	Ants	Plant polycultures, page 205 Rotate your crops, page 207 Traps, page 218 Diatomaceous earth, page 222
Large holes appear in the middle of leaves, and you see small, yellow beetles with black spots.	Cucumber beetles	Row covers, page 214 Hand-pick pests, page 217 Encourage beneficials, page 208 Insecticidal soap, page 221 BTSD, page 222 *Beauveria bassiana*, page 223 Spinosad, page 223 Neem, page 223 Horticultural oil, page 223 Sulfur, page 224 Pyrethrin, page 224

Symptom	Diagnosis	Solution
Shield-shaped insects feed on fruits. Fruits develop cloudy or light-colored spots, and the flesh below the spots is hard and white.	Harlequin bugs, stink bugs, tarnished plant bugs	Row covers, page 214 Plant polycultures, page 205 Hand-pick pests, page 217 Weed, page 210 Sanitize, page 210 Encourage beneficials, page 208 Beneficial predators, page 218 Kaolin spray, page 217 Garlic spray, page 220 Insecticidal soap, page 221 *Beauveria bassiana*, page 223 Neem, page 223 Horticultural oil, page 223 Pyrethrin, page 224
Large, irregular holes appear on the edges and sometimes in the middle of leaves. You may also find small black pellets of excrement. The soft tissue on the undersides of leaves may be eaten away. You may find holes bored into the fruit.	Caterpillars: beet armyworm, southern armyworm, fall army-worm, corn earworm, cabbage looper	Row covers, page 214 Plant polycultures, page 205 Weed, page 210 Sanitize, page 210 Hand-pick pests, page 217 Resistant cultivars, page 227 Encourage beneficials, page 208 Beneficial predators, page 218 Insecticidal soap, page 221 BTK, page 221 Neem, page 223 Horticultural oil, page 223 Sulfur, page 224 Pyrethrin, page 224
Small, bright-white insects fly away when disturbed. Large colonies on the undersides of leaves deposit patches of white residue. A clear, sticky substance coats the upper surfaces of leaves. A black coating that easily rubs off (sooty mold) may occur on lower leaves.	Whitefly	Blast with hose, page 217 Row covers, page 214 Vacuum, page 217 Move the air, page 210 Traps, page 218 Encourage beneficials, page 208 Beneficial predators, page 218 Insecticidal soap, page 221 Neem, page 223 Horticultural oil, page 223 Sulfur, page 224 Pyrethrin, page 224

Symptom	Diagnosis	Solution
Brown spots appear on leaves. Leaf edges turn yellow, and dry brown spots develop in the yellow areas. Leaves roll up, wilt, and drop off.	**Leaf-spot fungus**	Sanitize, page 210 Manage water, page 199 Resistant cultivars, page 227 Improve drainage, page 205 Move the air, page 210 Plant polycultures, page 205 Rotate your crops, page 207 Weed, page 210 Mulch, page 210 Create healthy soil, page 194 Baking soda, page 225 *Bacillus subtilis*, page 225 Sulfur, page 226 Copper, page 226
Thin, white or grayish white patches develop on the upper surfaces of leaves. Photo shows identical symptom on cucumber.	**Powdery mildew**	Sanitize, page 210 Resistant cultivars, page 227 Move the air, page 210 Plant polycultures, page 205 Weed, page 210 Mulch, page 210 Baking soda, page 225 *Bacillus subtilis*, page 225 Neem, page 226 Sulfur, page 226 Copper, page 226
Fluffy, white mold develops on the fruit or on the stems at the soil line. Sometimes black seed-like pellets appear within the mold. Photo shows identical symptoms on squash.	**Southern blight, white mold, stem canker, soft rot, crown rot**	Sanitize, page 210 Manage water, page 199 Resistant cultivars, page 227 Improve drainage, page 205 Move the air, page 210 Plant polycultures, page 205 Rotate your crops, page 207 Weed, page 210 Mulch, page 210 Create healthy soil, page 194 Solarize the soil, page 199

Symptom	Diagnosis	Solution
 Lower leaves turn yellow and develop brown blotches on their tips. Often, this symptom appears on only one side of the plant. Leaves curl up and die. The plant's growth slows. Look for black spots on the stems near the soil line. Slit a stem open; dark streaks inside confirm the diagnosis.	Fusarium wilt, verticillium wilt	Sanitize, page 210 Manage water, page 199 Resistant cultivars, page 227 Improve drainage, page 205 Move the air, page 210 Plant polycultures, page 205 Rotate your crops, page 207 Weed, page 210 Mulch, page 210 Create healthy soil, page 194 Solarize the soil, page 199

Rhubarb, Sorrel

Symptom	Diagnosis	Solution
Tiny black or gray, soft-bodied, pear-shaped insects, with two tubes on their rear ends hide inside tightly curled and crinkled leaves.	Aphids	Row covers, page 214 Blast with hose, page 217 Encourage beneficials, page 208 Beneficial predators, page 218 Insecticidal soap, page 221 Neem, page 223 Horticultural oil, page 223 Sulfur, page 224 Pyrethrin, page 224
You see large holes on the edges and in the middle of leaves where soft tissue has been eaten away. Leaves turn yellow. Note the excrement and silk left behind.	Caterpillars: imported cabbage worm, cabbage loopers	Row covers, page 214 Plant polycultures, page 205 Weed, page 210 Sanitize, page 210 Hand-pick pests, page 217 Resistant cultivars, page 227 Encourage beneficials, page 208 Beneficial predators, page 218 Insecticidal soap, page 221 BTK, page 221 Neem, page 223 Horticultural oil, page 223 Sulfur, page 224 Pyrethrin, page 224
Large, irregular holes appear in the middle of leaves. Look for slime trails, slugs, or snails nearby. They hide during the day and come out at night to raid your garden.	Slugs or snails	Row covers, page 214 Hand-pick pests, page 217 Copper tape, page 217 Traps, page 218 Iron phosphate, page 222 Diatomaceous earth, page 222

Symptom	Diagnosis	Solution
Small, dark spots develop on leaves. Then the centers of the spots fall out, leaving ragged holes. Leaves may be killed. Plants may be stunted.	**Leaf-spot fungus**	Sanitize, page 210 Manage water, page 199 Resistant cultivars, page 227 Improve drainage, page 205 Move the air, page 210 Plant polycultures, page 205 Rotate your crops, page 207 Weed, page 210 Mulch, page 210 Create healthy soil, page 194 Baking soda, page 225 *Bacillus subtilis*, page 225 Sulfur, page 226 Copper, page 226

PESTS AND DISEASES OF
Sweet Potatoes

Symptom	Diagnosis	Solution
Tiny green, black, or purple insects cluster on the undersides of leaves. The insects are pear-shaped, with two tubes on their rear ends. A black coating that easily rubs off (sooty mold) may occur on lower leaves.	Aphids	Row covers, page 214 Blast with hose, page 217 Encourage beneficials, page 208 Beneficial predators, page 218 Insecticidal soap, page 221 Neem, page 223 Horticultural oil, page 223 Sulfur, page 224 Pyrethrin, page 224
You see small beetles that are either metallic gold, or yellow with black spots. They skeletonize leaves (eat soft tissue and leave the tough vein tissue behind). Seedlings can be killed outright.	Golden tortoise beetles, cucumber beetles	Row covers, page 214 Hand-pick pests, page 217 Encourage beneficials, page 208 Insecticidal soap, page 221 BTSD, page 222 Beauveria bassiana, page 223 Spinosad, page 223 Neem, page 223 Horticultural oil, page 223 Sulfur, page 224 Pyrethrin, page 224
White grubs with brown heads feed on tubers and roots in the soil. The grubs make shallow channels in the tubers.	Beetle grubs, white grubs	Plant polycultures, page 205 Rotate your crops, page 207 Beneficial nematodes, page 220

Legless grubs with brown heads eat their way through the stems and roots, making tunnels and holes in tubers. Adults are weevils (long-nosed beetles).	Sweet potato weevil larvae	Row covers, page 214 Plant polycultures, page 205 Rotate your crops, page 207 Weed, page 210 Encourage beneficials, page 208 Beneficial nematodes, page 220 Insecticidal soap, page 221 Diatomaceous earth, page 222 *Beauveria bassiana*, page 223 Spinosad, page 223 Neem, page 223 Horticultural oil, page 223 Sulfur, page 224 Pyrethrin, page 224
Many small, round holes appear in leaves. You may also see tiny black beetles that jump like fleas. Be aware that their larvae live in soil and eat the roots.	Flea beetles, flea beetle larvae	Row covers, page 214 Encourage beneficials, page 208 Insecticidal soap, page 221 *Beauveria bassiana*, page 223 Spinosad, page 223 Neem, page 223 Horticultural oil, page 223 Sulfur, page 224 Pyrethrin, page 224 For larvae, see beetle grubs solutions, page 185
You see caterpillars that eat large holes in the middle and on the edges of leaves. You may also find small black pellets of excrement. Plants can be defoliated.	Caterpillars: loopers, hornworms, armyworms	Row covers, page 214 Plant polycultures, page 205 Weed, page 210 Sanitize, page 210 Hand-pick pests, page 217 Resistant cultivars, page 227 Encourage beneficials, page 208 Beneficial predators, page 218 Insecticidal soap, page 221 BTK, page 221 Neem, page 223 Horticultural oil, page 223 Sulfur, page 224 Pyrethrin, page 224

Symptom	Diagnosis	Solution
 Brown or green caterpillars hide in the soil and curl into a C shape when disturbed. They come out at night and mow down seedlings and plants just above the soil line. Tubers may have channels and scars near the stem end.	**Caterpillars: cutworms**	Row covers, page 214 Plant polycultures, page 205 Rotate your crops, page 207 Cutworm collars, page 214 Beneficial nematodes, page 220
Large colonies of small, bright-white insects form on the undersides of leaves. A clear, sticky substance coats the upper surfaces of leaves. A black coating that easily rubs off (sooty mold) may occur on lower leaves.	**Whitefly**	Row covers, page 214 Blast with hose, page 217 Vacuum, page 217 Move the air, page 210 Traps, page 218 Encourage beneficials, page 208 Beneficial predators, page 218 Insecticidal soap, page 221 Neem, page 223 Horticultural oil, page 223 Sulfur, page 224 Pyrethrin, page 224
You see small, fast-moving green insects, much bigger than aphids, on the undersides of leaves. They hop and fly when disturbed. Severe infestations cause leaves to curl and their tips and edges to turn brown.	**Potato leafhopper**	Row covers, page 214 Weed, page 210 Sanitize, page 210 Kaolin spray, page 217 Insecticidal soap, page 221 *Beauveria bassiana*, page 223 Neem, page 223 Horticultural oil, page 223 Pyrethrin, page 224
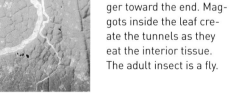 Silvery gray trails loop through leaves. The trails start small and get bigger toward the end. Maggots inside the leaf create the tunnels as they eat the interior tissue. The adult insect is a fly.	**Leafminer**	Row covers, page 214 Plant polycultures, page 205 Rotate your crops, page 207 Weed, page 210 Encourage beneficials, page 208 Beneficial predators, page 218 Neem, page 223 Horticultural oil, page 223 Sulfur, page 224 Pyrethrin, page 224

Symptom	Diagnosis	Solution
Leaves have large holes. Grasshoppers jump and fly about the garden.	Grasshoppers	Row covers, page 214 Plant polycultures, page 205 Rotate your crops, page 207 Weed, page 210 Encourage beneficials, page 208 Beneficial predators, page 218 Nosema spore, page 221 Neem, page 223 Horticultural oil, page 223 Sulfur, page 224 Pyrethrin, page 224
Large, irregular holes appear in the middle of leaves. Look for slime trails, slugs, or snails nearby. They hide during the day and come out at night to raid your garden.	Slugs or snails	Row covers, page 214 Hand-pick pests, page 217 Copper tape, page 217 Traps, page 218 Iron phosphate, page 222 Diatomaceous earth, page 222
Tan or dark brown spots develop on the upper surface of leaves. Leaves gradually turn yellow.	Leaf-spot fungus	Sanitize, page 214 Manage water, page 199 Resistant cultivars, page 227 Improve drainage, page 205 Move the air, page 210 Plant polycultures, page 205 Rotate your crops, page 207 Weed, page 210 Mulch, page 210 Create healthy soil, page 194 Baking soda, page 225 *Bacillus subtilis*, page 225 Sulfur, page 226 Copper, page 226

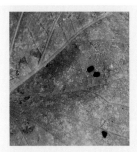

Symptom	Diagnosis	Solution
All the leaves on one side of the plant wilt, develop yellow patches, curl up, and die. Look for black spots on the stems near the soil line. Slit a stem open; dark streaks inside confirm the diagnosis.	**Fusarium wilt**	Sanitize, page 210 Manage water, page 199 Resistant cultivars, page 227 Improve drainage, page 205 Move the air, page 210 Plant polycultures, page 205 Rotate your crops, page 207 Weed, page 210 Mulch, page 210 Create healthy soil, page 194 Solarize the soil, page 199

Organic Solutions to Common Problems

FOR THE PURPOSES of organic gardening, "organic" means that a product you use on your plants comes from a naturally occurring substance (plant, animal, or mineral), and that it has not undergone any chemical change after being extracted from its original source. According to USDA regulations on organic food production, synthetic means that a product has been "formulated or manufactured by a chemical process," or that it has been chemically changed after it was extracted from "a naturally occurring plant, animal, or mineral source." Organic gardeners use no synthetic substances.

Each country uses its own rules to regulate organically grown food. In the United States, the organic certification program is administered by the USDA, through the National Organic Program (NOP). The rules formulated under this program for commercial organic farmers are complicated and stringent. You do not have to follow them, of course, but they do help you decide if and when to use a product in your vegetable garden. OMRI (Organic Materials Review Institute) labeling means that a product has been certified for use on organically grown plants.

SAFETY FIRST

Many of the organic solutions we recommend in the pages that follow are non-toxic, and some target specific pests while doing no harm to other creatures. But other products, while approved for organic gardens, are both toxic and non-targeted. Care is required. **We strongly encourage you to follow these five rules:**

1. **Always use the least toxic product first.**
2. **Keep all these products out of the reach of children and pets.**
3. **Read the label, and use a product only on the plant, or type of plant, for which it is labeled.**
4. **Follow the instructions on the label and dispose of the product properly.**
5. **Wear the recommended protective gear and clothing: respirator mask, goggles, gloves, long-sleeved shirts, and long pants.**

All pesticides available in the United States have undergone testing required by the Environmental Protection Agency. The safest products, such as deterrents and barriers, need no safety labels. The next level up on the toxicity ladder requires a "CAUTION" label. That's as far as we go in this book. One more level up requires a "WARNING" label. Use products labeled "CAUTION," or "WARNING," if you are striking out on your own, only after all other techniques have failed. Note: there is an even higher level of toxicity, requiring a "DANGER" label. These products should *never* be used on food plants.

Change Growing Conditions to Solve Problems

(top) Plant your lettuce, peas, and other cool-season crops to mature in shoulder seasons, the time before and after the heat of summer.

(bottom) A warm-season crop, corn thrives in the long, hot days of summer. If you live in a cool climate, look for cultivars with the shortest days to maturity.

Cool- and warm-season crops. Cool-season crops include artichoke, arugula, asparagus, beets, broccoli, Brussels sprouts, cabbage, carrots, cauliflower, chard, chicory, collard greens, endive, fava beans, garlic, kale, leeks, lettuce, mustard greens, onions, parsnips, peas, potatoes, radicchio, radishes, rhubarb, rutabaga, sorrel, spinach, and turnips. These crops do not fare well in the hotter months of the year, and many will bolt when it gets hot. Plant seeds of cool-season crops outdoors as soon as the soil can be worked in early spring. You can start seeds indoors in late winter so seedlings will be ready to go into the ground as soon as the last frost is over. Some will even survive light frosts. To grow cool-season crops in fall and winter, start seeds in late summer so the plants mature during the cool weather of autumn.

Warm-season crops include certain beans (green, lima, soy), cantaloupe and other melons, corn, cucumbers, eggplant, okra, peppers, pumpkin, squash (winter and summer), sweet potatoes, tomatillo, tomato, and watermelon. These crops do not thrive in cool weather, especially if the soil is cold. If you plant seeds of these warm-season plants in cold soil, they're likely to rot. Plant seeds of warm-season crops outdoors about two weeks after the average date of the last spring frost. You can start seeds indoors about six weeks earlier, but don't transplant seedlings outdoors until the weather is warm and settled. If you set out plants too early in spring, when days are cool and nights are cold, many will sit and sulk. They won't grow, their leaves will begin to yellow, and they'll be stunted. If you garden in a cool climate, then look for warm-season crops with the shortest days to maturity. A tomato that matures in 60 days as opposed to 90 or 100 days, for example, is the better choice for cool climates.

Modify effects of temperature. Have a look at your site, and consider the realities of your climate. What are the nighttime lows? Do you have microclimates in various locations you might use to advantage—or plan to avoid? For example, do you have a south-facing wall that will absorb heat during the day, in front of which you could plant a warmth-loving vegetable? Alternatively, are there shallow depressions in which cold air might pool during the night, causing plants to freeze?

If the temperature is too high for a plant's comfort, provide dappled shade with a small structure, a temporary covering of shade cloth, or by planting a small deciduous tree or shrub that casts its shadow on that area of the vegetable garden. Note also the direction of prevailing winds during the

Providing shade in the heat of a summer afternoon in New Mexico modifies the effect of high temperatures, and keeps lettuce from suffering leaf scorch.

(top) Because of cold winters, these artichokes in West Virginia should be covered with 6 inches of mulch after the aboveground foliage dies back in late autumn.

(bottom) Easy to build from recycled materials, cold frames effectively extend the growing season by creating a warm microclimate in your yard. The soil warms up earlier in the season, and the ambient temperature within the enclosed space is many degrees higher than the outside air.

growing season. Sometimes the wind can drop temperatures unexpectedly, and sometimes a hot afternoon wind can scorch your plants. Protection from strong winds may be necessary.

SOIL SOLUTIONS

Create healthy soil. Begin each growing season with a good in-ground or container soil mix. For your vegetable garden beds, mix one part topsoil that is free of weed seeds with one part mature, organic compost. If you don't have compost left over from last season, you can buy good organic compost at garden centers, but make sure it is weed-seed-free. Add 1 cup of high-nitrogen organic fertilizer to every 2 gallons of the soil/compost mixture. You can use your native garden soil in place of topsoil, but keep in mind that by digging up the garden bed, you disturb the living community of organisms there and undo some of the progress you made in previous years.

For plants or seeds in containers, mix one part commercially prepared potting soil with one part mature, organic compost. Add 1 cup of high-nitrogen organic fertilizer to every 2 gallons of the potting soil/compost mix. Do *not* use native soil or topsoil in place of potting soil. These become too dense in a container, leaving no air space—a critical component of healthy growing media. The roots will suffocate.

Composting is one of the most cost-effective garden activities you can pursue. You make healthy, crumbly compost from waste that usually goes into the landfill or down the drain. What could be better? What goes into compost? Garbage (kitchen waste that is free of animal products) and garden waste (clippings, shrub and tree prunings, leaves) are the primary ingredients. Everything you put into your compost pile should be free of weed seeds, diseases, pests, and chemicals. Over time the material in your compost pile

decomposes, helped along by the soil community, and becomes rich soil for your plants.

Good compost consists of two parts "brown" material (straw, dead leaves, twigs, and chipped branches, for example) to one part "green" material (grass clippings, kitchen garbage, green leaves, and weeds that are free of seeds, for example). Adding 10 pounds of chicken manure and two shovelsful of soil to each wheelbarrow-load of this mixture aids the decomposition process. Keep the pile dry in a wet climate and moist in a dry climate. For best results, maintain the proper proportions and turn the pile over once a week.

Sheet mulching (aka making "lasagna beds") simplifies the process of creating healthy soil while avoiding tilling and back-breaking labor. Here's how to do it. Cut vegetation to the ground. If you have a mower with a grass catcher, use it. And if the plants you cut are producing seeds, either burn what you have cut (assuming it is legal and safe to do so), or put the debris in black plastic garbage bags. Leave these bags in full sun for two weeks to let the material decompose. Then add it to your compost pile. Alternatively, you can put the material directly into your compost pile, but the pile must be hot enough (at least 145°F) to destroy the weed seeds. You do not want to turn any part of your property into a weed-seed repos-

(opposite, top) Garden and kitchen waste ("green" material), an egg carton and paper bags ("brown" material) make up the ingredients for compost in this "bin" made of straw bales.

(opposite, bottom) Garden debris in the first of these three bins decomposes to make a rich amendment for the garden. The gardener will move that material to the middle bin when it has decreased to half its size, and refill the first bin with more waste. When the material in bin two has decreased to half its size, she'll shovel it to the third bin, where it will finish becoming the rich nutrients her garden loves. By continually refilling the bins and moving the waste from one bin to the next, compost is available all season long.

itory. Next, flatten cardboard boxes (remove any packing tape, which will not decompose) and lay the sheets down over the ground. Make sure there are no gaps between pieces of cardboard, and that no light reaches the ground or vegetation. Spread 3 inches of mature organic compost or composted manure over the cardboard. Spread 3 inches of the soil mix you created over the compost layer. Plant your vegetables in this mix. Water thoroughly. Spread mulch.

Make raised beds. Raised beds are a really good idea, for several reasons. They are easier to plant. They warm up earlier in the spring than the surrounding ground, which gives your plants a head start. It is much easier to maintain good drainage in raised beds. Installing water delivery systems is simple, and watering the soil, not the foliage, is effortless. Weeds and their seeds are easily eliminated, without constant bending and pulling. Reaching your produce at harvest time is painless. At this point in our lives, we plant exclusively in raised beds or containers.

Create raised beds on top of cardboard, to prevent weed and grass seeds from germinating in them. Many materials can be used to make the sides of your raised beds: rocks, cinder blocks, lumber, recycled cement pavement that has been broken into chunks, slabs of stone, bender board, tree trunks, branches. We have even seen recycled radiators (that do not leak, of course) and sheets of discarded tin roofing. If you use recycled material, make sure it cannot leach pollutants into your garden or the ground water. Actually, you don't even have to build sides at all: mounding soil up into berms also effectively creates raised beds. After constructing the sides of the bed, lay down 1 inch of coarse (¼ inch) gravel on the bottom, on top of the cardboard, to help improve drainage. Then fill the bed with the soil mix you made. Containers also make excellent raised beds.

Use organic fertilizer. First, let's talk about fertilizers in general. All fertilizers, whether organic or not, have three numbers on the label (10-14-10, for example). These numbers indicate the percentage of three macronutrients that the fertilizer contains. The first number is the percentage of nitrogen (N), the second the percentage of phosphorus (P), and the third the percentage of potassium (K). Each macronutrient is important for plant health. And, in general, a balanced fertilizer (all three numbers the same—5-5-5, for example) meets the needs of most plants.

Organic fertilizers are as effective as, and have many advantages over, synthetic fertilizers. They feed the living community in the soil ecosystem, but it takes time for those organisms to break the material down so that the stored nutrients are accessible to plants. Because of this slow-release action, the nutrients are available to your plants for a long time. Typically, the benefits of an organic fertilizer last for the entire growing season. Organic fertilizers do not contribute to water pollution because their slowly released nutrients do not flee the garden. They stay put. Nutrient salts from synthetic fertilizers can build up in the soil, leaching moisture away from plants, which then dehydrate. Thanks to the slow-release process of organic fertilizers, these salts do not build up in the soil.

The potential downside to this lack of speed is that the nutrients in organic fertilizers are not immediately available to your plants—a good

(opposite, top) If you decide to delay planting until next season, spread 3 inches of mulch directly over the sheets of cardboard. This will prevent weed growth.

(opposite, bottom) Even the young students who tend this schoolyard garden in Santa Fe appreciate the benefits of raised beds: warmer soil, easily installed water delivery systems, good drainage, effortless weeding, and painless access to mature crops.

Nutrition Guidelines

Nutrient	Needed for . . .	Deficiency clues	Organic sources
Nitrogen	Vegetative growth, protein synthesis for new tissue	Lower leaves turn yellow, veins stay green. Leaves do not drop off.	Chicken manure, blood meal, alfalfa meal, cottonseed meal, fish emulsion
Phosphorus	Flower and fruit production	Leaves look purplish, veins turn purple.	Bone meal, rock phosphate, guano, greensand
Potassium	Flower and fruit production	Leaf edges turn yellow, with brown spots. Leaves turn brown and die.	Greensand, kelp, wood ashes, guano
Calcium	Numerous metabolic and physiological processes, cell elongation, and division	Blossom-end rot, growing tips die.	Lime, dolomitic lime, gypsum, greensand
Magnesium	Plant growth; a component of chlorophyll	Lower leaves turn yellow, veins stay green. Leaves do not drop off.	Epsom salts, dolomitic lime, greensand
Sulfur	Plant growth, especially roots and seed production	New leaves turn yellow, then whole plant yellows.	Epsom salts, gypsum, sulfur
Boron	Membrane function; a component of cell walls	Leaf edges curl under.	Seaweed (kelp), Borax
Chloride	Reproductive growth, root metabolism, and protein utilization	Stunted plants.	Seaweed (kelp)
Copper	Photosynthesis and plant growth	Leaves are pale green, tips die back and twist.	Seaweed (kelp)
Iron	Photosynthesis	New leaves turn yellow, veins stay green. Leaves do not drop off.	Seaweed (kelp), iron chelate
Manganese	Carbohydrate and nitrogen metabolism	New leaves turn yellow, veins stay green. Leaves do not drop off.	Seaweed (kelp)
Molybdenum	Nitrogen metabolism	Lower leaves turn yellow, veins stay green.	Seaweed (kelp)

reason to prepare your garden soil two weeks before you plant. In a nutritional emergency, you can always tend plants with an organic foliar spray, like fish emulsion or liquid seaweed. Plants can absorb nutrients through their leaves very quickly. For more on organic sources of nutrients, see the nutrition guidelines opposite.

Measure and modify pH. Soil pH measures the acidity or alkalinity of the soil, which in turn determines which nutrients your plant can take up from the soil to use for growth or to stay healthy. To measure pH, use one of the handy meters available at most garden centers. Changing the pH of your soil will treat clubroot and scab, two fungal diseases. For clubroot, raise the pH to between 6.8 and 7.5 (more alkaline) by adding lime. Do not plant in the area for six weeks. For scab (of potatoes and other root crops only), lower the pH below 5.5 (more acid). Pull mulch away, spread coffee grounds over the surface of the soil, and water them in. The coffee makes the soil more acid, but if you do not reach the target, then add sulfur. With lime, sulfur, and all purchased additives, follow the directions on the product label.

Solarize the soil. This is a pretty extreme measure, but it is sometimes necessary if you have had serious soilborne fungus infections that kill your plants. Here's how to do it. In the hottest, sunniest time of the year, remove all dead and dying plants, along with their roots and soil that clings to the roots. Turn over the soil, making sure it is not compacted. Mound the soil slightly and wet it thoroughly. Lay clear plastic, 1 to 6 mm thick, over the mound and weigh down the sides to hold it in place. The aim is to get the soil underneath the plastic very, very hot. After four to six weeks, remove the plastic. To garden here again, make sure drainage is good, and spread 3 to 4 inches of mature, organic compost over the area.

LIGHT SOLUTIONS

Modify the site. If your plant is getting too much light, as with transplant shock and sunburn, provide shade, especially on hot days. Plant a small deciduous tree that will cast dappled shade, or build a small trellis above the plant. For a temporary solution, throw a piece of 50 percent shade cloth over the plant until it becomes well established. Most of the time, if your plant is not getting enough light, it is a case of right plant, wrong place. Move the plant to a new location. If transplanting is not an option, try to prune or move surrounding trees, shrubs, or structures that block the light. And don't forget that you can always plant vegetables in containers and move them to a sunnier (or shadier) spot. If none of this is possible, then plan ahead next year to choose varieties that thrive in your circumstances.

WATER SOLUTIONS

Manage water. Wherever you live, if Mother Nature isn't providing adequate water, you'll have to provide it for your vegetable garden. Steady, consistent moisture is very often crucial for vegetables and fruits. Most require 1 inch a week. Never saturate the soil, or let it dry out completely between waterings. Wet foliage promotes fungal and bacterial infections, so always water the soil, not the foliage. Any one of the techniques pictured here is a good way to water your plants and keep them healthy. How do you know when your plant receives enough water? Set out an empty tuna fish can, begin your watering technique, and note the time it takes to fill the can with 1 inch of water. Now you know how long to water each week.

photo 353 / 88%
RGB

(top left) Tomatoes love the sun, but they enjoy a bit of relief under shade cloth on a hot day in New Mexico.

(bottom left) Containers make modifying the site a cinch. These pots are placed in the perfect light, near a water spigot, making life easy for the Santa Fe homeowner.

(top right) Rainbarrels harvest and store water from rooftops. They save money on your bill and protect the environment by controlling runoff.

(opposite, top left) Permeable soaker hoses deliver water directly to the soil, not the foliage, allowing water to soak deeply into the soil. Drain them before freezing temperatures strike, or they will burst.

(opposite, top right) Furrows (small channels made to carry water) have been used for thousands of years to irrigate vegetable crops. At watering time, fill them with water, and the plant roots will reach down into the soil as water soaks into it.

(opposite, bottom) Drip or trickle systems also deliver water to the soil, not the foliage. We recommend keeping these systems above ground, so that any necessary repairs are easily made. Again, drain the tubing when the weather turns cold.

Runoff water can also be harvested and stored in pools and fish ponds that enhance the landscape and provide irrigation in an emergency. Keep in mind that still water can harbor mosquito larvae. Prevent mosquito breeding by maintaining healthy habitat for fish and frogs, or use mosquito dunks from your local garden center.

(opposite, top) Swales are useful on sloping land. Dig a ditch across the land on the contour. Pile the soil excavated from the ditch on the downslope side to create a berm along the length of the ditch. The swale captures the rainfall or runoff from the slope above. Plant the berm with a variety of vegetables, herbs, flowers, and shrubs. These then obtain water from the swale.

(opposite, bottom) The dry streambed is a landscape feature designed to look like the gravelly bed of a stream in a dry season. When it rains, the streambed works like a ditch, directing the flow of runoff water to the garden. Even when there is no rainfall, the suggestion of the presence of water is a desirable result of this technique.

More and more, sustainably-minded people are harvesting runoff water from impervious surfaces (house, garage, and shed roofs; driveways, sidewalks, and patios). You can save this water and use it in the garden. A rainbarrel placed under a downspout from your roof's gutters can store up to 55 gallons of water for future use. More rainbarrels equals more water. Cisterns, either above or below ground, also capture rainwater. Above-ground swimming pools serve the same purpose as cisterns in rural Hawaii, where most households obtain all their water from these catchment systems. The systems funnel rainfall

Runoff water can also be directed to fill a sunken garden, like this one, or retention ponds or depressions. Such catchment systems hold water and allow it to percolate down to recharge groundwater. While water remains it can be pumped out to irrigate your vegetables whenever necessary.

from the roof into gutters, then downspouts, and finally into the pools. The water is pumped out to be used in the home as well as the garden.

Retaining water is slightly different from harvesting water. In this case, the land itself serves as a water catchment system. Water retention aims to prevent any water that nature gives you from leaving your property by implementing a system of swales, ditches, dry streambeds, or sunken gardens to capture, contain, and direct the water. Choose from several retention systems, but first, check your local or state regulations. In some places it is illegal to interrupt the flow of water from your property, whether by harvesting or retention.

Improve drainage. Before deciding you have a drainage problem, check the drainage. Dig a hole where you plan to grow vegetables. Fill the hole with water, and time how long it takes to drain completely away. If it takes more than an hour, then the drainage is not adequate. Try to locate the garden in an area with good drainage.

If you have no choice of sites, then improve the drainage. Dig a hole in the wet area, making sure you do not cut the roots of any plants you are trying to save. See if there is a layer of clay, rock, or other hard material preventing the water from draining away. If so, dig through the layer to create a drainage hole. Alternatively, you can dig a ditch to drain excess water away from the planting area. If you need a series of ditches, drains, or sump pumps, consult an engineer or landscape architect. Be aware that local and state governments regulate wetlands and water runoff, so check these regulations.

Watering the container garden. Overwatering is the number one killer of all potted plants, so keep the following tricks in mind. For starters, every pot should have a drainage hole. Add 1 inch of gravel to the bottom of each pot to improve drainage. Always allow the soil to drain before watering the plant again. And finally, put supports under the pot to keep the bottom of it at least 1 inch above the ground or standing water in a saucer.

PLANT POLYCULTURES

In a polyculture garden, unrelated plants grow next to each other. Think of it as the opposite of a field of corn, the classic example of a monoculture. A polyculture, with its variety of plants, provides three distinct advantages: it makes it more difficult for pestiferous insects to find your vegetables, it makes it more difficult for diseases to jump from plant to plant, and it attracts beneficial organisms from the wild. Not to mention that, like an English cottage garden, the mixed vegetable and flower bed can be quite aesthetically pleasing. All the plants discussed in "Encourage Beneficials" (page 208) should be included in a polyculture approach. And don't forget to plant marigolds. Read on to learn why.

Insects home in on your vegetable plants from great distances. Attracted from afar by the scent, the critters fly directly to their prey of choice. If you have several tomato plants growing close to one another, the insects easily find them. Instead, plant the same number of tomatoes, but scatter these around your yard. Surround them with other plants, thus masking the tomato scent. As insects approach their target, they switch from olfactory to visual cues. Thus, when the target plants are mixed in with a wide variety of other kinds of plants, the insects get confused and have difficulty finding the tasty treats they're after. In other words, they have to work hard to damage your produce.

Diseases caused by bacteria, fungi, and viruses move from plant to plant in a variety of ways. Bacteria are carried by insects, rain, or even your own clothing (if the plants are wet). Fungi spread by wind, or water splash from the ground. Aphids, leafhoppers, and thrips carry viruses from one plant to another. The closer together the plants of the same type are, the easier it is for disease to spread. It's just like people on an air-

Potato, chard, kale, calendula, and California poppy prosper together in this polyculture garden.

(opposite, top) A profusion of plants—broccoli, opium poppy, artichokes, avens—grow in close proximity in this coastal California garden. This plant diversity confuses insect pests, who cannot find their favorite host plants.

(opposite, bottom) A fungal pathogen decimated this row of beets. A polyculture approach minimizes such losses.

plane: when one person with a bad cold coughs, the entire cabin is exposed to the germs. Many others can get ill.

ROTATE YOUR CROPS

Because each plant family has its own suite of pests and diseases, moving your crops around from one season to the next protects them against the buildup of soilborne diseases and pests. For example, all brassicas, or cabbage family crops, are susceptible to clubroot, a fungus disease that lives in the soil. But no member of the potato family or squash family can get clubroot. So don't put the same kind of plant in the same place every year.

Here's a simple three-year rotation scheme for a standard vegetable garden. In year one, put brassicas (arugula, bok choy, broccoli, Brussels sprouts, cabbage, cauliflower, Chinese cabbage, collard greens, kale, kohlrabi, mustard greens, radishes, rutabagas, turnips) in Bed A, potato family crops (eggplant, peppers, potatoes, tomatillos, tomatoes) in Bed B, and squash family crops (cucumbers, melons, pumpkins, summer squash, winter squash, watermelon, zucchini) in Bed C. In year two, put squash family crops in Bed A, brassicas in Bed B, and potato family crops in Bed C. In year three, put potato family crops in Bed A, squash family crops in Bed B, and brassicas in Bed C. In year four, repeat year one. Things will eventually get more complicated, especially if more than three families get involved, but you can develop your own plan as you gain experience and knowledge.

Combining crop rotation and polyculture confuses some gardeners. How do you keep it simple? Randomly scatter the vegetables throughout your garden every year. There will be a small percentage of overlap from year to year, so that the randomized rotation scheme isn't 100 percent effective. But it's good enough. Another way to go, for the more technically minded, is to map out every square foot of your garden on paper, label each square foot with row and column (x and y) coordinates and make your rotation plan for each square foot. Either of these approaches will preserve the essential beneficial features of a polyculture garden and combine it with a rotation scheme.

Whatever your rotation plan, be sure to incorporate marigolds. Besides being very pretty, these low-growing annuals attract beneficial insects to your vegetable garden. Marigolds contain strongly aromatic compounds. To get a whiff of these, rub or crush the leaves. Their roots excrete these same compounds into the soil, repelling harmful nematodes. The soil where marigolds are (or were) growing is inimical to nematodes, but the adjacent soil is not protected. This means that planting marigolds *next* to nematode-susceptible vegetable varieties will not protect those vegetables against nematodes. But plant a susceptible vegetable in the same soil where a marigold *used* to grow, and it will be protected. Both French marigolds (*Tagetes patula*) and African marigolds (*T. erecta*) are effective against root-knot nematodes. French marigolds suppress a wider variety of nematodes.

ENCOURAGE BENEFICIALS

Wild creatures that help you in the garden are everywhere. Birds and insects provide pollination services. Many insectivorous birds help to get rid of insect pests for you. So do bats, frogs, toads, spiders, wasps, beetles, and nematodes. Some birds, beetles, and nematodes can harm your plants, however, so strive to maintain a healthy balance in the garden. Everything you do to encourage beneficial partners from the wild helps to create this balance.

A whole host of beneficial insects preys on or parasitizes the harmful insects that eat your vegetables. Ladybird beetles (aka ladybugs) and their larvae eat aphids, as do green lacewings, minute pirate bugs, and many more. There are even mites that love to hunt down and eat all those spider mites on your roses. Lure these helpers into your garden by growing plants that provide them with food, nectar, and shelter. Cosmos flowers, for example, attract hover flies. These flies do their best to look like dangerous bees or wasps, but they are harmless. They pollinate flowers, and their larvae are voracious predatory maggots that crawl over your plants and eat aphids.

To attract a large number of beneficial insects to your vegetable garden, add members of the carrot family (Apiaceae), the daisy family (Asteraceae), and the mint family (Lamiaceae) to your polyculture. The carrot family includes herbs such as dill, fennel, coriander (cilantro), parsley, and cumin, and flowers like Queen Anne's lace. The daisy family includes such herbs as tarragon and chamomile, and flowers like cosmos, sunflowers, anthemis, gaillardia, echinacea, bachelor buttons, and yarrow. The mint family includes herbs like thyme, rosemary, catnip, horehound, and sage, and flowers like catmint, agastache, and pycnanthemum.

(top left) French marigolds enhance your garden in three ways: they attract beneficial insects, they repel a wide variety of harmful nematodes, and they're very pretty.

(top right) Braconids and other tiny wasps lay their eggs inside caterpillars, like this tomato hornworm. When the eggs hatch, the larvae eat the pest alive from the inside out and make and attach cocoons to the outside of the caterpillar. Even tinier wasps lay their eggs inside aphids.

(bottom left) A hover fly pollinates a yellow cosmos. This small fly disguises itself as a bee to discourage predators, but it is quite harmless, and its larvae (maggots) kill and eat aphids.

(bottom right) Ladybird beetles (aka ladybugs) are a favorite and familiar beneficial insect. Both adults and larvae devour aphids and other small, soft-bodied pests. Fennel flowers, like this one, invite these small beetles into the garden.

Weed. Keeping the garden free of weeds is one of the best ways to keep your plants healthy. Weeds harbor pests and diseases, and compete with your veggies for sun, water, and soil nutrients. Pulling weeds up by hand is good exercise but can be a lot of work. Hand tools make the job easier. Make sure that you replace any mulch disturbed by weeding.

Mulch. Nothing works better than mulch to keep down weeds, to retain soil moisture, to keep water splash from spreading soilborne diseases to your plants, and to slowly add nutrients to the soil. Mulch insulates the soil, keeping it cool and curtailing evaporation, thus conserving water. When a drop of water hits mulch, the mulch splashes up, but not the soil, protecting the plant from disease. And as the mulch slowly decomposes, it feeds that biologically active medium that makes your plants so happy and healthy.

We highly recommend the use of mulch made from dead plant material. It suppresses weeds because it is nutrient-poor until it has decomposed. We do not recommend using compost as mulch, because good compost is nutrient-rich. If you put nutrient-rich compost on the surface of your soil, the weeds are going to have a field day. Cover compost with mulch (straw, pine needles, bark) that is nutrient-poor, and you'll keep the weeds at bay.

Sanitize. This is the term that plant pathologists apply to the act of cleaning out any pest- or disease-ridden plant material. It is the first thing you should do if you have heavy insect infestations or a rapidly spreading disease infection. During the growing season, prune, pick, or break off any part of the plant that is badly affected. Clean tools thoroughly and wash your hands before handling any healthy plants.

In the case of some diseases (late blight, clubroot, any virus disease) you should remove the entire plant, roots, and any soil clinging to the roots. Dispose of infested or infected plant material in such a way that it cannot affect other plants. Burn it, if it is legal and safe to do so, or put it in black plastic garbage bags and send it to the landfill. Some people who know how to maintain a hot compost pile (at least 160°F) can add this kind of material to their compost. But if you have any doubt about whether your compost pile is that hot, it is better to just get rid of the plant material.

At the end of each growing season, clean up leftover plant material of all annuals and biennials. If perennials have died to the ground, clean up all the above-ground plant parts. Dispose of this material where it cannot infect other plants. Many pests can live over the winter in the garden if you do not get rid of their cozy habitat, so don't give them the chance to be around in the spring. Fungal spores, insect eggs, and bacteria lurking on old dead leaves lying on the ground can quickly infect your new plants and ruin your produce all summer long.

Move the air. Air movement is important for both pest and disease control. It hinders fungus infections from spreading rapidly through dense foliage. It also encourages insects that are not strong fliers to leave the premises. To provide air movement, thin plants so that they are not too crowded. Remove objects and structures that prevent air circulation around your plants. Indoors or on the patio, don't hesitate to use fans, especially in container gardens.

(top) Gardeners from Berkeley to Boston have discovered that straw makes a cheap and effective mulch. Its disadvantages are that it tends to blow away in high winds, and it decomposes a little too quickly.

(left) Shredded bark of Douglas fir or redwood makes a very good mulch. It decomposes slowly, stays put in wind, and is moderately priced.

Solve Pest Problems

(top) Up close and personal. Deer really appreciate just about everything we grow in our gardens, including Japanese maples.

(bottom) Possums share our habitat in many places. This L.A. momma has clearly succeeded in adapting to an urbanized environment and provides well for her many babies.

Unpredictable events that affect your vegetable garden's productivity sometimes involve visits from troublesome wildlife. Deer, raccoon, and rabbits steal into the garden as we sleep, or as we look the other way, to gobble our ripe vegetables from under our noses. How dare they? And what can, or should, we do about it? Read on and find some answers.

We call them pests, but they are really wild creatures that roam their circumscribed world searching for food, water, mates, and a safe place for their young. As we humans develop more and more habitat for ourselves, the raccoons and rabbits, the gophers and birds, the deer and the antelope wander into our backyards. Their habitat shrinks every day, and by necessity they find themselves in ours.

Sharing with wildlife reaps its own rewards. We love to invite wildlife of all sorts, including mammals, into our garden. Squirrels frolic, birds sing and lighten our spirits, and eat insect pests that damage plants. Even when we discover our guests have crossed the line from friend to foe, we often decide to look the other way. But when they've overstayed their welcome, it is sometimes better to discourage them or limit their access.

Not all insects are pests. Many are not only beneficial but essential to the health of the vegetable garden. Soil would be much less productive without their contribution to the decomposition of organic matter. Helpful insect predators eat damaging insect pests, and most of our food plants are pollinated by insects. Though some insects devour our fruits and vegetables without our permission, it is still a good idea to consider your control options carefully. Think about whether you really need to do anything at all. If you are losing too much produce, choose non-toxic solutions first. Begin by encouraging ben-

Troublesome Wildlife Problem-Solving Guide

Symptom	Diagnosis	Solution
Leaves are missing, or have large chunks bitten out of them. Plants can be mowed to the ground.	**Deer or other large mammals, like elk or your neighbor's goats**	Grow highly aromatic herbs among your vegetables (rosemary, thyme, lavender) Row covers, page 214 Fence, page 214 Fright tactics, page 217 Nets, page 217 Garlic spray, page 220 Pepper spray, page 221 Deer repellent spray, page 221
Fruit has been stripped off the plants and partially eaten. Plants are broken, and debris litters the ground.	Raccoons	Fright tactics, page 217 Nets, page 217 Garlic spray, page 220 Pepper spray, page 221
Tubers and roots are chewed, fruit is gnawed open, and seeds are eaten. Parallel grooved tooth marks confirm the diagnosis.	**Rodents (squirrels, rats, mice, marmots) and rabbits**	Fright tactics, page 217 Nets, page 217 Garlic spray, page 220 Pepper spray, page 221 Traps, page 218
Holes appear in the ground under plants. Roots are eaten away. Stems are chewed. Plants may disappear.	**Gophers, voles**	Make raised beds, page 197 Wire mesh, page 214 Traps, page 218
Corn husks are shredded, and kernels are eaten, but ears are not stripped off. Leaves have triangular holes along edges. Plants are not broken. Sweet berries, cherries, sunflower and other seeds may be missing.	Birds	Row covers, page 214 Fright tactics, page 217 Nets, page 217

eficial insects, birds, and soil microorganisms for the valuable services they provide. Next, find ways to avoid or exclude pests entirely. Finally, consider using one of the toxic (albeit organic) remedies we have listed here, but only as a last resort. Safety is an issue even when you use remedies approved for organic gardening. Have a look at page 191 for a definition of organic as applied to garden remedies and information about safety labels.

All the remedies listed here are certified for use on organically grown food. The most toxic remedies are listed last and should be turned to only if all else fails. Choose the remedy that works for your situation.

Row covers. Row covers are made from a lightweight, white fabric that you can drape either directly over your plants (floating row covers) or over a rigid frame (rigid row covers). The fabric excludes pests, but it breathes and allows light to reach the plants.

Cutworm collars. Cutworms are caterpillars that hide in the soil by day and come out at night to ravage your seedlings and eat leaves of older plants. To make a cutworm collar, take cardboard tubes from toilet paper or paper towel rolls and cut them into 1- to 2-inch-tall sections. Tuna fish cans with the top and bottom removed also work well. Place these cylinders around each small seedling, directly on the ground with the seedling in the middle. Cutworms won't climb over these barriers.

Tar paper. A simple device made from this product protects your plants from cabbage maggots, carrot maggots, onion maggots, and other kinds of flies. The adult insect is a fly that lays its eggs in the soil at the base of its host plants; the eggs hatch into maggots that eat the roots and tunnel into radishes, turnips, carrots, and so forth. Cut

3- or 4-inch squares of tar paper or some similar flexible material. Punch a ¼-inch hole in the center of each square, and make a straight cut from one side of the square to the center hole. Slide one of these squares around the base of seedlings with the seedling nestled securely in the central hole. Since the fly cannot get to the soil, she can't lay her eggs.

Wire mesh. If you live in an area where gophers, voles, or other burrowing rodents are a problem, you can line your planting holes with ¼-inch wire hardware cloth to keep them away from the roots of your plants. Essentially, you make a basket out of hardware cloth, bury it in the ground, and plant your seedlings inside the basket. You can make this basket as big as you like. This device is especially valuable for root crops like carrots, beets, and potatoes.

Fence. Deer are major garden pests in many areas, and a fence is the best choice to keep them out. Deer are excellent jumpers. Your fence needs to be 8 feet tall. It also has to be very sturdy, or deer will push their way through to get their favorite food. You can always add extensions to a shorter fence to achieve the height you need. Run wire or some other visible material between the extensions and the fence. An alternative to such a tall fence is to enclose your vegetable garden with two shorter, parallel fences 4 feet apart. Most deer won't jump into such a narrow space. Electric fences are another alternative, but we prefer to keep things simple and low-tech in the

(opposite, top) This floating row cover is draped directly over plants. The fabric is weighted down along its edges but is still loose enough that plants can push it up as they grow.

(opposite, bottom) With rigid row covers, a frame of PVC pipe, wood, or metal holds the fabric up and away from the plants. Remove the cloth as plants grow and become restricted by the structure.

garden. If you opt for the electric fence route, choose photovoltaic cells to charge it.

In other areas, rabbit fencing will be necessary, but as rabbits are neither high jumpers nor powerful, a 2-foot-high fence of 1-inch chicken wire will keep them out. Be sure to peg the chicken wire to the ground with long, metal, U-shaped pins that you can buy at most garden centers. If rabbits learn where the gaps are between the pins and begin to dig under the fence, then bury the chicken wire about a foot deep.

Kaolin spray. Kaolin is clay that you purchase as a dry powder and mix with water to spray on your plants. The clay coating repels insects but does not kill them. Apply when the foliage is dry, and keep in mind that rain will wash it away. This product leaves a white coating on plants but is safe to use until one day before you harvest. Garden centers carry the product under various trade names.

Nets. Throw lightweight nets made from plastic over plants or around fruits that are plagued by birds or deer.

Hand-pick pests. Some people find this a yucky proposition, and if you are one of them, then wear gloves or use kitchen tongs to pick up slugs, snails, large caterpillars, and other pests. Plop all the pests you catch into a wide-mouthed jar of soapy water in which they will drown. Knock beetles off plants into the jar. Scrape adult scale insects off with your thumbnail. For boring insects, slit open the stem with a sharp knife and remove the pest, or insert a thin, flexible wire into the hole and hook the pest to drag it out.

Copper tape. Remove slugs and snails from the garden bed, and then place copper tape along the border of the garden, around a container, or along the edge of a raised bed. Slugs and snails will not move across copper.

Blast with hose. Adult insects often fly away before you can get them, but you can wash their eggs and larvae off with a strong blast from the hose. Wash away aphids, whiteflies, mites, and others about once a week to keep their populations from building up. Do this in the morning on a clear day, so that the leaves and stems have a chance to dry out.

Vacuum. Using your household vacuum cleaner or a shop-vac works pretty well on whiteflies and other insects that are somewhat weak fliers. Scoop them right out of the air, and you'll avoid sucking the plant's leaves into the vacuum cleaner hose.

Fright tactics. It makes us a bit sad to think about scaring animal visitors away from the vegetable garden, but sometimes they are just doing too much damage to share your produce with them. A barking dog that is outside will scare away deer, raccoons, rodents, and birds. Motion-activated sprinklers deter deer, cats, and other small mammals, but you will need to move it from time to time, or the animals learn to tip-toe around them. These will also scare raccoons for awhile, but sometimes they learn to dismantle them. The recorded sounds of birds of prey that go off at random intervals scare away birds and some rodents. Garden centers and hardware stores sell gizmos that produce ultrasonic sounds, beyond the range of human hearing, that frighten

(opposite, top left) A cardboard toilet paper tube makes a great cutworm collar for this chili pepper.

(opposite, top right) Birds cannot peck, damage, or eat fruit enclosed by netting.

(opposite, bottom) Deer fencing needs to be both tall and sturdy. Sometimes necessity creates an opportunity to add an attractive feature to your garden, as this homeowner in Washington State has done.

animals. Each unit can be adjusted to different frequencies, to affect raccoons, squirrels, rabbits, or deer.

Traps. Earwigs are beneficial insects as well as pests, so don't do anything about them unless they are clearly damaging your plants. The simplest method we know of to remove and kill earwigs is a moist, rolled-up newspaper. Roll it fairly loosely and secure it with a rubber band. Moisten it slightly and lay it on the ground in the evening. The earwigs hide in there overnight. Retrieve it in the morning, close up the ends, and roll it tightly so the earwigs cannot escape. Seal the paper, along with its hidden earwigs, in a plastic bag and put that in the garbage.

Sticky bands and stem wraps work like old-fashioned flypaper. Purchase commercially prepared sticky goo that is made to mire insects. Paint this goo on pliable plastic, cardstock paper, or metal strips. Wrap the strips around the stems of your plants, and the insects get stuck as they climb the stems. This prevents ants from bringing aphids to your plants. You can also lay these strips along flat edges of a raised bed and see what you catch. Once the goo is littered with insect carcasses, replace the strips with fresh goo.

Sticky cards work just like bands and stem wraps except that they catch flying insects. You can buy a kit or make your own, from the same commercially prepared insect-trapping goo that you got to make sticky bands. Yellow attracts insects, so these ready-made cards are always yellow on one side. If you make your own, paint one side of a 4- by 5-inch piece of plywood or masonite yellow and cover it with the goo. Attach the unpainted side to a stick, and sink the stick into the ground next to your troubled plant. When the sticky side is covered with carcasses, scrape the goo off and paint on fresh goo.

There are a few things you can do to discourage rodent populations. The best solution is a cat that enjoys hunting outdoors, though this is admittedly a non-targeted solution. Songbirds beware. If that's not possible, your local humane society frequently loans or rents Havahart traps. When the animal is captured, you take the pest to a more appropriate habitat and release it. Other kinds of lethal mammal traps are often as non-targeted as prowling cats, which means that you can accidentally kill animals you would rather not harm.

Capture slugs and snails by placing upside-down pots or boards in strategic locations around the garden. Prop them up on pebbles, so that the critters will seek hiding places beneath them. Then you can easily find and destroy them, or move them far, far away.

Beneficial predators. This may be the best remedy for any insect pest problem. Not only do you use a completely non-toxic solution, you encourage your healthy garden ecosystem to flourish. Sometimes we want to go further than encouraging beneficials (see page 208). We actually want to buy the eggs or the insects or the mites themselves and release them in the garden. There are lots of predatory or parasitic insects and mites that kill and eat specific garden pests. Most of the beneficial organisms that you purchase arrive as eggs, but a few are adults. Unless otherwise specified, always release these beneficial organisms in the evening. They're more likely to settle down and stay put in the dark. Spread them around the vegetable garden; many will turn to cannibalism if they can't find enough prey to eat. The ones presented here are a good place to start.

Ladybird beetle (aka ladybug). These popular little red beetles with black spots are a joy to see in the garden. They eat soft-bodied insects like aphids, mealybugs, and scale. Place them toward the base of plants, because they like to crawl up toward the light. If there is not enough to eat, they will leave.

Green lacewing. When you purchase these as eggs, they will be mixed with other material, such as brown rice hulls and moth eggs, to keep them alive. Wash active aphid and other pest populations off your plants, and then sprinkle the lacewing mixture over plants throughout the garden. When the eggs hatch, the lacewing larvae crawl across plants, consuming up to 10,000 aphids a day. You won't see them, but you should notice a decrease in harmful soft-bodied pests. As well as aphids, green lacewing larvae eat mealybugs, scale, spider mites, caterpillars, whitefly larvae, and a wide variety of moth eggs.

Praying mantid. This wonderful bug eats beetles, caterpillars, grubs, aphids, grasshoppers, and almost anything else that crawls by. Purchase an egg case, and place or hang it at least 2 feet off the ground. The egg case holds about 200 eggs, and when they hatch the baby praying mantids will venture out into the garden. Praying mantids will overwinter, reproduce, and persist in the vegetable garden year after year if they are happy.

Parasitoid wasps. Several kinds of parasitoid wasps are available for purchase. Braconid wasps kill caterpillars of all kinds by laying their eggs inside the creatures and eating them from the inside out. Trichogramma wasps parasitize moths. Purchase containers with cards that hold about 4,000 moth eggs, inside of which the wasps are developing. Uncap the container and place it in the fork of a tree, or carefully remove the card and hang it on a branch with a string or tape. Protect the eggs from ants, and place the container or the card where it will be protected from rain.

Delphastus. This small, shiny black beetle, about a quarter the size of a ladybug, eats whitefly eggs

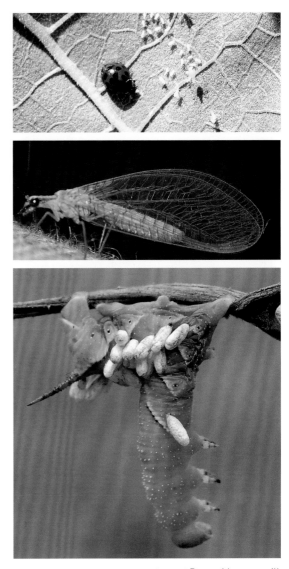

(top) What a boon to gardeners. This ladybird beetle devours aphids all day long.

(center) A green lacewing takes a break from her busy schedule of laying eggs.

(bottom) Braconid wasps will soon emerge from these cocoons, hanging on the carcass of a tomato hornworm. The new wasps will hunt down caterpillars, lay their eggs inside, and begin the cycle again.

Ants tend aphids the way we tend livestock. They bring aphids to your plants and then "milk" them, as we would cows or goats, for the clear, sticky, sugary substance (honeydew) they excrete.

Encarsia formosa. This tiny wasp, about the size of a pencil point, parasitizes the eggs of whitefly. The product you buy is a card filled with wasp eggs. Remove cards from the container, separate along perforations, and hang them on branches of plants where whiteflies are present. Unlike the other beneficial predators listed here, the purchased product should be placed in the garden when it is sunny and warm.

Predatory mites. These beneficials seek out and kill pest mites, particularly spider mites. Purchase adult mites in a medium, such as corn grit or vermiculite. The mixture will come in a bottle. Shake the mixture out of the bottle on the day you receive it, spreading it out on leaves where the good mites are likely to find pest mites.

Beneficial nematodes. These microscopic garden partners kill adults and larvae of about 200 different species of pests that live on or in the soil during some part of their life cycle. The product usually contains nematode larvae of two species mixed with a moist storage medium (typically gel, vermiculite, or peat moss). Since the package you buy contains living nematodes (aka roundworms), it must be handled carefully. Keep it refrigerated until you are ready to use. When you are, mix the product with water and spray on the soil. Nematodes survive in your garden for about five years if they have enough to eat, so this is a very cost-effective remedy.

Garlic spray. The strong odor and flavor of garlic repel a range of garden pests, from insects to deer. Whether you make it yourself or purchase one of the many commercial preparations for garden use, garlic spray is easy to use, relatively non-toxic, and, best of all, it actually works. It's usually prepared as a liquid, which you spray on your plants. It kills some beneficial insects too, so don't just use it routinely as a general preventive.

and larvae, but if whiteflies are not present they will also feed on spider mites. Both the adult beetle and larvae are predators. Wash the plants to knock pests off, and then sprinkle the tiny beetles in different locations around the garden. These beetles prefer to spend their time in the upper portion of your plants.

Mealybug destroyers. As their name implies, these small orange-headed black beetles love mealybugs, but they also eat aphids, immature scale, and immature whitefly. Carefully shake the beetles directly onto infested plants on the same day you receive them. Since ants are attracted to the clear, sticky substance secreted by aphids and mealybugs, ants will actually attack the mealybug destroyers. Place sticky bands around the stem of your plants to control ants before you buy and release mealybug destroyers.

Instead, use it when you know that pests have shown up. There are lots of recipes for making your own garlic spray. Most use several cloves of garlic in a quart of water, whirled in a blender and strained. Put this in a spray bottle and apply it to your plants. If you add liquid soap as a spreader-sticker, be aware that the soap will make the product even more effective at killing all insects, including your beneficial ones. No safety label required. See "Safety First."

Pepper spray. Chili peppers contain capsaicin, a compound that gives them their fiery taste. We humans love that heat in Thai or Mexican cuisine, but deer and other garden pests don't like it at all. Like garlic spray, pepper spray is easy to make yourself, or you can buy commercial preparations. It is not toxic, and it works as a repellent, just like garlic. You can even combine the hot chili peppers with garlic if you want. Pepper spray is non-targeted, so it will kill beneficial organisms as well as pests. No safety label required. See "Safety First."

Deer repellent spray. Commercial preparations of deer repellents usually contain a mixture of putrescent egg solids (rotten eggs), capsaicin (chili pepper oil), and garlic. This mixture apparently smells and tastes as bad to deer and other mammals as it does to us. However, it will not deter a really hungry critter. Also, rain washes it away, so be ready to reapply, or when the offending mammal returns, there may be nothing nasty left. No safety label required. See "Safety First."

Vegetable oil. Coating corn silks with vegetable oil prevents corn earworms (caterpillars) from crawling inside the ear of corn. After the silk turns brown, which is your signal that pollination has occurred, put several drops of oil on the silks of each ear. If you apply the oil earlier, the oil prevents pollination. If you wait until the silks start to dry up, the earworms are likely already inside. No safety label required. See "Safety First."

Insecticidal soap. Soap (technically, potassium salts of fatty acids) kills all insects and mites, including beneficial friends, by penetrating the cuticle layer (skin) and causing the organism's cells to collapse. Soap is not a poison. It kills only when it is wet and you spray it directly on the insect or mite. Therefore, spray only insects or mites that you *know* cause damage to your plants. Otherwise you may kill beneficial insects and mites by mistake. Once you identify the critter as a pest, spray it with the soap. You can buy a ready-made product at garden stores or online, or you can make your own insecticidal soap spray. Mix a tablespoon of liquid soap with a quart of water in a spray bottle. Do not use a detergent, as it may damage your plants. No safety label required. See "Safety First."

Nosema spore. This bioinsecticide is a very effective control for grasshoppers. A microscopic protozoan parasite (*Nosema locustae*), nosema is mixed with bran and made into a bait grasshoppers like to eat. After they ingest it, they get sick and die. If they manage to lay eggs after they get infected, they will pass the infection on to the next generation, so the disease can persist for years. Nosema is highly targeted and safe to use. It does not affect children, dogs and cats, birds, honeybees, or butterflies. It kills only grasshoppers and crickets. Since adult grasshoppers can fly from vegetable garden to vegetable garden, nosema is extremely effective when an entire neighborhood uses it. No safety label required. See "Safety First."

BTK. *Bacillus thuringiensis* var. *kurstaki* is a living bacterial parasite that is suspended in water and sprayed on stems and foliage. It kills all caterpillars and only caterpillars, no matter what we call

This cutworm will grow up to be a night-flying moth if the BTK doesn't get to it first.

them. Armyworms, cutworms, earworms, and corn borers are all caterpillars, and all are larvae of butterflies and moths. The caterpillar chews on your plant, ingests the bacteria, stops eating almost immediately, and dies several days later. Apply this bacterial spray on dry but cloudy days. BTK's efficacy diminishes in intense sunlight and high heat, and rain washes it away. Reapply as needed. Best results are achieved if you use it about once a week. This product is available at garden centers, usually in ready-to-use spray bottles but sometimes as a liquid concentrate or dust. The product label does not always list inert ingredients, so test the product and wear protective gear, in case you are allergic to an unnamed ingredient. Safety label: CAUTION. Please read "Safety First," page 191.

BTSD. The San Diego variety of BT (*Bacillus thuringiensis*) is a highly targeted bacterial parasite that must be ingested by the critter as it eats your plants. Therefore, though BTSD kills beetles and weevils, it does not kill predators that do not eat plants, such as ladybird beetles (aka ladybugs) or other beneficial beetles. The living bacteria are suspended in water and sprayed on stems and foliage. The beetle chews on your plant, ingests the bacteria, stops eating almost immediately, and dies several days later. Apply on dry but cloudy days. BTSD's efficacy diminishes in intense sunlight and high heat, and rain washes it away. Reapply as needed, but best results are achieved if you use it about once a week. This

product is harder to find than BTK. Look for it at garden centers and online, in ready-to-use spray bottles or as a liquid concentrate or dust. The product label does not always list inert ingredients, so test the product and wear protective gear, in case you are allergic to an unnamed ingredient. Safety label: CAUTION. Please read "Safety First," page 191.

Iron phosphate. Two natural elements found in soil, iron and phosphorus, combine to make this product. It attracts slugs and snails, which eat it and die. It usually comes in the form of little white pellets that you scatter on the ground. Combine these elements with oxygen and you get fertilizer, so, as it dissolves, this product also feeds the soil. Research has shown that it may affect aquatic animals (slugs and snails are mollusks, like clams, oysters, and octopuses), so do not use it near or dispose of it in water. Iron phosphate causes eye irritation, so be sure to wash up thoroughly after handling it. Safety label: CAUTION. Please read "Safety First," page 191.

Milky spore. This bacterial disease kills Japanese beetle larvae and their relatives. It does not kill unrelated beetle larvae. The bacteria are cultivated in laboratories and carried in dust or granules that you spread on the ground beneath plants infested with the beetles. Since this product does not kill adult beetles, they can still fly in and damage plants. You'll get better control if your neighbors use the product too. Milky spore is available at garden centers and online. Safety label: CAUTION. Please read "Safety First," page 191.

Diatomaceous earth. This powdery, white grit kills any small creature that crawls across it. When insects, slugs, and snails encounter this material it is, for them, like crawling across shards of glass. The product is made from diatoms, ancient microscopic plants that have skeletons of glass (silicon dioxide). Scatter the dust-like grit on the ground in the area where you have a ground-crawling pest problem. Wear a respirator mask, goggles, gloves, long-sleeved shirt, and long pants because this product irritates skin and eyes and can cause lung damage. The powder is ineffective if wet. Keep it dry by spreading it under a board or flower pot that is slightly raised on small pebbles. Find the product, labeled as an insecticide (not the one for swimming pool filters), at garden centers. Safety label: CAUTION. Please read "Safety First," page 191.

Beauveria bassiana. This fungus's spores germinate when they land on the body of certain insects and then grow through the insect's cuticle layer (skin), producing toxins that kill. It takes the pest several days to die. Once it has, the fungus often grows over the carcass, creating a white mold. This mold continues to produce spores that infect other insects. Keep in mind that if you have used any sort of fungicide (including baking soda) within the last 24 hours, this product will not work. The fungal spores are suspended in a liquid that you spray on the pest and the plant. As long as the solution is fresh when the pest crawls across it, the critter ought to become infected. Typically you will need to spray several times, about five to seven days between doses. Since this product kills some beneficial insects (including bees), make an effort to spray only when you *know* that insects are actively damaging your plants. Do not use it on or near water, as it may be toxic to fish. The best time of day to spray is early morning or early evening. The garden should be cool and moist, so water first if it is dry. Look for this product at garden centers and online. Safety label: CAUTION. Please read "Safety First," page 191.

Spinosad. This bacterial toxin kills beneficial insects as well as pests, so use it only if you *know*

you have a serious pest problem. The living bacteria are suspended in a liquid solution that you spray on your plants. The insect eats the leaves or stems and ingests the bacterium and its toxic substances. Spinosad remains toxic on plant foliage up to a week, so it could easily kill your wild insect partners. Do not spray it on water. Tests are incomplete, but it may be toxic to fish. It is best to use this product early in the morning or late in the afternoon. You may need to spray about once a week until the pest population diminishes to acceptable levels. Spinosad is frequently premixed with iron phosphate and is available as a ready-made liquid spray or as a powder that you mix with water. Safety label: CAUTION. Please read "Safety First," page 191.

Neem. This oil is extracted from the seeds of *Azadirachta indica*, a tree that is native to India. It works as a pesticide in several unusual ways. It repels some insects, sending out a signal that says, "Do not gather here." It prevents other insects from molting, so they cannot mature. And in still others, it stops egg laying. Research, including concerns about its safety and side effects, continues. Therefore, do not use neem when bees and other beneficial insects are active in the garden. And do not use it on or near water. Neem oil is available at garden centers as a ready-to-use product that has a surfactant in it. You mix it with water and spray it on your plants. The effect on insects takes time, so be patient and make observations. You may need to repeat applications about every seven to 14 days, depending on what you see. Safety label: CAUTION. Please read "Safety First," page 191.

Horticultural oil. This oil coats and smothers insects, mites, and their eggs and larvae. It kills all insects and mites, including beneficials, so do not use this product unless you *know* you have a serious pest problem. Horticultural oil has been marketed under various names over the years, including dormant oil and superior oil. Some formulations are made from petroleum products (and some of these are allowed on organically grown plants), but we recommend you use only those products made from vegetable oil, even if they are hard to find. If the label does not say that the product is made with vegetable oil, do not use it on your food plants.

Do not swallow the product or allow it to come in contact with your skin, because it can cause an allergic reaction in some people. It can also cause eye irritation and difficulty breathing. Wear a respirator mask, goggles, gloves, long-sleeved shirt, and long pants; and keep children and pets away while spraying. In addition to protecting yourself, some plants need to be protected from horticultural oil. Test spray a small area or a single plant to see how it reacts, before going further. Do not use this product if the temperature is higher than 85°F or below freezing (not too likely in the summer growing season, we know). Make sure plants are well hydrated before using horticultural oil. Spray the plants thoroughly, because this product works only by direct contact with the pest. Find horticultural oil in ready-to-use spray bottles at garden centers, or make your own: add a tablespoon of liquid soap—not detergent—to a cup of vegetable oil. Put a tablespoon of this concentrate in a gallon of water to make your spray. Safety label: CAUTION. Please read "Safety First," page 191.

Sulfur. Sulfur is a yellow mineral mined from the earth that kills insects, including beneficial ones, by disrupting their metabolism. You should use sulfur only if you *know* you have a serious problem and other, more benign, techniques have failed. Sulfur has side effects and poses potential health hazards, particularly for people with allergies. Wear a respirator mask, goggles, gloves, long-sleeved shirt, and long pants; and keep children and pets away when spraying. Since sulfur kills your wild and purchased beneficial insect partners, use it while temperatures are cool and insects are less active. Keep it away from ponds, streams, and lakes, as it will kill fish. It can also harm plants under two conditions: when it is too hot (above 80°F), and if you have sprayed with horticultural oil within the last month. Finally, if you use sulfur fairly regularly, it will build up in the soil and make it more acid. Spray all above-ground plant parts thoroughly. To kill insect eggs, you need to spray before eggs hatch, and you may need to reapply every seven to 14 days because the product washes off in the rain. Observe your plants for continued signs of insect damage. Do not use it more often than you have to. Sulfur is available as a ready-to-use spray or as a concentrate or dust that you mix with water. Safety label: CAUTION. Please read "Safety First," page 191.

Pyrethrin. This product is a naturally occurring insecticide/miticide made from the dried flowers of *Chrysanthemum cinerariifolium*—that's right, a relative of our old friend, the garden mum. The dried flowers are ground into a powder that can be mixed with water and sprayed on plants. The product paralyzes insects and mites on contact, and it remains potent for several days, affecting any creature that walks over the sprayed area. Pyrethrin kills most insects and mites, so it will kill your beneficial partners, as well as pests. Don't use it unless you have a severe pest problem. Some manufacturers add a synergist to increase pyrethrin's toxicity. Wear a respirator mask, goggles, gloves, long-sleeved shirt, and long pants; and keep children and pets away when spraying. Spray the plants thoroughly. Don't forget the undersides of leaves. Look for pyrethrin at garden centers as a ready-to-use spray or as a concentrate that you mix with water. Safety label: CAUTION. Please read "Safety First," page 191.

Solve Disease Problems

Luckily for all gardeners, diseases on plants are fairly uncommon. If something has gone wrong in the garden, 80 percent of the time it is a problem with the plant's growing conditions. Changing those conditions solves the problem. But when a plant does not get what it needs for a prolonged period, it is under stress. Just like people, when a plant is under stress it is vulnerable to diseases. To avoid plant stress, be sure to give your vegetables what they need by following the guidelines in each plant portrait.

If despite your best efforts, your plant does get "sick," 80 percent of the time the problem is a fungus infection. Fungal spores are everywhere. There is no avoiding them, nor would we want to. Fungi are beneficial partners in human health (think of penicillin, an important antibiotic derived from bread mold) and in the garden. The healthy soil ecosystem teems with fungi. Indeed, mycorhizzal fungi are essential for plant nutrition. Because of their crucial role in any healthy ecosystem, it is a good idea to keep fungi happy and healthy. Nevertheless, some fungi are pathogens and harm plants. As plant caretakers, it is our job to keep these diseases in check.

Remember, "Safety First." Please have a look at page 191 for a definition of "organic" as applied to garden remedies and information about safety labels. Before using any of the remedies that follow, please revisit the growing conditions that have contributed to the occurrence of disease in the garden. Changing growing conditions is truly one of your most effective solutions. Reread each vegetable's portrait. Is there anything that was missed that would make your plant happier and healthier? Correct the growing conditions before using remedies.

Preventing fungal, as well as bacterial and viral, infections is by far the best approach, so use two all-important techniques before reaching for a remedy. Water the soil, not the foliage. Most fungi and all bacteria need a thin layer of moisture on the foliage to gain access to and infect your plants. Sanitize. Clean up all infected plant parts and get them out of the vegetable garden.

All the remedies listed here are preventive measures, not cures. All are certified for use on organically grown food. Choose the one that fits your circumstances. The remedies are listed from least to most toxic, so please use them in the order presented.

Baking soda. An oldie but goodie, baking soda inhibits fungal spores from germinating and causes the cell walls of fungi to collapse. It has no known side effects and is non-toxic to mammals, insects, and fish, but it can burn the leaves of some plants. Spray a few leaves, and wait a day or two to see what happens. If you see no adverse reactions, use it in a wider application. Spray your plants thoroughly, covering all sides of the leaves, stems, and fruits. Repeat every two weeks as needed. Rain will wash it off. You can buy ready-to-use spray bottles at garden centers, or you can make your own baking soda spray: add a tablespoon of baking soda, 2 ½ tablespoons of vegetable oil, and a teaspoon of liquid soap (not detergent) to a gallon of water. Safety label: CAUTION. Please read "Safety First," page 191.

Bacillus subtilis. This naturally occurring strain of bacterium kills fungal pathogens that land on your plants. In addition to competing with fungi for nutrients and space on plant surfaces, this living bacterium also attaches itself to cell walls of fungi and eventually kills them. Tests have shown that it is non-toxic to humans, birds, fish, and other aquatic organisms. However, some people have allergic reactions to this product, so wear a respirator mask, goggles, gloves, long-sleeved shirt, and long pants when applying it. The bacteria are suspended in a liquid that you spray on all plant parts (foliage, flowers, stems, and fruits). You may need to reapply it about every two weeks, or whenever rain has washed it away. Safety label: CAUTION. Please read "Safety First," page 191.

Trichoderma harzianum. This beneficial fungus prevents fungal infections (but does not cure existing ones) by growing into colonies around the roots of your plants and outcompeting pathogenic fungi. In addition to fighting off the bad guys of the fungi world, TH seems to promote healthy root growth. Use it on seedlings if you see signs of damping off, a fungal infection that causes roots to rot and seedling to collapse. Remember that the fungus in the product you buy is alive, so use it right away. TH is available as a powder that you mix with water, which you then use to water your seedlings. The soil temperature should be above 50°F. Find it at garden centers. Safety label: CAUTION. Please read "Safety First," page 191.

Neem. In addition to being an insecticide (see page 223), neem oil also prevents fungal spores from germinating. Neem is thought to be non-toxic to mammals, but do not use it on or near water, or when bees and other beneficial insects are active in the garden. Buy a commercial preparation that has been prepared with a surfactant, so that the oil will mix with water. Mix the preparation with water and spray plants thoroughly about every seven to 14 days, as needed. Look for neem oil at garden centers. Safety label: CAUTION. Please read "Safety First," page 191.

Sulfur. In addition to killing insects (see page 223), including beneficial ones, this yellow mineral prevents fungal spores from germinating. Research has shown that it is as effective as synthetic fungicides. Sulfur kills beneficial insects and fish, so use this product only if your plants have a serious fungus infection. It is somewhat toxic to mammals and can cause breathing problems for anyone with asthma or other allergies. It can also harm plants under two conditions: when it is too hot (above 80°F), and if you have used an oil spray within the last month. Lastly, sulfur can build up in the soil if you use it regularly. Sulfur is available at your garden center as a ready-to-use spray or as a concentrate that you mix with water. Spray your plants thoroughly. To keep fungal spores from spreading, you may need to apply it every seven to 14 days. It will wash off the plant in the rain. Safety label: CAUTION. Please read "Safety First," page 191.

Copper. Copper is a natural element that has been used as a fungicide and bactericide for centuries. It prevents fungal spores from germinating, and it kills bacteria. Copper is somewhat toxic to humans, and highly toxic to aquatic invertebrates, fish, and amphibians. Do not use it on or near water. Wear all your protective gear—you know the drill—respirator mask, goggles, gloves, long-sleeved shirt, and long pants. Make sure your children and pets are indoors. If your plants remain wet for too long after you use copper, it can also damage plants. Standards set for certified organic food production allow copper to be used up to one day before harvest. Copper is available at your garden center as a ready-to-use liquid spray, as a powder, or as a dust. To use the powder, you will also have to buy a spreader-sticker, and then mix both products with water, according to the directions on the label. In fact, some liquid sprays require a spreader-sticker, as well. To use the dust, you will need specially made duster guns. Spray or dust plants on a dry morning. Safety label: CAUTION. Please read "Safety First," page 191.

APPENDIX

Choosing the Right Cultivar

The word "cultivar" (short for "cultivated variety") entered the English language in 1923. It applies to plants selected or bred for their desirable traits. For a plant to receive a cultivar name, it must have special identifiable characteristics, the characteristics must remain stable and, when propagated properly, the plant must retain these characteristics. As you might guess, this is not easy. Plant breeders work for many years to breed plants for desirable qualities.

A cultivar name follows the scientific name of a plant. A cultivar name is always capitalized and often in single quotes. The scientific name of the green bean, for example, is *Phaseolus vulgaris*. 'Blue Lake' is a specific cultivar of the green bean. Each vegetable seedling that you purchase from your local independent garden center will have a cultivar name and an informative tag or label. Seed packets will also list the cultivar and have a lot of information printed on the back.

The information included on these tags, labels, and packets is important. Read it. You'll learn the plant's temperature range and its light and water needs. If the plant requires either acid or alkaline soil conditions, you will learn it here.

Always look for the days to maturity. How long it takes for a vegetable crop to become harvestable is an especially important consideration. You need this information to calculate when to sow the seed or get your seedlings in the ground. Start counting on the day you put seeds or seedlings outdoors in the ground.

Resistant cultivars. Always choose disease- or pest-resistant varieties. Many cultivars have letters in caps inserted after the name or somewhere on the package. These abbreviations tell you which resistance has been bred into the plant. TMV, for example, means the plant is resistant to tobacco mosaic virus, N to root-knot nematodes, F to fusarium, V to verticillium wilt, and PM to powdery mildew.

Inspect your vegetable seedlings at the store for diseases and pests, and buy only healthy plants. It is very easy to infect your garden by unwittingly bringing infected plants or seeds

home and putting them in the ground. Reliable seed companies go to great lengths to ensure that their seeds are free of diseases and pests, but seed handed to you by a neighbor (or seed that you saved yourself) may not be so safe. It pays to be careful. You don't want to infect your garden if you can possibly avoid it.

Here are some other terms you might encounter on a cultivar's tag. Knowing what they mean will help you make your decision.

Annuals. Most vegetables are annuals. They germinate from seed, grow their green foliage, flower, set seed, fruit, and die in a single growing season.

Biennials. Some vegetables are biennial, which means they take two years to complete their life cycle. Cabbage, carrots, onions, and beets are familiar garden vegetables that are biennials. They germinate from seed, grow their foliage, and store food in a large below-ground food storage structure (carrots, beets, and onions) or in above-ground foliage (cabbage) all in the first year. In the second year, they use the stored food to flower and make seed, leaving you with nothing to eat. As a result, biennials are always grown as annuals, so that we can harvest and eat all the stored food before the plant uses it up.

F1 hybrid. Plant breeders create F1 hybrid vegetables using traditional plant breeding methods of sexual reproduction (these are *not* genetically modified organisms). The breeders carefully inbreed two lines of zucchini, for example, to create zucchini line A, and zucchini line B. After several generations of inbreeding, and culling out the weak and deformed, the breeder crosses line A to line B. All the seedlings of this cross will be highly uniform and have superior hybrid vigor, growing faster and bigger and producing better fruit. These hybrid traits are advantageous to us.

One disadvantage is that F1 hybrids cannot breed true from seed in the second or succeeding generations. The plants you grow from the seed you purchase will be extremely uniform, like purebred puppies. Second-generation plants grown from seed made by the first generation will not be uniform at all; all their genes will segregate and no two will be alike, kind of like a litter of mongrel puppies. You can save seed of these hybrids to grow more plants, just be aware that they will never come true to type.

F2 hybrid. This kind of hybrid (common in corn, for example) is just like an F1 hybrid, except more complicated. Instead of two inbred lines, the breeders use four lines. Again, these hybrids are extremely uniform, very vigorous, and high yielding, but they do *not* come true from seed in the second or succeeding generations.

Genetically Modified Organism (GMO). Genetic engineering combines genes from unrelated organisms, bypassing sexual reproduction completely. The new creation is a genetically modified organism. Plant breeders use genetic engineering for many purposes. For example, genes from the bacterium *Bacillus thuringiensis* have been inserted into the chromosomes of corn to make plants toxic to the corn earworm. Genetically modified plants are not certifiable as organically grown.

Heirloom. Heirloom cultivars are always open-pollinated and have been developed over many generations. Many are "land races," distinct, easily recognized varieties developed long ago by a particular group of gardeners/farmers in a specific place. The Tess's land race currant tomato from Maryland is an example. You can save seed from the plants you grow, and they will come true to type, as long as they have not been cross-pollinated by a different variety.

Open-pollinated. These cultivars are developed by selecting seedlings with particular desirable traits and allowing them to cross freely among themselves. Open-pollinated varieties always come true from seed—meaning that you can save your own seed year after year and grow these varieties. You must be careful, of course, not to allow two different varieties of a vegetable (say, pattypan and yellow crookneck summer squash) to grow too close to each other, or else the bees will make hybrids for you by moving pollen from one kind of squash to the other. When this happens, your seedlings will be like a litter of mutts—you have no idea how they will turn out. Flying saucers with crooked necks?

Perennials. Perennials are plants that stay alive year after year. Some perennial vegetables, such as artichokes, remain evergreen in a wide variety of climates but will die back to the ground and sprout again in spring if the winter is too cold. Still others, like asparagus and rhubarb, die to the ground sometime during the year, and then sprout again after a rest period. Tomatoes, long-lived perennial vines native to subtropical and tropical Peru, die where winters are cold. So, north and south of the subtropics, we treat tomatoes as annuals.

Plant patents. Plant patents (note PBR or PVR or the phrase "It is unlawful to propagate this plant" on plant labels) have long been a source of confusion. The relatively recent emergence of genetically modified plants has only muddied the waters. We are not lawyers, but this is what our researched has revealed. GM plants that have been patented may *not* be propagated in any way. In fact, you are not permitted to grow them without paying a fee to the patent holder; this fee is usually built into the cost when you buy the plant. Plants that arise from traditional breeding programs may always be lawfully propagated, no matter what the tag says. You may propagate a plant from seeds, divisions, cuttings, or whatever for your personal use; however, you may not *sell* plants you propagate from a patented plant. You may also always collect seeds from a patented plant and sow them in your garden next year—as long as you do not *sell* the plants that grow. You may, however, sell the produce that comes from the plant. It is the plant that is patented, not the vegetable or fruit.

Finally, choosing the right cultivar is a matter of taste. Aesthetic and/or flavor considerations can play into your decision. Some are simply more beautiful than others. 'Bright Lights', for example, is an extremely ornamental chard, as well as delicious. Ordinary chard is not so pretty but still good to eat. Select vegetables that are attractive for inclusion in your flower beds, or in pots on your balcony or patio. Also, be aware that many vegetables taste different when grown under different conditions. Tomatoes are a prime example of this; their flavor varies widely depending on where and how they are grown. You won't know exactly how a vegetable is going to taste until you grow it and taste it for yourself.

Resources

For Information on Regulations for Organically Grown Food

USDA, Alternative Farming Systems Information Center, Publications
nal.usda.gov/afsic/pubs/ofp/ofp.shtml

For Organic and Biological Remedies

Applied Bio-nomics
Victoria, BC
Canada
appliedbio-nomics.com

Beneficial Insectary
9664 Tanqueray Ct.
Redding, CA 96003
insectary.com

Biofac Crop Care, Inc.
Box 87
Mathis, TX 78368
biofac.com

W. Atlee Burpee & Co.
300 Park Ave.
Warminster, PA 18974
burpee.com

Evergro Canada
growercentral.com

Henry Field's Seed
& Nursery Co.
415 N. Burnett St.
Shenandoah, IA 51602
henryfields.com

Foothill Agricultural Research
550 Foothill Pkwy.
Corona, CA 92882

Gardener's Supply Co.
128 Intervale Rd.
Burlington, VT 05401
gardeners.com

Gardens Alive!
5100 Schenley Pl.
Lawrenceburg, IN 47025
gardensalive.com

Harmony Farm Supply
Box 460
Graton, CA 95444
harmonyfarm.com

Hydro-Gardens
Box 25845
Colorado Springs, CO 80936
hydro-gardens.com

The Natural Gardening Co.
217 San Anselmo Ave.
San Anselmo, CA 94960
naturalgardening.com

Nature's Control
Box 35
Medford, OR 97501
naturescontrol.com

Orcon
5132 Venice Blvd.
Los Angeles, CA 90019
organiccontrol.com

Peaceful Valley Farm Supply
Box 2209
Grass Valley, CA 95945
groworganic.com

Richters
Box 26, Hwy 47
Goodwood, ON L0C 1A0
Canada
richters.com

Rincon-Vitova Insectaries
Box 1555
Ventura, CA 93002
rinconvitova.com

For Seeds and Plants of Disease- and Pest-resistant Cultivars

Adams County Nursery, Inc.
Box 108
Aspers, PA 17304
acnursery.com

Ames' Orchard and Nursery
18299 Wildlife Rd.
Fayetteville, AR 72701

W. Atlee Burpee & Co.
300 Park Ave.
Warminster, PA 18974
burpee.com

C & O Nursery
Box 116
Wenatchee, WA 98807-0116
c-onursery.com

Cumberland Valley
Nurseries, Inc.
Box 471
McMinnville, TN 37111

Farmer Seed and Nursery Co.
818 NW 4th St.
Faribault, MN 55021
farmerseed.com

Henry Field's Seed & Nursery Co.
415 N. Burnett St.
Shenandoah, IA 51602
henryfields.com

Freedom Tree Farms
Box 69
Pelham, TN 37366
freedomtreefarms.com

Gurney's Seed & Nursery Co.
110 Capital St.
Yankton, SC 57079
gurneys.com

Harris Seeds
355 Paul Rd.
Rochester, NY 14624
harrisseeds.com

Johnny's Selected Seeds
310 Foss Hill Rd.
Albion, ME 04910
johnnyseeds.com

J. W. Jung Seed Co.
335 S. High St.
Randolph, WI 53957
jungseed.com

Kelly Nurseries
1708 Morrissey Dr.
Bloomington, IL 61704
kellynurseries.com

Miller Nurseries
5060 W. Lake Rd.
Canandaigua, NY 14424
millernurseries.com

Nichols Garden Nursery
1190 N. Pacific Hwy.
Albany, OR 97321
nicholsgardennursery.com

One Green World
28696 S. Cramer Rd.
Molalla, OR 97038
onegreenworld.com

Park Seed Co.
Box 31, Cokesbury Rd.
Greenwood, SC 29647
parkseed.com

Pinetree Garden Seeds
Box 300
New Gloucester, ME 04260
superseeds.com

Plants of the Southwest
3095 Aqua Fria St.
Santa Fe, NM 87507
plantsofthesouthwest.com

Raintree Nursery
391 Butts Rd.
Morton, WA 98356
raintreenursery.com

Renee's Garden
6060A Graham Hill Rd.
Felton, CA 95018
reneesgarden.com

Southern Exposure Seed
Exchange
Box 170
Earlysville, VA 22936
southernexposure.com

Southmeadow Fruit Gardens
10603 Cleveland Ave.
Baroda, MI 49101
southmeadowfruitgardens.com

Stark Bro's Nurseries &
Orchards Co.
Box 10
Louisiana, MO 63353
starkbros.com

Stokes Seeds, Inc.
Box 548
Buffalo, NY 14240
stokeseeds.com

Territorial Seed Co.
Box 157, 20 Palmer Ave.
Cottage Grove, OR 97424
territorialseed.com

Thompson & Morgan, Inc.
Box 1308
Jackson, NJ 08527
tmseeds.com

Victory Seeds
Box 192
Molalla, OR 97038
victoryseeds.com

For Fertilizer, Irrigators, and Other Gardening Equipment

Gardener's Supply Co.
128 Intervale Rd.
Burlington, VT 05401
gardeners.com

Gardens Alive!
5100 Schenley Pl.
Lawrenceburg, IN 47025
gardensalive.com

Harmony Farm Supply
Box 460
Graton, CA 95444
harmonyfarm.com

The Kinsman Co., Inc.
River Rd.
Point Pleasant, PA 18950
kinsmangarden.com

A. M. Leonard, Inc.
Box 816
Piqua, OH 45356
amleo.com

Mantis Garden Tools
1028 Street Rd.
Southampton, PA 18966
mantis.com

The Natural Gardening Co.
217 San Anselmo Ave.
San Anselmo, CA 94960
naturalgardening.com

Ohio Earth Food, Inc.
5488 Swamp St. NE
Hartville, OH 44632
ohioearthfood.com

Peaceful Valley Farm Supply
Box 2209
Grass Valley, CA 95945
groworganic.com

Smith & Hawken
target.com/smithandhawken

The Urban Farmer Store
2833 Vicente St.
San Francisco, CA 94116
urbanfarmerstore.com

Recommended Reading

The following books were particularly helpful to us and our vegetable garden. Those marked with an asterisk (∗) focus solely on organic gardening techniques.

Agrios, George N. 2005. *Plant Pathology*. 5th ed. Elsevier Academic Press.

∗ Bradley, Fern Marshall. 2007. *Rodale's Vegetable Garden Problem Solver*. Rodale Books.

——, et al. 2009. *Rodale's Ultimate Encyclopedia of Organic Gardening*. Rodale Books.

Brenzel, Kathleen Norris, ed. 2007. *Sunset Western Garden Book*. 8th ed. Sunset Publishing Corp.

∗ Coleman, Eliot. 1995. *The New Organic Grower*. Rev. ed. Chelsea Green.

∗ Deardorff, David, and Kathryn Wadsworth. 2009. *What's Wrong With My Plant? (And How Do I Fix It?)*. Timber Press.

∗ Ellis, Barbara W., and Fern Marshall Bradley, eds. 1996. *The Organic Gardener's Handbook of Natural Insect and Disease Control*. Rev. ed. Rodale Press.

Gillman, Jeff. 2008. *The Truth About Garden Remedies*. Timber Press.

——. 2008. *The Truth About Organic Gardening*. Timber Press.

Grissell, Eric. 2001. *Insects and Gardens*. Timber Press.

Lowenfels, Jeff, and Wayne Lewis. 2010. *Teaming with Microbes*. Rev. ed. Timber Press.

Mollison, Bill, and Reny Mia Slay. 1997. *Introduction to Permaculture*. Rev. ed. Tagari Publications.

Smith, Edward C. 2009. *The Vegetable Gardener's Bible*. Storey Publishing.

Useful Conversions

inches	centimeters
¼	0.6
½	1.25
¾	1.9
1	2.5
1¼	3.1
1½	3.8
1¾	4.4
2	5.0
3	7.5
4	10
5	12.5
6	15
7	18
8	20
9	23
10	25
12	30
15	38
18	45
20	50
24	60
30	75
32	80
36	90

feet	meters
1	0.3
1½	0.5
2	0.6
2½	0.8
3	0.9
4	1.2
5	1.5
6	1.8
7	2.1
8	2.4
9	2.7
10	3.0
12	3.6
15	4.5
18	5.4
20	6.0
25	7.5

temperatures

$$°C = 5/9 \times (°F - 32)$$
$$°F = (9/5 \times °C) + 32$$

Acknowledgments

We have so many people to thank, the list could be endless. Thanks as always to Regina Ryan who continues to guide us with her amazing knowledge and insight. We are very grateful to everyone at Timber Press for their professionalism and dedication to publishing such beautiful and informative books. Tom Fischer, Franni Bertolino, Emma Alpaugh, and Kara Wilde have all provided exceptional expertise for which we cannot fully express our appreciation. Kona Ink—Rebecca Cantrell (aka Bekka Black), Judith Heath, and Karen Hollinger—we could not have done it without your sharp editorial eyes, your relentless support, and your dedication to the work. You are still the best critique group on the planet. We had amazing assistance everywhere we went over the past year, capturing images for this book. Janette Heartwood, Ronn Patterson, Jeanne Deardorff, Terry Thomas, Ana Perez, Jeanne Leighton, Paul Miller, Betsy O'Neil, Denise Fort, Oksana Fort, Melissa Kaplan, Kris Maltrud, Charles Jaeger, Debra Sharp-Hartman, and Ruth Murphy all provided safe havens as we traveled the country to take photographs. For our generous and kind friends and family, who help us every day, we hope to return (or pay forward) all their countless kindnesses. We owe much to Weezie Jenkins and Steve Connor, Steve and Louise Carroll, Barbara Smith and Randy Deardorff, Lauren Wadsworth, Sarah Wadsworth, Jake and Annod Bickley, Barbara Ansley-Vensas, and David Vensas for the loving support provided every step of the way.

Index

About the authors

David Deardorff and **Kathryn Wadsworth** are freelance writers, photographers, and garden coaches, offering consultation on plant selection, landscape design, garden problem solving, and plant identification. Deardorff's PhD in botany and years of experience as a plant pathologist inform their shared expertise: together they have nurtured plants in their nurseries and gardens in the Desert Southwest, the Pacific Northwest, and Hawaii. They travel extensively, holding popular workshops and lectures across the country, and have appeared on numerous radio shows throughout the United States, including *Martha Stewart Living Radio*, Joe Lamp'l's *Growing a Greener World*, Ken Druse's *Real Dirt*, and Ciscoe Morris's *Gardening with Ciscoe*.